Disabling Relations

In the series *Dis/color*, edited by Cynthia Wu,
Julie Avril Minich, and Nirmala Erevelles

ALSO IN THIS SERIES:

Akemi Nishida, *Just Care: Messy Entanglements of Disability, Dependency, and Desire*

James Kyung-Jin Lee, *Pedagogies of Woundedness: Illness, Memoir, and the Ends of the Model Minority*

Milo Obourn, *Disabled Futures: A Framework for Radical Inclusion*

Sona Kazemi

Disabling Relations

Wounded Bodyminds and Transnational Praxis

TEMPLE UNIVERSITY PRESS
Philadelphia • Rome • Tokyo

TEMPLE UNIVERSITY PRESS
Philadelphia, Pennsylvania 19122
tupress.temple.edu

Copyright © 2026 by Temple University—Of The Commonwealth System
  of Higher Education
All rights reserved
Published 2026

Cataloging information is available from the Library of Congress.

ISBNs are 978-1-4399-2248-4 (cloth), 978-1-4399-2249-1 (paper), 978-1-4399-2250-7 (ebook).

The manufacturer's authorized representative in the EU for product safety is
Temple University Rome, Via di San Sebastianello, 16, 00187 Rome RM, Italy
(https://rome.temple.edu/).
tempress@temple.edu

♾ The paper used in this publication meets the requirements of the
American National Standard for Information Sciences—Permanence
of Paper for Printed Library Materials, ANSI Z39.48-1992

Printed in the United States of America

9 8 7 6 5 4 3 2 1

Contents

	Preface	vii
	Acknowledgments	xvii
	Introduction	1
1.	Ripping the Wound: A Transnational Disability Theory and Praxis	23
2.	Gaping Wounds: Disablement in the Iran-Iraq War	42
3.	Rotten Wounds: Madness and Disability in Prison	65
4.	Bleeding Wounds: Punitive Limb Amputation, Disability as Punishment for Poverty	99
5.	Burning Wounds: Acid Attack, Disabling Gender-Based Violence	128
	Conclusion: Healing Wounds: Transnational Disability Praxis and Active Witnessing	173
	Notes	185
	References	197
	Index	215

Preface

> Men make their own history, but they do not make it as they please; they do not make it under self-selected circumstances, but under circumstances existing already, given and transmitted from the past. The tradition of all dead generations weighs like a nightmare on the brains of the living.
>
> —Karl Marx, *The Eighteenth Brumaire of Louis Bonaparte* (1852)

This book bears witness to the veterans and civilians wounded in the Iran-Iraq War (1980–1988) by conventional and chemical weapons, the disabled political prison survivors incarcerated in the 1980s in Iran, the disabled survivors of punitive limb amputation (PLA) under sharia law, and the women survivors of acid attacks. It throws light on the capitalist, theocratic, patriarchal, and imperialist social relations as they lead to disability, and finally, it offers a materialist and transnational theorization of disability. By foregrounding the stories of disabled survivors of violence, I strive to understand and bear witness to their experiences of becoming and remaining disabled, as a historical process mediated by power relations and how they come to terms with their disability, which I call "disability consciousness."

The seeds of the questions I address in this book were planted during my life as a young girl living under sharia law in post-revolution Iran, and later, during my work as a disability rights activist in the United States and Canada. Growing up in the 1980s and 1990s in a society that had gone through a revolution and a war in less than a decade meant encountering wounded bodyminds everywhere: in battlefields, institutions, nursing homes, prisons, and psychiatric hospitals. By "wounded," I mean individuals who have become disabled as a result of violence inflicted on them through the horrors of war: chemical weapons of mass destruction, shrapnel shells, minefields, displacement; and through the political violence unleashed by the Islamic revolution: crushing dissent, purges, torture, forced conversion, execution, and unmarked mass graves. I grew up haunted by two wounded groups comprising the generation before me, those who were killed in the war, or came back disabled, as well as those imprisoned, tortured, or killed by the newly established regime.

In other words, these two wounded groups, as Marx (1852) put it, "weighed like a nightmare" on my brain. The first group comprised wounded individuals, disabled veterans, and civilians who had acquired a physical or psychological injury either during the war between Iran and Iraq, or later, in nursing homes, hospitals, and asylums, where they were shelved away. The second group consisted of dissidents who had become disabled or mad, fighting the regime in prison cells, solitary confinement, and torture chambers. As a child, I didn't have the vocabulary or analysis to describe, let alone explain, what had happened to the generation before me. It wasn't until I became a graduate student in disability studies that I realized that the disability I had witnessed in those wounded bodyminds was not just a biomedical or health issue but a sociopolitical wound, an injury that was caused by the violence of war and political suppression and sustained by denial, inadequate care, structural neglect, and state terror. This reminded me of a quote by John Phillips where he states, "The wound as an event which brings the knife and the flesh together can be reduced to neither knife nor flesh" (2006, p. 109).

After joining the disability studies program at York University in Canada, my own rotten wound found a place to open its mouth. I started questioning everything I had witnessed growing up in Iran. I found myself wondering why, as a seven-year-old child, I had to cover my hair and body to go to school; why there were no boys in my school; why girls and women sat in the back of the bus; why only women had to follow the Islamic dress code and wear a veil/hijab/headscarf and not men; why my Bahá'í friends couldn't go to university; why fathers could behead their daughters with impunity; and why some men threw acid in the faces of women who had rejected them, and walked with impunity, or served minimal sentences while going home for the weekend? Why couldn't women become judges, and why was their testimony worth only half that of men in court? Why were labor unions crushed, criminalized, and their members arrested? Why was the civil society, even charities helping child laborers, under attack and their members imprisoned? Why did many poor and neglected war veterans who couldn't provide for their families set themselves on fire? Why were poor people—who had resorted to theft to survive—subject to amputation in town squares while the bigger thieves ruling the country embezzled millions with impunity? Why were the rich disabling the poor? Why were dissidents being tortured and left disabled in prisons? Why was a person executed every seven hours?

After leaving the country in search of a better life, these and many more unanswered questions led me to seek an education in disability studies. However, the existing theories and models in the field seemed disinterested in the wounded bodyminds that I had witnessed. By the time I started my graduate program, many critical antiracist movements had challenged the whiteness of the existing disability studies discourse, but the field had not yet moved past the deadlock of Western contexts, and it mostly remained concerned with congenital disabilities or those acquired by accident in the United States, U.K., Canada, and Australia. I felt devastated and my wound reopened its mouth. The bodyminds wounded by the violence of war, incarceration, torture, PLA, gender-based violence, and systemic neglect came back to haunt me.

On the bright side, as a person in self-imposed exile in Canada, I was relatively safe away from the watchful eyes of the theocratic state, the Islamic Republic of Iran (IRI). Free from censorship, I was able to read the real stories of the war, not the official war narratives that the state manufactured to legitimatize itself and justify its involvement in the war. Additionally, in Toronto, I had a chance to meet many former political prisoners from Iran and families of the executed or forcibly disappeared prisoners and form lifelong friendships with them. Over the years, I read many of their memoirs, testimonies, blogposts, and books, and spoke with them over numerous gatherings, dinners, trips, phone calls, and commemoration events. I eventually found myself organizing with them as an ally, as part of their transnational movement, called *Jonbesh-e Edalatkhahi* or *dadkhahi*,[1] or the Justice-Seeking Movement,[2] demanding justice for the wounded prisoners as well as those executed and forcibly disappeared. I also became increasingly involved in disability advocacy, migrant justice, and gender equality projects and started collaborating with refugee and immigrant women with disabilities to serve our communities, teaching each other how to apply for student loans, seek better employment, and go to college.

In a matter of years, I had become a social justice activist, a willing and active witness who wanted to do something about what I was witnessing as opposed to just watching with indifference. I mobilized with many wounded individuals and communities and became an ally to several movements in Iran and Canada. In my doctoral program, I got a chance to revisit the tough questions I'd had when encountering the wounded generations of war veterans and political prisoners that haunted both my lived experience and consciousness. Faced with disability studies' lack of interest or theory to analyze the experiences of acquiring a disability through war, torture, and incarceration, this time, as a scholar in the United States, I wrote this book, telling four distinct stories of the wounds caused by war, incarceration, PLA, and acid attacks in Iran, an enormously complex society with a long history of struggle for democracy and the rule of law and liberation from tyranny.

How I Inherited the War with Iraq and the 1979 Revolution

During the Cold War, after stemming the world's rising communist revolutions, the United States adopted the redundant strategy of "the enemy of my enemy is my friend," and perceived the surge of religion as a force to resist socialist dreams that were still breathing across the world, including in the Middle East and North Africa (MENA). Western countries, led by the United States, smoothed the overthrow of the monarchy in Iran and trusted that Ruhollah Khomeini, a Shia cleric, would, as he pledged, be a good ally to the United States (Milani, 2012). However, the West didn't get what they had hoped for; the Islamic revolution of 1979 altered the world order by destabilizing the MENA region and revitalizing Islamic fundamentalist groups, militias, and movements that were previously less active during a long period of left-wing inclinations in the 1960s and 1970s. In other words, the Iranian Revolution (along with the Camp David Accords, the Siege of Mecca, the Soviet invasion of Afghanistan, and Iraq's invasion of Iran), as Hamit Bozarslan notes, "marked a decisive move towards the domination of Islamism in the Middle East [and] paved the way for decades of war, violent contest, and massive state repressions" (2012, p. 2). Many misinterpret militant Islamist regimes, such as the Islamic Republic, Taliban, or nonstate actors like ISIS (i.e., self-proclaimed Islamic State of Iraq and Syria), as "indigenous" forces resisting the U.S. empire and its allies. However, the truth is that they mistake competition to reach global hegemony for "resistance." The Islamist forces, whether states or proxy militants, "compete" with the U.S. empire; they need to replace the current empire in order to become one themselves. This gross misunderstanding is unfortunately prevalent in the left-leaning and progressive circles of Western media and academia.

After taking absolute power in 1979, the Islamic regime began summarily eliminating political dissidents, activists, journalists, and ethnic and religious minorities, killing thousands in only the first decade after the revolution (Abrahamian, 1999, 2008; Akhavan, 2017; Bakhash, 1984; Makaremi, 2015). The new tyrannically religious regime imprisoned, tortured, and/or executed almost every person who opposed them—many being dumped into unmarked mass graves, depriving family and loved ones of their right to bury and properly mourn their dead. Khomeini's government not only persecuted those who had access to firearms and engaged in outright armed struggle against the new dictatorship but also targeted anyone who even sympathized ideologically (not necessarily militantly) with any competing political party or organization. Overall, the IRI's anti-Western agenda, ideological antagonism toward the United States and Israel (Sadjadpour, 2019), pursuit of nuclear weapons (Albright & Burkhard, 2021), export of its Shia revolution to the rest of the region, animosity toward Sunni Muslim nations, and total dependency on Russian (Rumer, 2021) and Chinese neocolonialism[3] (Davar, 2020) have come at a colossal cost to the Iranian people. Examples include wasting resources for completely unnecessary nuclear adventures and funding terrorism (Byman, 2008) that has brought upon Iranians nothing but isolation, instability, poverty, and economic sanctions.

The IRI's imperialist behavior in the region, while still brutally suppressing its own people and eliminating its dissidents abroad, is not a secret to anyone. At this point, Iran has outmaneuvered the United States in Iraq, funded and armed numerous militia groups across the MENA region, and interfered with many nations' affairs, such as Lebanon, Yemen, Palestine (Gaza), Iraq, and Syria. The regime has done this by infiltrating those nations' weak governments, providing weapons to terrorist groups (e.g., Hamas, Houthis) to sustain their Shia influence, and weakening the central government to fight a proxy war with its rivals, while supporting its ally dictators to stay in power and shed more blood (such as Bashar Al-Assad in Syria) (Borshchevskaya, 2023; Sadjadpour, 2019). The IRI's imperialist ventures would not have been possible without Russian and Chinese support. The Soviets have had a manipulative relationship with Iran for centuries, leading to the ratification of tremendously despotic contracts that benefitted them and harmed the Iranian side. Even China, a relatively new economic superpower, has been engaged in neocolonial aggression in the region, just like Anglo-Americans have for centuries.

My grandfather was a Royal Persian Army colonel when the 1979 Iranian Revolution took place. Luckily, he survived the mass executions of high-ranking military personnel carried out by the new Islamic regime in the days immediately following the revolution. In 1980, he retired as he did not want to be part of the new regime that had the blood of the people on their hands. However, when the war with Iraq began, he asked the new chiefs to let him fight along with other soldiers; he believed he had been trained for twenty years for a moment like this—to defend and protect the nation. But they denied his request, saying that they did not need strategic, tactical, and technical advice from experts; instead, they explained that all God's army needed was a shield made of human bodies. Using the masses as cannon fodder—a fundamental aspect of war in a class society—is the brute-force strategy of deploying combatants from the lower classes as an expendable resource in the face of enemy fire. My grandfather subsequently went into a long depression after seeing the young generation perish on the battlefield due to a lack of effective leadership, military knowledge, and rational decision-making based on national interests. More than five hundred thousand people died in that war between 1980 and 1988 on both sides, with Iran suffering the greatest losses. Nearly half a million more Iranians were left with permanent injuries, severe disabilities, and enduring recalcitrant trauma (Hiro, 1991; Katouzian, 2010; Mikaberidze, 2011; Murray & Woods, 2014). Most of the survivors who incurred disabilities were shelved away in institutions, a fate all too similar to that faced by dissidents who suffered in the state's notorious prisons.

In 1985, my grandparents sold everything they owned and paid a smuggler to import their teenage son into Canada so he would avoid the military draft during the war. Without the communicational and technological advancement that we enjoy today, they had to wait for months, not knowing where he was or what he was encountering, or if he had anything to eat while traveling secretly through the lands and deserts he had never visited. Now, decades later, both grandparents still start sobbing every time they remember those days. Losing a child to exile was an enormously painful experience for them. Not knowing if they would ever see my uncle again, the feeling of absolute uncertainty took over their lives. This emotional turmoil intensified day after day while they were deprived of contact until he had reached a place safe enough to get in touch with them. My grandmother, for the first time in her life, became so distressed that she started taking psychiatric medication, as she could not sleep without having nightmares. My grandfather, on the other hand, could not even eat an apple without distress, not knowing if my uncle had anything to eat while crossing barbed wires and mountains in the dead of night.

Three grueling months later, in the winter of 1986, the phone rang and my uncle told my grandparents that he had arrived safely in Montreal. They were, of course, overjoyed that he had successfully made it to a haven in Canada, but they were equally, bitterly mournful, not knowing if they would ever see him again. The relationship between the IRI and the West had grown increasingly chaotic, and there was no way of knowing whether it would even be possible, let alone safe, for him to ever return. Suddenly, my grandparents were overwhelmed with the realization of what it meant for their son to be exiled to such a faraway place—he was on an entirely different continent and they were separated by thousands of miles of mountains, deserts, and oceans. They were trying to grapple with these mixed feelings and the loss that they were experiencing when another phone call gave them another shock: their daughter was pregnant, but she wanted to have an abortion.

My grandparents pleaded with her to reconsider and insisted that they would raise the baby. Perhaps they were secretly happy for another child who could fill some of the void that my uncle's absence created. They convinced her to keep the baby, and I was born months later in the summer of 1986, right in the middle of the Iran-Iraq War when my mother, scared by the horrific sound of an Iraqi bomb being dropped in Esfahān, went into labor. She managed to deliver me, a premature baby, in the hospital the next day. I grew up amid continuous strife and terror, war outside and within Iran's borders, and relentless bombings like the one that literally terrified my mother into early labor. Bombs were my birth song.

Growing up I knew that my generation had inherited a revolution—a revolution standing on the ruins of dictatorship and rooted in political dissent, socialist dreams, and un/armed struggles by several competing political groups, coalitions, and organizations. Gradually, I came to realize what it meant to be born in the MENA region—a golden imbroglio of ancient history, art, glorious and tyrannical dynasties, peoples' resistance, social movements, a gluttonous oil industry, sectarian wars, political Islam (Islamism), competing Eastern and Western interests, and never-ending conflict. These conflicts were started and sustained by both corrupt local leaders and foreign powers, who could profit from the chaos the Iranian people had to endure.

In 1978, the Soviets invaded Afghanistan, killed thousands, and displaced millions. Then, in 1995, the Taliban seized power, amid the turmoil that followed the withdrawal of Soviet forces from Afghanistan in 1989. The Soviets were defeated by Islamic fighters known as the Mujahideen, who were, according to the Cold War's proxy-war logic that "the enemy of my enemy is my friend," supported by the U.S. government. Rival factions of Mujahideen subsequently branched off, precipitating the rise of the Taliban and the opposing Northern Alliance. With the help of Pakistan, Saudi Arabia, and the United States, these Islamist fighters established an Islamic state and ruled over the country in a dictatorial style for six years until they were defeated by the U.S.-led coalition in 2001. Their reign was characterized by a fundamentalist interpretation of sharia law that involved gender apartheid (e.g., prohibiting women from leaving the house without a male chaperone, forced veiling),[4] PLA, stoning, public flagellation, execution, segregation, and authoritarianism. Unfortunately, they again came to power twenty years later in August 2021 as soon as the United States withdrew from Afghanistan. The global community has largely remained silent and indifferent as the Taliban has reestablished its Islamic state and gender apartheid system, seeking legitimacy from the rest of the world to sustain itself.

When I was seventeen (in 2003), the United States attacked Iraq. Iraq's invasion by the United States gave ample space to the Islamic Republic to rise as a regional imperialist power. Using the country's frail state, the IRI crept into Iraq and formed numerous Shia militia groups to exert regional control and engage in asymmetrical warfare with its sworn enemy, the United States. Many years later, in 2011, the horrors in the region took a new turn with Russian and Iranian involvement in the Syrian civil war to save Bashar al-Assad's dictatorship, and its transformation into a proxy war by their simultaneous alliance and rivalry (Borshchevskaya, 2023). By involvement, I mean the bold use of military power against the Syrian opposition forces and bringing militia (many of whom were Afghan asylum seekers or even Pakistani nationals) into Syria and arming them. Tehran's tentacles continue to grow today and the state is committed to expanding its theocratic empire all over the region by its dedicated efforts to access nuclear weapons, wipe Israel off the map, and oust America from the region.

Iran is not only surrounded by various hostile national factions of Islamic fundamentalists (like the Taliban) but is also ruled by a tyrannical religious government, the IRI (Abrahamian, 2008; Milani, 2012). The state's terror is totalitarian in scope and Machiavellian in application. Since the establishment of the Islamic regime, sharia law has extended to the most intimate aspects of citizens' lives, with Islamic religious police—the so-called Guidance Patrol, or morality police—having full impunity to patrol and enforce. They are particularly brutal when it comes to modesty and strict dress codes, especially for women, who must properly cover their head with a hijab. Perhaps the term morality police rings a bell; in 2022, the twenty-two-year-old Kurdish Iranian woman Mahsa Zhina Amini was beaten to death in the morality police's custody after being arrested for "bad veiling." Ironically, her tragic death breathed life into the dusty lungs of feminism all around the world, when women from her hometown, Saqqez, took off their hijabs, burned them in a bonfire, and, inspired by the decades-long Kurdish women's movement, chanted "Woman, Life, Freedom." Soon, the wave swept through the country, and the Iranian people poured onto the street. This time a scene different from what the forty-four-year-old revolution had imposed on the country emerged from the ashes of a myriad of crushed protests over the years: dancing women throwing their hijabs into a bonfire, and with that, the weight of second-class citizenship, sexual apartheid, and gender segregation. Dissimilar to the March 8, 1979 demonstrations, where most men didn't accompany women protesting mandatory hijab, men followed women, supported them, and stood by their side. They also chanted "Woman, Life, Freedom," which encapsulated everything that the Iranian people desired—everything the Islamic Republic has actively tried to destroy and repress. As expected, a violent crackdown ensued, resulting in tens of thousands of arrests, many deliberately shot in the face at close range losing their sight (Engelbrecht, 2022), and hundreds of deaths, including children. Additionally, over a hundred protesters were sentenced to death after cursory trials for the all-encompassing crime of "corruption on Earth"; some have already been hanged. In its report to the UN Human Rights Council, the UN fact-finding mission stated that there has been a systemic weaponization of rape against Iranian women protesters who got arrested to punish them for saying "Woman, Life, Freedom" (Amnesty International, 2023; The Independent International Fact-Finding Mission on the Islamic Republic of Iran, 2024).

For me, twenty-two-year-old Zhina's death was a bitter reminder of what had happened to me twenty-two years earlier when I was a teenager.[5] I was also arrested, abused, questioned, terrorized, and imprisoned in a dark, dirty cell for going out without a proper hijab (according to the state's standards). My conditional release was granted only after my father desperately begged the police and wrote a statement promising that he would make sure I would never again leave the house in such "offensive clothing." During the twenty years I spent living directly under the theocratic fundamentalist regime, I came to realize that there is a very fine line separating modest humility defined by the IRI from dictatorial humiliation exclusively subjected upon the bodies of women. It is precisely through the subjugation, corporeal violence, and policing of bodies that a regime such as the Islamic Republic asserts and maintains power. Sovereign dominance over a population through coercion, direct violence and terror, uncontested imposed social standards, or rendering particular bodies incapable of resistance is at the core of what Michel Foucault (1976) coined as "biopower," and it functions through the control of all the vital processes by which people live and die. It can also result in willing submission, unquestioning acceptance, self-policing, and moral norms.

However, the "Woman, Life, Freedom" uprising has changed everything, posing the biggest challenge to the IRI's legitimacy since its inception. Control over women's bodies and sexuality is of utmost importance to the regime and one of its key pillars. If this pillar collapses, so will the Islamic Republic's rule. Under the regime's rule in Iran, hijab is not just a piece of fabric but an insurance policy for Islamic gender policing, male supremacy, second-class citizenship for women, and means for the implementation of gender apartheid.

I survived the morality police, but Zhina did not. My commitment in this book is to amplify her lost voice, an ethnic and religious minority young woman like me, whose only "crime" was not bad veiling—but being a woman. Zhina's unheard voice, along with other voices, will be articulated through my active witnessing.

In the sea there are countless treasures,
But if you desire safety, it is on the shore. —Sa'adi

Acknowledgments

Growing up as the only child and cared for by my parents and four grandparents, who were actively involved in raising me, I usually felt special and confident. My paternal grandparents believed that I had remarkable communication and advocacy skills and that I should become a lawyer. My father never stopped reminding me that I needed to get a Ph.D. and write many books. My mom, on the other hand, believed that whatever I'd decide to do with my life, I'd do it well. Negin Yadranji, Morteza Kazemi, Manouchehr Yadranji, Parvin Rohani, Najibeh Rohani, and Sattar Kazemi became the island from which I departed, the ocean in which I learned how to swim, the waves that never gave up on hitting the tall cliffs of hopelessness, and the sun that showered me with unconditional love. They each had their own vision for my future career, but because of a forced migration at the age of twenty, my life took a different turn. When I started graduate school, my mentor Rachel Gorman gave me a book called *We Lived to Tell*, which entailed three women political prisoners' memoirs who had experienced imprisonment and torture in the 1980s in Iran. Reading that book, along with Rachel's persistent encouragement to get in touch with my own embodied, communal, intergenerational, and experiential knowledge as a source, launched me on a new theoretical path as an emerging scholar and made me confident enough to keep writing academic papers and contributing to my field. However, I never even contemplated writing a book, but in 2018, after starting my first postdoctoral fellowship at the Ohio State University, Margaret Price, another legendary mentor of mine, casually uttered the following words at a housewarming party, "I can help you write your book." Turning my head toward her, I smiled carelessly and appreciatively, meaning that I was thankful for the offer but that the idea was unthinkable.

That night Margaret planted a seed in my head that Rachel had already prepared the fertile ground for. My other mentors, Amy Shuman, Nirmala Erevelles, and Wendy Hesford, never ceased expecting me to write a book. Their expectation convinced me not only that I could, but that I should, write a book.

A few months after Margaret's offer to help me write my book, which was the equivalent of saying "I'll help you go to space," I found myself on the phone asking Rachel to brainstorm with me for developing the book's outline. Then I reached out to my network of torture, acid attack, and prison survivors and human rights activists and started interviewing them. Shahla Talebi, a prominent anthropologist who experienced nine years of political imprisonment and torture in Iran, before and after the revolution, graciously offered to fly across the country and stay with me for several weeks so we could think through my questions and get in touch with her former prison inmates and interview them. Weeks, months, and years passed while I cried, laughed, and died on the phone and Skype listening to the stories of my interviewees who were generous and brave enough to rip and share their gaping, burning, rotten, and bleeding wounds with me. My best friends, Hemachandran Karah and Efrat Gold, never stopped cheering for me while worrying about my well-being, knowing deep down that I needed to do what I was doing. My furry daughter, Pashmak, begged for food and purred next to me while I was typing. The late Bonnie Burstow's fierce spirit and memory accompanied me on this voyage just like Bonnie herself used to do as mentor, radical role model, and a revolutionary feminist ally.

My body ached while my heart bloomed like an orchid during some interviews and withered away during others. Some nights I would collect pieces of myself that had fallen on the ground, pick them up, and go straight to my mom where she would put me back together with a magical glue that only she possesses and pat me on the back saying that I needed to continue on my path as the path couldn't wait and that I was the only one who could pave it with my steps.

Every single night, I would row back to the harbor where my life partner, Mike, would be shining light from the lighthouse eagerly waiting to lend his firm shoulders, sharp intellect, loving heart, and courageous ears to the treasure of stories I had collected that day.

I want to sincerely thank Masoumeh Ataei, the acid attack survivor whose beautiful face is on the cover of this book you are holding today, who shared with me not only her story but her embodied resilience and courage as a sister, friend, and ally.

Legendary Shekoufeh Sakhi's existence in the world taught me that we can love and care about others no matter what the external contingencies are.

Nasrin, Homayoon, Ali, Masoud, Siamak, Mersedeh, Shahin, Mehdi, Iraj, Nazli, Soudabeh, Rahman, Minoo, Nadia, Zahra, Farzaneh, Roya, Giti, Shahrnoosh, Monireh, Nezhla, Babak, Tahmineh, Shohreh, Hossein, Ebrahim, Reza, Assad, Fereydoon, Nader, and many other former political prisoners who endured years of imprisonment and torture in the 1980s in Iran, you became torches without whom I would not have found my way.

My students at the University of Toronto, Ohio State University, and University of Wisconsin-La Crosse easily convinced me that it was worth crossing three continents to become their teacher. They showered me with care, love, compassion, and gratitude, as they listened to and read parts of the manuscript over the years and gave me invaluable feedback.

Anonymous reviewers of the manuscript reminded me at times that my own voice should be highlighted and not get buried in other people's arguments. I thank them for their confidence in the intellectual value of my theoretical contributions and for empowering me as a scholar.

Shaun Vigil, this book would not have come into fruition without you. Thank you for your faith in me and commitment to this project.

Last but not least, let me say that I have built my contribution to the field of disability studies on the shoulders of the giants like Nirmala Erevelles, whose presence, activism, and scholarship have carved and sustained much needed space for marginalized scholars like me.

DISABLING RELATIONS

Introduction

When violent practices that render bodies from the global south disabled get naturalized, those bodies and their disabilities get fetishized. Fetishization of disabled bodies from the global south takes place through local blocks of power such as the state and its sponsored institutions in the global south, as well as global hegemonic forces such as popular culture, media, and even academies of the global north. In this book I ask: How do we learn to defetishize disability in our everyday lives? How do processes of patriarchy, imperialism, and religious fundamentalism rework the dialectics of disability and shape our capacity to understand history and think about a revolutionary future? This book uses the global context of class and ideology—inherent within the capitalist economy and the global and regional-imperialist politics in the Middle East and beyond, situated around the disabling effects of the rise of Islamists to power in Iran after the 1979 revolution as well as the aftermath of the Iran-Iraq War (1980–1988) in particular—to understand how disabled bodies are produced and sustained through the violence of imperialist and theocratic social relations.

Striving to resist an easy conceptualization of disability in the violent intersection of power, social relations, ideology, and the human bodymind, I offer an analysis of disability produced/sustained/appropriated by the imperialistic architects of state violence in the current historical context where we continue to bear witness to the proliferation of disability in geopolitical spaces and where there are no simplistic ways to explain whose side we are on. I aim to reshape how we theorize disability via postcolonialism/neocolonialism/imperialism in transnational contexts—a theoretical shift that I think the field of disability studies (DS) could benefit from.

I conceptualize disability as integral to global class relations as well as global ideological structures rather than as additive dimensions to them. This book attempts to explicate these relations, focusing less on what disability identity is or should be in the global south, and more on how disability is produced transnationally, always constituted within the historical relations of global class struggle. Even though the production of disabled bodies as a historical process is located within global class relations, the discourse/language around it is usually hidden. According to Erevelles (2011), when historical and social relations that create disability are overlooked, disability gets fetishized: "The very category of disability operates as a commodity fetish that occludes the violence of the socio-economic system" (p. 67). Here, I extend this by arguing that the very category of disability also occludes the violence of other exploitative social relations, such as theocracy, fascism, patriarchy, and their consequences, including domestic violence, incarceration, gender-based violence (GBV), female genital mutilation, and torture.

The disablement of global south bodies is often somehow fetishized/naturalized (e.g., reducing people to numbers or associating a region with conflicts) as the only description we can expect from peripheral and disappearing regions like the Middle East, which continue to burn in never-ending conflicts. Erevelles (2011) defines fetishization of disability as the processes by which the sociopolitical relations and economic agenda behind the production of disabled bodies become mystified. I analyze how the disablement of global south bodies in wars, state repression, genocides, and sweatshops are persistently naturalized—that is, attributed to the natural state of affairs in those regions, with the inevitable consequence that they cannot be connected to the violence of ongoing fundamentalism and imperialism(s). Furthermore, I develop a theory and praxis for a revolutionary understanding of disability, contextualized within transnational, nonideological, and class-conscious disability activism. This book has five main foci: (1) bearing witness to wounded/disabled survivors of war, incarceration, torture, punitive limb amputation (PLA), and acid attacks, by actively defetishizing their disability and disability consciousness; (2) formulating a transnational disability theory; (3) further developing the conversation in DS about the creation of disability by violence in the global south through four different case studies; (4) demonstrating that transnational disability theory, through a defetishizing process, has a revolutionary capacity to produce nonideological forms of consciousness, knowledge, and praxis; and (5) application of transnational disability theory by foregrounding the inseparability of disability and care as a dialectic and theorizing what I call "infrastructures of care" (Kazemi & Karah, 2023) in each case of disablement.

By defetishizing, I mean carrying out a thorough analysis of these categories to unveil the social relations (e.g., patriarchy, theocracy) behind their creation and to name the processes (e.g., poverty, incarceration) that render people disabled through violence. For instance, in the case of war survivors' disabilities, the process of defetishization can take place by listening to what the veterans have to say about the war and by refusing to believe the "official narrative" (Radstone & Schwarz, 2010, p. 133) imposed by the state. With the aim of producing a form of knowledge based on the material reality under which disabled people live, I shift the analysis and pave the way for a revolutionary understanding of disability and its relationship with the state, the capitalist economy, and class society, contextualized within transnational political consciousness and activism.

The questions that I ask in every chapter are centered around defetishizing the wounds of the disabled people whose stories I narrate, as well as the disability consciousness that they may or may not have developed as part of the defetishization process. This process involves (a) listening to the first-hand experiences of disabled survivors; (b) unmasking the social relations behind the creation and sustenance of their disability; (c) identifying ideologies involved in the disabling processes (e.g., punishment, dying, getting disabled for or by the state); (d) shifting our analysis from the familiar/normative, and paving the way for a nuanced and nonideological understanding of disability in global contexts; (e) contributing to the theorization and application of the principles of disability justice (Berne, Morales, & Langstaff, 2018) in transnational contexts by foregrounding the infrastructures of care in each case; and (f) producing a form of knowledge based on the material reality under which disabled people live, as opposed to ideological abstraction (e.g., living martyrs, angels, saints).

This book also contributes to DS by proposing and applying a new disability theory and praxis from the standpoint of a Middle Eastern feminist woman war survivor. It uses dialectical and historical materialism (DHM) (Marx & Engels, 1932/1998) as a theoretical framework and as a tool of analysis to collect and interpret data from the case studies I have conducted for this purpose. My research methods include ethnographic fieldwork, interviews, digital studies of human rights documents' archives, social media, and political commentaries, as well as sixteen years of participatory action research as part of my transnational community organizing, solidarity building, archiving, and activism with the survivors of state terror.

Critical Concepts

State Violence

As Jasbir K. Puar (2017) notes, one of the shortcomings of the dominant DS discourse is that it rarely questions how disabilities are produced (e.g., by state violence), for it assumes that we should solely theorize disability *after* it occurs or just ignores the process of the production of disability entirely. This approach masks the ways in which disability is produced and thus fetishizes disability. Also, it is not a secret that the state is an undertheorized concept in DS literature. One way in which I engage in defetishizing disability is by theorizing the state not just as a disabling apparatus (i.e., the embodiment of disabling social relations that injures its subjects) but also as a socioeconomic class, whose constituents are people. I explicitly say people to demystify the state, so as to interrogate its disabling mechanisms such as its judiciary system, intelligence gathering, terror, mass incarceration, and unaccountability, all of which are enacted by decision-making humans. I pay close attention to how authoritarian, imperialist, and theocratic states in the global south mobilize their biopower to control, rule over, and punish their populations using religious ideological justification. One way in which the state exerts control over people is by keeping them afraid for their lives, freedom, and health (i.e., fear of losing their status of not being in pain, not being tortured). Sluka (2000) argues that the problem of state terror is particularly relevant in the twentieth and twenty-first centuries, as a result of the state's diminished legitimacy in the face of extreme class hierarchy and social inequality. When the masses resist the elite's absolute power, and when the elite realize that the masses negate their power, the elite deploy force to maintain the asymmetrical power relation between them. One example is the state-sanctioned disablement of racialized and impoverished communities via resource deprivation (Gilmore, 2007). Through four studies with their own theoretical constructs, I engage with different forms of state violence in Iran under the Islamic Republic regime in order to understand how people become disabled in the hands of their own states through war, incarceration, torture, gender based violence, and punitive limb amputation.

Imperialism

While settler-colonialism has received increasing attention in DS,[1] imperialism, whether global (e.g., United States, China, and Russia) or regional (Iran and Turkey), has remained largely unexplored.[2] The dominant DS discourse demands that we engage with "post"-colonialism as a *past* that has passed, which highlights what Gorman (2018) calls "the past-to-present ideology of harm." This means that people are only expected to grieve past harms, and not their present miserable lives and conditions—if they are current, they are therefore not part of the colonial harms. We are asked to grieve but then stop and focus elsewhere, which means avoiding gazing at imperialism and assenting to the continuation of economic exploitation, maiming, genocide, and forced migration. To enable the world to grieve and resist this forgetting, this book exposes how imperialist relations (both global and regional) produce dead and disabled bodyminds in global contexts.

Colonialism implies the actual occupation and control of other nation-states. However, in modern times, direct occupation of land is not even necessary. Imperialism, or the indirect occupation and control of other nations, arises as a socially organized mechanism of control and conquest (Steinmetz, 2005; Konkle, 2008). "Imperialism [is] a non-territorial form of empire in contradistinction to colonialism as a territorial one" (Steinmetz, 2005, p. 2). Steinmetz (2005) iterates the difference between imperialism and colonialism as follows: "Modern non-territorial empire, also known as imperialism, has a much more sweeping agenda of controlling the world or a region for reasons that include economic ones alongside security, glory and order" (p. 8). Furthermore, David Harvey (2004) argues that Rosa Luxemburg and Vladimir Lenin presented their definitions of imperialism as a form of space production,[3] albeit with its own "terminal contradiction" (p. 62), as a solution for the crises inherent to capitalism. Lenin (1916) defines imperialism as "capitalism at that stage of development at which the dominance of monopolies and finance capital is established" (p. 265). On the other hand, Marx and Engels (1932/1998) write, "The class, which is the ruling material force of society, is at the same time its *ruling intellectual force* [my emphasis]. The class, which has the means of production at its disposal, consequently, also controls the means of mental production" (p. 26). Gorman (2005) reveals that the same social relations that determine our experience of becoming disabled organize *the way we think* about disability, which means that official DS discourse is also mediated by structures of power. In other words, our systems of thought about disability are determined by the structures that rule over our consciousness. Throughout this book, I discuss imperialism not only as a form of indirect occupation and economic control but also as a form of cultural and intellectual domination. The examples include cultural imperialism, academic imperialism, and feminist imperialism as dominating social relations that affect our bodyminds and disable us in profound ways.[4] I engage with imperialism not as an essential, rigid, fixed, and unchanging predisposition of a certain nation-state, like the United States. Rather, I demonstrate that imperialism is a social relation and behavior that any nation-state, like Iran, Iraq, and Turkey, or even institutions perceived as progressive like academia, can embody and perform.

Bodymind

In this book, I follow Margaret Price's (2015) conceptualization of "bodymind" as it pertains to the physical and mental disabilities discussed in each case study. My goal is to underline the fully integrated nature of the body and mind and the inseparability of the two in the harshest of circumstances such as torture, war, acid attack, and limb amputation. Additionally, following a Marxist tradition that has recently been disfavored in the humanities and social sciences, I place no ontological separation between the mental and physical entities, as well as no demarcation between mental and physical "labor," which is described as "sensuous human activity." Unlike Hardt and Negri's (2001) turn to Spinoza and basing their theory of human labor on bifurcations of mind and body, reason and passions, assertion and affectability, I consider the body's power to think as not autonomous from its power to act, feel, or produce. In other words, I propose a dialectical (inseparable, nonidentical) relationship between sensation and consciousness.

Rooted in Buddhist philosophy, pioneered by traumatologist Babette Rothschild (2000), and further developed by Margaret Price (2015), Eli Clare (2017), and Sami Schalk (2018), "bodymind" is an approach to cognize the relationship between the human body and mind as a single, integrated unit. Both the terminology and the notion of "bodymind" attempt to tackle the duality of body (and) mind and resist the traditions that ascribe their separability. The term "bodymind" is often encountered in mad studies and DS, referring to the intricate and often inseparable relationship between the body and the mind, and how these two units cannot be dissected. By "bodymind," Margaret Price (2015) means "a socio-politically constituted and material entity that emerges through both structural (power- and violence-laden) contexts and also individual (specific) experience" (p. 4). For Price, the body and mind are connected, and to use them as one word is to resist the dominant notion that emphasizes their distinction as two separate entities according to the Cartesian dualism.

However, Price warns against tokenization of the term as lip service, or just a rhetorical sentiment, as opposed to a meaningful theoretical engagement. Eli Clare (2017) uses "bodymind" in his work as a way to resist common assumptions that the body and mind are separate entities, or that the mind is "superior" to the body (p. xvi). Sami Schalk (2018) utilizes "bodymind" to recognize that "processes within our being impact one another in such a way that the notion of a physical versus mental process is difficult, if not impossible to clearly discern in most cases" (p. 269). Schalk emphasizes the utility of the term "bodymind" as it relates to disability and race. In analyzing histories of race, gender, and disability, Schalk notes that it is important to recognize the nonphysical impact of various oppressions. For Schalk, the term "bodymind" "is particularly useful in discussing the toll racism takes on people of color" (p. 5). In relation to transgenerational trauma in people of color, Schalk uses "bodymind" to demonstrate the intertwined nature of the psychological and physical toll of oppression and its resulting stress on both mental health and the physical body.

Global South

The conceptualization of the global south that I take up in this book is not restricted to national boundaries; instead, it refers to the regions in Asia, Africa, Latin America, and even parts of Eastern Europe whose economic and political structures have been distorted by the colonial and imperialist process carried out by global north countries (United States, Western Europe, Russia, and China), as well as to Black, Asian, Latinx, and Indigenous peoples in North America, Europe, and Australia. I also conceptualize the global south as places that may have never been colonized by the global north but are affected by their imperialist presence and neocolonialism, such as Iran. Iran was only occupied for just under a year by the Anglo-Soviet forces as part of the joint invasion of the neutral Imperial State of Iran by the United Kingdom and the Soviet Union in August 1941 (Ward, 2014). It should be noted that the "third world"/majority world/developing world/global south is not a homogeneous concept, for it comprises several states, several lands, several nations, or even stateless nations (e.g., Kurds, Palestinians), where people speak several different languages and practice several different cultures, customs, religions, and forms of resistance.

Wounding

Several DS scholars have tried to differentiate between a disability that one is born with, or a disability acquired by accident, and a disability imposed as a result of structural violence. Disability theorists such as Kelly Fritsch (2015) and Kateřina Kolářová (2015), who draw on the work of Jasbir Puar (2009), have suggested using the word "debility" rather than disability to refer to the ways in which disabled bodies are "targeted for death" or other forms of violence. On the other hand, Rachel Gorman (2016) frames this as a dialectic of disability—disablement wherein disability catalogs the mobilization of both state entitlements, through disability rights and benefits, as well as state violence, through imperialist wars or precarious immigration status. Additionally, Mary Jean Hande (2017), conceptualizes this phenomenon as "bodies and minds... *broken down* by poverty, never-ending war and work, state violence, highly exploited and 'disposable' labor, and poorly resourced and rapidly privatized public services" (p. 5, italics are mine). Judith Butler (2004) defines becoming injured as "[having] the chance to reflect upon injury, to find out the mechanisms of its retribution, to find out who else suffers from permeable borders, unexpected violence, dispossession, and fear, and in what ways" (p. xii). In this book, I instead use the term "wounded" to refer to disabled people who have become disabled as a result of violence. The wounded/injured people whose stories I tell never got a chance to do the list of things Butler (2004) suggests. They were mostly robbed of the opportunity (at least immediately) to even comprehend (in conventional ways) what happened to them. For me, every wound is a disability but not every disability is a wound.[5] By using "wound," I propose that a focus on "wounded bodymind" or "bodymind disabled by the violence of unequal power relations" may provide a way out of the closure of context and the collapsing of social relations that occurs in current formulations of disability identity in the global north. If disability is claimed as an identity in the global north, and DS is an approach to explore its meanings, then I argue for the necessity of conceptualizing "wound" at this juncture, in order to move beyond the erasure of disabled people in the global south.

"Wound" is an indicator of injury—a spectator and evidence that an injury has transpired. The word "wound," woven into every chapter's title in this book, indicates an injury, a deep scar created by deliberate violence of social relations and structures of power mediated by historical processes and modes of consciousness. What I intend to do in every chapter is defetishize disability via the historical materialist lens through the analytical category of the "wound"—the materialization of the flesh (Spillers, 1987) that resists fetishization. Wounds are not only knowingly caused but are also sustained by incessant violence, lack of support, indifference, and even (inadequate or harmful)[6] care. For instance, a war injury can be caused by the violence of militarism, and then sustained by scarce care and support from the state and society.

In this book, Chapter 1 is titled "Ripping the Wound: A Transnational Disability Theory and Praxis," where I unpack the problem of wounding and injuring by violence and offer a historical materialist conceptualization. Chapter 2, "Gaping Wounds: Disablement in the Iran-Iraq War," demonstrates the open mouth of the wounds in the veterans and civilians who continue to endure the injuries they sustained during the war and suffer from the acute negligence and abandonment they experienced from the state and society after they returned. Additionally, the title shows that the mouth of the wound is still open, that the affected populations received no acknowledgment whatsoever from the global community when they were hit by unconventional chemical weapons. Chapter 3 is titled "Rotten Wounds: Disability and Madness in Prison," to signal the forgotten state of Iranian political dissidents who metamorphosed into "mad" prisoners under brutal torture, while the local and global communities remained unconcerned. The title suggests that not only were the dissidents tortured and driven to madness but they were also forced to put up with an ableist and sanist world inside and outside prison. Chapter 4 is titled "Bleeding Wounds: Punitive Limb Amputation, Disability as Punishment for Poverty" to indicate the cruel nature of state-sanctioned amputation of people convicted of petty theft, whose empty and poor hands or fingers were sawed off. I call their wounds *bleeding*, as a metaphor for becoming empty of itself; a poor hand is an empty hand that has nothing to lose but its blood. The last case study in Chapter 5 deals with throwing acid on women's faces to disfigure, disable, and blind them. I call the chapter "Burning Wounds: Acid Attack, Disabling Gender-Based Violence," to emphasize the experience of acid burns as a lifelong journey of suffering, medicalization, "curative violence" (Kim, 2017), reconstructive surgeries, solitude, resilience, and survival. In the Conclusion, I discuss the meaning of what I call "active witnessing" as a transformative care practice embedded in transnational disability praxis.

Whose Disability (Studies)?

Moving away from the limitations of the social model[7] of disability, far more nuanced analyses of disability as it intersects with other social relations, such as class and immigration status, and other axes of oppression, such as race, gender, sexuality, and ethnicity, are now available. We now understand disability as being in a multifaceted relationship with structures of power, exploitation, governance, and supremacy. Disability activists and scholars have begun to refuse to understand the meanings of disability without first locating it in a complex matrix of other sociopolitical struggles, historical dis/continuities, and identities. Those leading this major shift are grassroots movements like *Sins Invalid* (2015), who dreamed of disability justice coming into being as a radical possibility along with many community writers, performers, poets, and activists.[8]

In the past decade, contributions have been made to DS[9] as it intersects with state violence, especially by queer, trans, Black, Indigenous, people of color (QT/BIPOC),[10] and transnational feminists.[11] Postcolonial DS scholars, such as Helen Meekosha (2011), Shaun Grech (2009, 2012, 2016), and Karen Soldatic (2014, 2016), have made significant contributions to the field, arguing for the globalization of DS as a field of knowledge that fights exclusion and oppression. Meekosha (2011) insightfully observes that the "universalizing and totalizing tendencies of disability studies scholars have pushed the experience of people from the global south to the periphery" (p. 667). Meekosha (2011) states, "Southern countries are, broadly, those historically conquered or controlled by modern imperial powers [Western Europe and North

America], leaving a continuing legacy of poverty, economic exploitation and dependence" (p. 669). To analyze disability in a global framework, Meekosha (2011) suggests one should take into account the power imbalance between the south and the north, and argues in favor of southern DS, which recognizes (neo)colonialism as a "disabling" process.

Southern DS scholars[12] investigate the relationship between disability, colonialism, and development, and attempt to address the unequal power relations between the Western world (Western Europe and North America) and the rest of the world; between the global south and the global north; between former colonies of Western Europe and Western Europe itself; between "third" world and "first" world. An important shortcoming of postcolonial DS is that it rarely engages with the modern-day forms of colonialism by Russia and China in Eastern Europe, Africa, Asia, and the Middle East. It usually only speaks of post- and neocolonialism as it pertains to the former colonies of Europe and not anywhere else.

Postcolonial disability theories[13] are not adequate in dealing with imperialist and nationalist violence. The global south, for many, encompasses only the former colonies of Europe, although there are countries in the Middle East region that are either post-empires interested in irridentism and revivalism of the past (like Turkey, the last remnant of the Ottoman Empire)[14] and/or have never been colonized by any European power (like Iran) (Kazemi, Gold, & Karah, 2024).[15] Ordinary people in these countries, namely Iran and Turkey, are constantly overpowered by two forces. One is the military and political presence of superpowers like the United States, China, and Russia, as well as their own states' regional-imperialist ventures. Turkish and Iranian states justify their imperialistic behavior in the Middle East region and beyond under the guise of defending the security of the nation-state from hostile forces (Kazemi et al., 2024). Middle Eastern people usually suffer at both ends, "resisting their own suppressive expansionist states on the one hand, and the U.S., Chinese, and Russian imperialism on the other. Therefore, applying a same-size-fits-all approach is not appropriate especially for a field like DS that is supposed to challenge normalization and normative conceptualization without paying attention to the context" (Kazemi et al., 2024, p. 5).

Since the start of the current century, postcolonial criticism has seen mounting concern for an emerging "post-postcolonial" turn or moment and the insufficiency of postcolonial critique for addressing new configurations of power in a globalizing era. Many works, such as Gayatri Chakravorty Spivak's *A Critique of Postcolonial Reason* (1999), Hardt and Negri's *Empire* (2001), and the *Cambridge History of Postcolonial Literature* (2012), have sought to reflect on postcolonial critique, concluding that it no longer has the efficacy to explain and critique the current reality of the world. Concurring with them, while staying committed to DS as a discipline that resists normalization of disciplinary lenses, I defy the universalizing tendency of postcolonial theory to perceive every global southern context as a former colony of Europe. Elected states (democratic or engineered) as well as populist, and even revolutionary, governments can and do commit extreme atrocities against their own citizens. Therefore, universalizing colonialism as the only type of state violence robs our chance to tell alternative stories in which Indigenous—and even elected—states commit violence against their people (Kazemi et al., 2024).

We need to discuss the shortcomings of the postcolonial critiques in DS and develop a nuanced analysis of "imperialism" as a *social relation* that many nation-states engage in, including those that have never been colonized by a European power (Kazemi et al., 2024). Imperialism is usually interpreted as only a U.S.-specific or Western characteristic, rather than an exploitative relation between any two countries or groups of people, like Russia-Ukraine, or China-Sri Lanka. One of my aims in this book is to problematize the narrow and limited definition of "imperialism" in the field.

Transnationalizing Disability

Significant attempts have been made by Meekosha (2011), Erevelles (2011), Gorman (2016), and Puar (2017) to widen the scope of this field and intervene in mainstream DS to disrupt its colonial and imperialist discourse, through their antiracist and feminist approaches. Building on their interventions, I move from reading popular DS accounts pertaining only to the United States, United Kingdom, Canada, and Australia to "Other" parts of the world. I (re)theorize disability by trying to unveil how representations of (the global northern) subjects in disability rights and culture movements have disallowed a focus on disablement caused by war, imperialism, theocracy, nationalism, PLA, GBV, and torture (Gorman, 2016; Kazemi & Karah, 2022).

Some DS scholars[16] have tried to widen the scope of the field to research disabilities that are created in the non-Western parts of the globe. For instance, Eunjung Kim (2011) recognizes that theorizing imperialism requires an exploration of its multiple meanings without diluting their political, ethical, and aesthetic significance. Kim discusses the imperialist domination of Korea by the Japanese, the United States, and the Soviets across different timeframes to problematize a narrow definition of the term "imperialism." From her transnational analysis, we learn that imperialism is not specific to one nation in a timeless and fixed status but a context-specific social relation. My own struggle with the theorization of Iranian imperialism in the Middle East region has taught me how hard it is to resist these dominant notions and discourses that the only version of imperialism is U.S. or "Americanized" like everything else.

Transnational disability analyses are only adequate if they include a comprehensive analysis of transnational social relations between the global north and global south, as well as power dynamics within each of them. This analysis includes studying how disability proliferated through violence; how the global north is implicated in producing disability in the global south (Meekosha & Soldatic, 2011; Puar, 2017); and how nationalist/ideological forces (such as nation-states) in the global south are also implicated in this violence. As argued by Erevelles (2011) and Gorman (2016), among others, what has been left unquestioned in the mainstream knowledge produced by DS are the historical and economic conditions that situate *becoming* disabled in a violent context of social and economic exploitation. Throughout this book, I seek to contribute to remedying this gap by proposing an approach to transnational disability rights that integrates local and global analyses of class, historicity, gender, ideology, nation-building, and racialization, while it critically intervenes into local, national, and transnational regimes.

My analysis in this book will add a new dimension to the works mentioned earlier, including Erevelles and Gorman's analyses, by demonstrating how *remaining disabled* is an additional layer of struggle that is often imposed upon the survivors after they become disabled, where there is a deliberate absence of civil society (e.g., NGOs) and lack of accessible healthcare and adequate support from the state. For example, as I demonstrate in Chapter 2, the war veterans' disabilities become exacerbated due to chronic negligence by the state, in addition to the lack of access to housing, employment, and healthcare. I also contribute to their analyses by proposing new ways in which we can develop transnational disability solidarity and praxis (Kazemi & Karah, 2023) that go beyond our local settings and comfort zones and cultivate new spaces of multilingualism (Kazemi & Karah, 2021c) and multiculturalism within disability activism and advocacy.

Although in a seemingly contradictory manner, two recent books, Eunjung Kim's *Curative Violence* and Jasbir K. Puar's *The Right to Maim*, represent the possibilities of DS to be in conversation with other disciplines such as transnational studies. I say contradictory because Kim problematizes the "cure" discourse as it tries to eliminate disability, chronic illness, diversity, and nonnormative sexual expression, or lack thereof, while Puar problematizes the production of disability by colonial violence. This tension is not new and has existed from the beginning in the field. This dialectical tension should not and cannot be resolved. In my own conceptualization of "madness" in political prisons in Chapter 3, I resist any theorization of madness that would come across as sanist. Nevertheless, I avoid glorifying and romanticizing the bodymind's response to torture whose main goal is to destroy human dignity (Bernstein, 2015). I suggest that we welcome these tensions, work through them, and take advantage of their existence as opportunities for developing a more nuanced understanding of disability. To further contribute to the nuances of this complex dialectic of cure-pride or the "elimination" versus "production" of disability in Chapters 2, 4, and 5, I discuss the curative politics in the context of war, legal limb amputation, and acid attacks. In all the chapters, I strive to bring nuance to the dialectic of cure-pride or prevention versus production of disability by transnationalizing my case studies, thinking through poverty, religion, gender, and war, while resisting easy conceptualization of disability that further fetishizes it.

Chapter Overview

In Chapter 1, I introduce a new model for DS that I term "Transnational Disability Model (TDM)," based on DHM. I do so, in general, to shift our current analysis of disability/wound/trauma/madness and, in particular, to grasp the reality of violence (e.g., war, incarceration, acid attack) and its resultant wounds in the global south. Developing my disability model in this chapter, I pave the way for a revolutionary understanding of disability and its relationship with the nation-state, contextualized within transnational class consciousness and activism and, more generally, capitalism. I call this revolutionary because unlike poststructuralist theories that "intentionally mystify the violent relations of disablement, white supremacy, and hyperexploitation of labor, which glosses/obscures the class antagonisms that structure disability," DHM makes a revolutionary organization of disability appear possible, necessary, and not merely utopian (Gorman, 2016; Hande, 2017, p. 7). Additionally, I discuss the ways in which we can organize ourselves against violence; develop solidarity for each other's struggles, as political actors and agents; and resist becoming ahistorical cultural egos, disjointed from others, drifting in a social vacuum.

In Chapter 2, I present a case study of "gaping wounds," the disablement among the Iranian survivors of the Iran-Iraq War. The word "disablement," as used here, covers two states: the acquisition of disability due to the violence of war and living with that disability under conditions of little to no care. This chapter depicts an important case of disablement in the global south and invites the reader to witness the two important processes of "acquiring" and "living with" a disability under deficient care in a class-based society, ruled by a theocratic state. I discuss how the ideological category of "living martyr," manufactured by the state, has hindered the way for disabled veterans to seek and receive support (e.g., medical intervention, accommodation, housing) and has fetishized their disabilities by concealing the structural violence they face as neglected citizens. Additionally, the social and structural pressure to take on and perform the identity of a "living martyr" (Kazemi, 2024a) has only contributed to their further disablement, mental health crises, suicide attempts, and even death. Furthermore, to impose a sense of competition for resources among disabled veterans and to prevent any possibility of solidarity between them, the state uses a dysfunctional "percentage" allocation system that determines the extent of benefits disabled veterans receive based on the severity of their disability. I call this system "soma-technologies of disability measurement" and explain its harmful implication for the veterans' lives.

In Chapter 3, I discuss the theocratic state's entitlement to disabling dissidents and torturing them into believing in the legitimacy of the state as a form of biosovereignty (Bargu, 2016). I demonstrate how disabling processes such as *Tavvabism*, *Muslimization*, or *Saming* are all processes of exercising biosovereignty intended to turn political dissidents into empty living beings. Furthermore, Agamben (2002), following Primo Levi (1959), argues that the complete witness of Auschwitz is not the survivor who writes but rather the Muselmann who has virtually lost the capacity to speak. Drawing on Agamben's conceptualization of the complete witness in Chapter 3, I discuss the disabling conditions under which Iranian political prisoners were forced to live, "repent," lose their political selves, and become "surviving egos" (Sakhi, 2014) and, in some cases, humans with autonomy and agency. I discuss how the political prisoners were incarcerated, tortured, and put under extreme psychological pressure to either repent or recant in public. Drawing on Levi's conceptualization of Muselmann as the "true" witness of Auschwitz, I explore whether the "true" witnesses of those prisons are the "mad" prisoners who have lost the capacity to speak. I investigated the processes and relations involved in how some prisoners went "mad" and some remained "sane."

In Chapter 4, I examine PLA in Islamic sharia law and its relationship to economic inequality and poverty. I analyze the case of PLA using the TDM, while asking theoretical and philosophical questions in regard to "disability as punishment." Why is amputating people's limbs a punishment for theft? Is disability *the* worst punishment? And why? Additionally, I discuss how poverty leads to disability and then disability leads to poverty, homelessness, stigmatization, and eventual death. I also ask how the theocratic state is implicated in disabling the poor. In this chapter, I engage with the political economy of PLA under theocratic-kleptocracy, leading to disability, as a form of corporal punishment for poverty and a fetish to conceal the existing inequalities. I also discuss the theocratic state's entitlement to disabling the poor as biosovereignty whereby the state officials who steal with impunity (wealthy thieves) disable the poor (convicted of petty theft) under the guise of spiritual cleansing of the society. Through this torturous process, disability is imposed and produced on the body of a poor person who is already disenfranchised and marginalized by the theocratic state that "cures" crime by producing disability.

In Chapter 5, I discuss the case of acid attacks in Iran. Going over a survivor's testimony collected in several interviews and analyzing her stories using the TDM, I conceptualize "burning wounds" that are caused by GBV by shedding light on the processes and social relations behind the survivors' "disfigurement" after acid was purchased, handled, and thrown on their faces. I strive to understand how and when (if) the survivors developed a new feminist and/or disability consciousness in the face of the violence that they endured by examining how they *became* and *remained* disabled under inadequate support from the society and from the state. In this chapter, I engage in the defetishization process by highlighting and theorizing the role that the Islamic Republic of Iran plays in disabling women and then masking and justifying their disability by upholding sharia law, protecting perpetrators, and enforcing patriarchal laws to further marginalize the victims. In this chapter, I also discuss the dilemma of thinking about cure and disability consciousness by seeking transnational solidarity and support while simultaneously working toward the elimination of ableism (Kazemi & Karah, 2021a, 2023).

Each chapter engages with the dialectic of disability and care and contributes to transnational cases of disability justice including collective care, access intimacy (Mingus, 2011), and interdependence (Mingus, 2010). Equally, to transnationalize our understanding of disability, the discussion on infrastructures of care in each chapter contributes to disability justice (Berne et al., 2018) framed in transnational thought, care, and activism by offering new conceptual tools including the living martyr, biosovereignty as disablement, and soma-technologies of disability measurement.

Although all these case studies are contextualized within Iran, disability and state violence connect with other regions and states. This is to say that while I draw on Iran as a Muslim-majority Middle Eastern country, the theoretical analyses in this book can be applied to many other cases of disability and violence in the world. After all, war, incarceration, GBV, PLA, and disabling state violence are relevant to many contexts, while the theory and willingness to analyze them from disability studies' perspective is rare or even absent. Furthermore, many global cases of disability caused by violence, including environmental destruction, toxic chemicals, female genital mutilation, police brutality, and unsafe working conditions, can also be explained using the conceptual tools I develop in this book.

In the Conclusion, I discuss what it means to engage in "healing wounds" and to be an active witness, not as an identity, but as a process of engaging in witnessing as praxis with a revolutionary potential. I explain my ethical and political commitment to this project both as a researcher and as a witness. In doing so, I ask what it means to be a "present" witness; what it means to develop political consciousness in relation to witnessing; and finally, what transnational disability praxis is if we were to consider active witnessing as a constituent of the infrastructures of collective care.

The Necessity of "Double-Critique"

> White men may be trying to save brown women from brown men, but brown men may indeed oppress brown women, and brown women (elite and otherwise) may also collude in sustaining structures of misogyny. (One may try, among other variants, Muslim and non-Muslim in this sentence.) As these lines suggest, another way to approach the question of coercion is to strain, and always to register the costs of that straining, in a colonized world, against coercion within the culture colonized without exempting colonial culture or imperial institutions. The precarious, precious enterprise of double-critique means, then, that feminist concern ... cannot be postponed. (Sadia Abbas, 2013, p. 189)

Magic circles are a somewhat close-knit community of seemingly likeminded people and something all of us end up connecting to (Kazemi & Karah, forthcoming). In many ways, stories that do the rounds in such communities shape our desires, aspirations, and even a propensity for ideological persuasion. Karah (2019) calls such an ever-present, and yet transient, narrative a "magic circle." The circle feels magical as it can bring familiarity and comfort, no matter what the external contingencies are. The academic world, particularly the modern humanities and social science establishment, relies on such magic circles to draw boundaries between ideological positions.

Poststructuralist DS theorists have drawn on the theories of Foucault and Butler to confront essentialist understandings of the human, binary thinking, and dualism, and to deconstruct "able-bodied"/"impaired" distinctions. Karah and I have argued that compartmentalizing knowledge is an imperialist enterprise and that it prevents disciplines from speaking to one another. Belonging or being alienated to schools of thought, communities, and disciplines is a matter of becoming a fortress of moral rectitude (Kazemi & Karah, forthcoming).

For example, as a feminist scholar in the North American academy, I constantly struggle to have my experiential- and embodied-knowledge recognized. This struggle for being heard, and to not be erased, is embedded in the fact that I am an immigrant, racialized, and mad/disabled woman who was born and raised in the Middle East. My encounter with feminism, as a movement, and not as an academic discipline, happened long before I immigrated to North America. I was born in Iran, an enormously complex society run by a theocratic state, which has gone through many upheavals, such as the Constitutional Revolution,[17] the 1953 coup, the 1963 White Revolution, the 1979 Islamic Revolution, an eight-year-long war with Iraq, and several (brutally suppressed) oppositional movements to the present conditions. I find it increasingly difficult to diffuse my vote into the knowledge spectrum. This is partially due to the colonized and imperialist notions of womanhood, gender, and sexuality that are widely held by the Western academy assuming that "they" know what "we" think. This is what Alatas (2003) calls "academic neo-imperialism" or "academic neocolonialism," and what has dire consequences for non-Western social movements.

For immigrants and exiles in the West, who know their homeland better than the residents of their host land, this poses a challenge. For instance, since the start of the protests against the mandatory hijab in 2017 in Iran, many Iranian women, in both the diaspora and the country, have tried to side with the protesters, even virtually, hoping they could invoke solidarity and alliance from the members of their host societies, such as North America and Western Europe. To my surprise, a minuscule number who support Iranian women's feminist struggle against the mandatory hijab have sided with us, especially before Mahsa Zhina Amini's protests in 2022. In 2019, I wrote a letter to the National Women Studies Association (NWSA) in the United States demanding a solidarity statement for the Iranian women receiving decade-long prison sentences for "bad veiling."[18] NWSA promised a response to my letter, but they never followed through. Can we say that academe's strategic silence was partially responsible for Mahsa's death? This is one out of many moments where Sadia Abbas's (2013) words that begin this section become urgently imperative. We rightfully critique white men pretending or wanting to "rescue" brown women from brown men, but we refuse to care about brown women being actively oppressed by brown men. Once the white man is not in the picture, we abandon the brown women, if not actively collude with brown men to maintain the structures of misogyny by justifying the status quo under the veil of "cultural relativism," "resisting Orientalism," and above all "silence."

Why do progressive people, in this case feminists, hesitate to express solidarity for women living under gender and sexual apartheid regimes? I have two hypotheses as to why women, especially Western leftist, critical, or progressive women, have mostly remained silent. One reason could be the fear of generating or further perpetuating Muslim-phobia in the West. I deliberately refrain from using the word "Islamophobia" because Islam is not a race or ethnicity but a set of ideas. Fearing people is problematic, but critiquing ideas is necessary for a progressive human society. I use the word "Muslim-phobia" to problematize hating and discriminating against people, and to simultaneously protect the right to freedom of expression and critiquing ideas. Furthermore, in the current political landscape, many think it is politically incorrect to defend women's right to resist sharia law in a Muslim-majority country. Does the phrase "Muslim majority" mean that (the majority of) people actually practice Islam in those contexts, such as in Iran? Even if that is the case and some people practice their religion, does this mean that the state can prosecute women who do not want to observe this misogynist law? One could say, perhaps, secular and non-Muslim Middle Eastern women cannot even exist in the (both liberal and critical/leftist) Western imagination (read colonized notion). Why can leftist, Marxist, atheist, non-Muslim or even secular-Muslim women not exist in the Western imagination of Middle Eastern women? Why are Kurdish guerrilla fighters in military uniforms holding AK-47s, who fought and defeated ISIS, never portrayed as Middle Eastern women, and why are women in hijabs portrayed as such?

Moreover, poignantly, some on the left, with their anti-U.S.-imperialism politics, naively assume that the enemy of their enemy is their friend, meaning anyone and any community who opposes the same enemy is their ally. Therefore, since the Islamists (especially Shia governments like Iran) appear to be anti-imperialists (read anti-U.S. hegemony but also pro-Islamic hegemony), then they must be aligned with their political agenda. In the process, they presume closeness with sometimes the most reactionary and fundamentalist forces—overlooking the pain and suffering they have caused in their own communities wherever they have gained footing (Moghissi, 1999). This makes it almost impossible for exiled women like me to individually flourish. We can neither garnish solidarity for women's movements in our native land, nor get legitimacy in the land of exile, where we never find an ecosystem to talk about new forms of imperialism(s) as a power relation that is not merely America-centric. That imperialism is not specific to one nation in a timeless and fixed status but a context-specific social relation.

Zeynep Korkman (2023) and Ladan Zarabadi (2023) have also talked about a similar problem they have encountered when attempting to translate the oppressive pro-Islamist policies of Recep Tayyip Erdoğan in Turkey and the oppression of women under the gender apartheid in Iran for the skeptical audience in North America, only familiar with these contexts in the frame of Islamophobia. They have noted and warned against what they call the "mistranslation" of feminist struggles in transnational contexts into the critical Western feminist and often U.S.-centric realms. Korkman (2023) has talked about how the Islamic authoritarian states, particularly the Justice and Development Party or AKP in Turkey, have weaponized the progressive politics in North America, which problematize anti-Muslim and anti-Black racism, by presenting themselves as "racialized" and "oppressed" entities, marginalized by the Western imperialism and white supremacy, while they have gotten away with violence against women, queer people, and minorities like the Kurds in Turkey. Zarabadi (2023) has, on the other hand, critiqued the mainstream media representation of the "Woman, Life, Freedom" movement, observing that many within the North American academic and progressive circles have naively assumed that the real reasons behind the "Woman, Life, Freedom" uprising were the U.S.-imposed economic sanctions, skyrocketed prices of gas and groceries, and inflation, while the real reason was actually a feminist struggle for gender equality battling the inherently misogynist Islamic theocracy. In short, both Korkman and Zarabadi warn against the instrumentalization and co-optation of anti-imperialist politics in North America by authoritarian or theocratic states like Turkey and Iran to appear "oppressed" and victimized by U.S. imperialism, while subjugating their own populations, expanding their military presence in the Middle East and North Africa, and forging superficial alliances with progressive forces in North America who may not be familiar with those contexts. One example of this is how many Islamic fundamentalist groups showed support for the Bernie Sanders's presidential campaign while the only thing they had in common was their critique of the U.S. empire.

Furthermore, women's recent uprising in Iran came as a surprise to many in the world. A good many academics from the West expressed their surprise on social media on seeing Muslim-majority women from Muslim-majority[19] countries burning the hijab. Unlike other groups who are rarely identified by the religion believed by the majority in their specific contexts, "Muslim women" are categorized by their religion. In the Western world, we do not call Western women "Christian women," although the religion that the majority in the West believe is Christianity. Why is it that non-Western women's identities are interpreted as "fixed and rigid" and frozen in time and space, unlike Westerners whose identities are understood as fluid, temporal, dynamic, and everchanging?

Why is it that progressive Western women rarely show solidarity for Iranian women's struggle against Islamic fundamentalism and for equality, freedom, justice, and rights? Why do feminists not speak up against the atrocities that Afghan, Syrian, or Iranian women are forced to experience? I wonder what it is about their struggle that does not attract Western progressive/ leftist women's attention. Or if it does, what prevents them from declaring solidarity?

In 2001, the George W. Bush administration, to justify the early phases of the war on terror, tried to convince the world it was on a "feminist mission" to rescue Afghan women. This pity for Middle Eastern women, and fear of the Middle Eastern men, has become a common trope in the right-leaning Western literature and culture, especially after September 11, 2001. Perhaps many think that if they declare support for women yearning for freedom from patriarchal and misogynist rule and condemn the Islamic states that imposes that rule, they would be promoting Muslim-phobia, or that their solidarity message would be co-opted into the "saving" or "rescuing" rhetoric that warmongers like the Bush administration used to justify the invasion of Afghanistan.

Can we move outside pity/fear tropes, which are usually the spinning wheels of the liberal ideology encountering the "Orient"? According to right-leaning conservatives, Middle Eastern women are inherently oppressed and content with their oppression, as patriarchy and misogyny are integral to their "culture." On the other hand, "apologists explain that those whom the Western media calls terrorists are simply those who oppose Western racism; the left explains that the regimes, which denounced the United States, are the regimes that stand against imperialism" (Gorman, 2018). Therefore, women like me, who are secular (Muslims), do not exist, and indeed cannot exist, in the conceptual universe of the Western left, and therefore it is impossible for the Western left to grasp the contradictions that women like me face. The anti-imperialist wars and patriarchal nationalisms that characterize my reality, as a victim of both kinds of state terror, are invisible.

In progressive circles, we hear Israel being characterized as a racial apartheid state (like South Africa) and criticized widely but not Iran. Is this because Israel is an American ally and Iran an American enemy? Do we adjust our anti-imperialist politics by recentering America as our moral compass? We rightfully critique American friends, like Saudi Arabi and Israel, but stay silent when it comes to Iran and Syria. If we are decentering the Western hegemony, we shouldn't recenter it with binary assumptions like the "enemy of my enemy is my friend." In fact, this is what the Iranian state does: bifurcation of everything into Western and "original" or "Indigenous."

Iran engages in imperial expansion and *competes* with the West, although some frame it as a country "resisting" the Western hegemony. DHM teaches us that imperialism is a relation and not a predisposition specific to the West. Iran can also be and is an imperialist power. Just because Iran is not considered an ally to the American and European imperialist powers, some feminists assume that somehow there is an imperial expansion of Iran in the region without actual imperialism. This becomes oppressive to women like me who have resisted global imperialism as well as the Iranian state's terror both in forms of regional imperialism and theocratic nationalism.

It is time to acknowledge that we live in an era where there is an increasing pressure to reduce our analyses to postclass and postgender approaches. Lacking a proper class analysis, we run the risk of being reduced to being categorized as just "ideas"/"ideologies" such as our religious beliefs (Mojab, 2001). This can lead to the only legitimate way of differentiating identities through religion. For example, just because I was born in the Middle East, I am considered a Muslim woman, no matter what I believe in, or what my politics are. This reduction of every woman who lives in a Muslim-majority country or region is another form of feminist imperialism or imperialist feminism. This assumption that since you're born into a Muslim family then you must not be resisting or fighting the existing Islamic state and sharia law in that place is a colonization of people's identities. Not to mention how many religious minorities, such as the Yazidis, live in the Middle East and experience horrific methods of discrimination by Islamists, the most recent one being the genocide and sexual slavery at the hands of ISIS in 2014 (Brincka, 2022).

My goal here is not to deny Muslim-phobia or racialization of Muslims, or undermine Western feminists' solidarity with their Muslim sisters in the West who experience harassment, racism, and discrimination because of their faith, their hijab, or the color of their skin. In fact, I acknowledge that we live in an era where anti-immigrant rhetoric has become a public discourse with serious implications for immigrants and asylum seekers who risk their lives just to escape the horrors of war, famine, and political prosecution. In the wake of the 9/11 attacks, Muslim-phobia has mobilized the "white affects" (Gorman, 2018) to rise for reaffirmation of their supremacy by constructing Islam and Muslims as the de facto enemies of the Western states and nations. On the other hand, though, we rarely question Islamic ideology, Islamic countries, and the problems their citizens face under sharia, in which there is no Muslim-phobia; instead, there is the Islamic state terror, discriminatory Islamic laws, punitive measures (*Hodoud*, such as corporal punishment), stoning of women accused of adultery, gendered violence (which often goes unpunished), discrimination against the followers of other religions, and so on. Why are these problems rarely discussed? Are we afraid of being accused of Muslim-phobia or Orientalism? Muslim-phobia is not a problem in the Middle East where Muslims constitute the majority. Rather, it is a form of discrimination practiced in places where Muslims are among the minority groups, such as in the West. Therefore, portraying Muslim-phobia as a universal phenomenon is to recenter the West as the only place that needs to get rid of prejudice and violence. Nevertheless, we should note that the racialization of Muslimness or Islamic practices like veiling and assuming its association with backwardness is neither specific to the Western context nor specific to the post-9/11 era. Even in the 1960s to mid-1970s, the veil was assumed by many progressive women as a sign of backwardness in Iran. On the other hand, oppressive measures have been regularly used against the Muslim population in non-Western contexts such as Myanmar, China, India, etc.

The alienation and Othering of Muslims and women with the veil, for instance, should be critiqued without hindering our way to critique the veil; the meanings attached to it in any given time and space; its instrumentalization by the state to ensure women's second-class citizenship, like in Iran and Afghanistan; and its weaponization against the women who wear it. We should be able to critique the veil in any context without the fear of being called an Islamophobe or a racist. We should go past the binary of Islamophilia and Islamophobia by being able to critique the oppressive Islamic practices as well as any interpretation of Islam that is oppressive. If we criticize the gender wage gap in the West, no one would accuse us of enticing Christianity-phobia or Western-phobia. Instead, they might even praise us for tackling a gender equality issue. So why is it that questioning anything sexist or oppressive in non-Western contexts is received with hesitation or as an attack on Islam, Muslims, or the culture? Homophobia and sexism are not anybody's culture but rather oppressive attitudes and practices that should be named as such and questioned.

To question the Islamic state terror is to decolonize our epistemologies around what social justice means in every society. If we shut down any conversation around questioning the Islamic ideology's horrific consequences for people who are forced to live under the Islamic law, then we fail abysmally to properly scrutinize what constitutes injustice in Islamic societies of the global south. To resist disabling relations, including Islamic imperialism, embedded in any state ideology, and to follow DHM, I will not refrain from criticizing Islam both as an ideology and class (read, a way of governing the state at all levels). Carrying out this project, my greater goal and humble intention is to work toward building a world free of poverty, prisons, gender inequality, corporeal punishment, and ableism. In other words, this book is a contribution to the abolition of prison, torture, gender inequality, and any law that permits and demands punishment for the poor, be it sharia or any other law.

1

Ripping the Wound

A Transnational Disability Theory and Praxis

In this chapter, I develop a theory, which I term the transnational disability model[1] (TDM), predicated on the foundation of the Dialectical and Historical Materialism (DHM), geopolitics, and a Disability Studies (DS) lens. By DS lens, I mean paying close attention to how social relations produce disability or how social/economic relations mediate mechanisms of disability production, such as war, gender-based violence (GBV), torture, etc. The theoretical constructs that I engage in building the TDM are: dialectical historicity (preexisting conditions leading to unavoidable results/forms), class, nation-state, violence of capital (or capitalist relations) along with other violent social relations (such as imperialism, nationalism, patriarchy), and ideology. The Marxist theoretical framework of DHM sheds light on the ways in which the world actually operates. I discuss the importance of organizing ourselves against violence, as political actors, and resist becoming, what Bannerji calls (2000, p. 42), "cultural sel[ves], floating non-relationally in a socio-historical vacuum." In this chapter, I talk about how this newly formulated theoretical perspective can become a transnational form of collective political consciousness, as a revolutionary response, stemming from lived experiences of violence. This chapter guides us toward answering one of the questions this book seeks to answer: How can we read disability transnationally using DHM by engaging the dialectics of local and global politics?

Dialectical and Historical Materialism

In this book, I refuse to disarticulate culture from hegemony, to reduce all political issues into cultural ones, or to convert culture into a private matter. Marx argued that history is not just a combination of events that form the past. Instead, ideas have social origins and could be manipulated for political purposes. In *The German Ideology* (Marx & Engels, 1932/1998), the foundational conception of DHM was conceived of as a method of social inquiry and of recording history. Marx defined historical materialism as a way to understand the material conditions of humans through history. By understanding the material conditions of humans through history, Marx argued, human beings can come to understand their current social and political conditions. He criticized Hegel for "mystifying" social relations. For instance, Hegel gave an independent existence to the "state," while Marx argued that the state is just made up of people (Tucker, 1978). He developed DHM as a way to demystify human relations and understand history as a result of the "sensuous activity of [hu]man[s]" (Marx & Engels, 1932/1998, p. 25). Marx argued that capitalism reduced all human/social relations to material relations of commodity production and exchange, despite any appearance that such relations might be intimate or personal.

Marx perceived the distinction between "a sense of self or being, and the world that being inhabits" as wrong. He disagreed with both idealists and materialists, even though they each insisted that they respectively constituted independent separate approaches. On the one hand, idealists had mastered the "theorization of cultural self, of the sense and imaginative cultural beings" (Bannerji, 1995, p. 18). On the other hand, the materialists theorized the world as constitutive of "organizations or structures." Marx's project was a combination of the two stances. For Marx, "the project consists of an interjective and constitutive theorizing of the two moments—of the self or consciousness as being in the world, and of the world as history and structures made by the self with forms of consciousness" (Bannerji, 1995, p. 19). In other words, Marx argued that humans (as material and cultural selves) make history and structures of their world with forms of consciousness extended from the past. Here, the use of the word, "interjective," refers to the unity of the self and consciousness, meaning they affect, adopt, and constitute each other as two components in one relationship. As such, Marx's understanding of self and consciousness did not involve a "dichotomy between the two." Instead, he theorized them as a unity—constituted by two components that are inseparable from each other.

Marx (1845/1976), as he argued in the *Theses on Feuerbach*, believed that knowledge is not separate/separable from the physical body, and therefore not separate/separable from the material world. As he himself said, Marx was out to change the world, not just interpret it. In formulating the approach of DHM, he developed a new knowledge adequate for creating change "with a centrally-situated agent or subject, without whom no transformative politics would be possible" (Bannerji, 1995, p. 19). From the standpoint of Marxist disability theory, the task is to use DHM to present a dialectical and reflexive understanding of disability, difference, subjectivity, and agency. The key in understanding DHM, and using it, is to understand how it relates to history, ideology, and social structures, such as class and capital.

Materialisms and the Wound

Materialist analyses are not new to DS. Several British disability scholars, who are also among the founders of the social model of disability, have utilized this framework extensively (Barnes, Mercer, & Shakespeare, 1999; Morris, 1991; Oliver, 1990; Thomas, 1999). Among the most popular recent theorizations of disability are the new materialist approaches, which include relationality, affective economy, and intercorporeality theories to understand new assemblages/bodies/subjectivities.[2] Challenging the autonomous, independent, and rational subject that the humanist tradition is founded upon, posthumanist and postconventionist theorists such as Deleuze and Guattari (1987) have suggested replacing static being with active becoming, clear-cut categorized subjects with assemblages, and independence with interdependence. For Deleuze and Guattari, identity and subjectivity are partial and transitory, leaking linkages between bodies, as opposed to private possessions of each body. By transgressing anthropocentrism and the autonomous individual, posthumanists argue for interconnectedness of species including humans and problematize the hierarchical order among species and within humans with a non-disabled, "rational," and independent human at the top. Some DS scholars have found posthumanist ideas useful to contemplate a different world for disabled people in which their presence is celebrated in reciprocal relationships, care assemblages, and interdependent networks, and not frowned upon, followed by marginalization and erasure. One way in which posthumanist theories have been co-opted into DS is in the field of disability and care relations (Fritsch, 2010; O'Brien, 2005; Shildrick, 2009), disability prosthesis as extension of the body (Gibson, 2006), theorization of embodiment by Michael Feely (2016), Karen Barad's agential realism (2007), and Robert McRuer's (2006) Crip Theory, among others.

If we consider my work with acid attack women survivors in Chapter 5, a posthumanist would suggest that these women have become injured and wounded by a chemical substance that has transformed them into a disfigured "Body-Without-Organ," a living organism without subjectivity. A disfigured, burned, and often blind survivor of an acid attack might be seen as an assemblage that is neither flesh nor acid but a wound. Furthermore, over the course of my transnational activism, along with the survivors and other women from across the world, we have come together to fundraise for one survivor's eye surgery who has lost both eyes to an acid attack by her ex-father-in-law. A posthumanist theorist might suggest that not only the survivor is an assemblage, but other women in this transnational activist network, who support her, are also assemblages in an interdependent and intercorporeal relationship with her.

While I find this exciting. I fear that the celebrated interdependence does not happen outside global, local, or even interpersonal power relations. What if other women suddenly withdrew from her fundraising campaign? If so, she would be left with a state that provides nothing for her and a society that will forever treat her with pity at best, and disgust, at worst. Her relationship with the world that surrounds her under a theocratic and misogynist state that considers her half-human limits her subjectivity to a victim. Therefore, the material conditions under which she must live are mediated by power relations no matter how radical she and her allies are or how resiliently she strives to survive. Besides, the interdependence celebrated by the new materialists is usually predicated on taken-for-granted contexts including Western countries where most people live above the poverty line and have access to a minimum of services, such as clean water, relative safety, and due process. People in Western countries rarely fear for their safety when talking about their lack of access to services or protesting injustice. Their chance of landing up in prison for voicing their concerns is low. Neither do they usually need a visa to travel to other countries, meaning they mostly have the privilege of global mobility, denied to many in non-Western contexts.

The Iranian woman survivor of the acid attack for whom we are fundraising was prevented from accessing her bank account when the security forces found out that she had recorded a short video about her life and sent it to a journalist outside Iran. Also, when she found out about the only surgeon in the world who could perform the needed surgery on her blind eye, her visa application to the U.K., where the surgeon is based, was denied twice. Therefore, what we mean by interdependence could lose its presumed effectiveness when we are talking about the global south where local and global blocks of power hinder your freedom, mobility, and access.

New materialisms toggle between idealism (a conception of reality not grounded in the concrete) and mechanical materialism (identifying an aspect of the concrete but not grasping its relations with other aspects of the concrete, and/or not grasping how these unfold and change over time). Plateaus and assemblages are moving but inaccessible and intangible for many whose lives these theories are supposed to change. Marx taught us that philosophers have interpreted the world; our job is to change it. It seems what Deleuze and Guattari do is frame and interpret reality from multiple, yet bourgeois angles. The question is whether we can situate these "becomings" outside transnational power relations such as global class relations (i.e., realpolitik[3] and imperialisms). Or do these complex high theories only apply to the global north and not "those who continue to inhabit the uninhabitable [and] are so perversely outside the Western bourgeois conception of what it means to be human that their geographies are rendered—or come to be—inhuman, dead, and dying" (McKittrick, 2013, p. 7)?

Throughout Chapter 5, I was cautious about celebrating the acid attack survivors' "becoming" and my work with them. Instead, I paid attention to how they were rendered disabled by the society that nurtures a perpetrator, who thinks that disabling someone is the worst punishment for them. It's at this moment that her disability should not be treated like an always-already existent condition but a violent wounding (as becoming) that occurs in an inhumane encounter between a patriarchal and misogynist social and a woman's bodymind. By "social," I mean not just the person who throws the acid but an amalgamation of the religious state, patriarchal culture, and misogynist and ableist social norms that enables him to do so with impunity if not admiration.

Becoming wounded is not a positive event—sometimes it is a disaster, according to the survivors who frame it as "dying every day and re-inventing ourselves to stay alive" (personal communication with an acid attack survivor, 2019). This becoming cannot be celebrated and treated as pride. This is disabling material violence mediated by material social relations. The critical significance I place on historical materialist conditions and unequal power dialectics is necessary to foreground the social relations/encounters between bodies/subjects/organisms that occur in the fluid and the always incomplete process of becoming-in-the-world. In the case of violent encounters that I discuss in this book, bodies/subjects/organisms encounter one another, often in violent collision. Correspondingly, as Erevelles (2011) has taught us, some dismemberments into the Body-without-Organs are not just discursive but instead inform a brutal materiality that coheres with the hierarchical binary of Self/Other. To this binary I add the interrogator/prisoner and perpetrator/victim, disjointed and yet at the same time tied via the local and transnational social relations.

A Dialectical and Historical Materialist Lens

Conscious of the danger of invoking an ableist aesthetic, I join other Marxist feminist DS scholars such as Erevelles (2011), Hande (2017), and Gorman (2016) in arguing that new materialist theorizations are exciting, however, we need to also angle the analytical frame purposefully toward considering the ideological, political, economic, and historical contexts that allow and want people to "become" disabled. Hande observes that "Of particular importance for identity politics and oppression around... disability is that red [DHM] theory which 'demonstrates that the fragmentation of the social is an effect of the alienation of labor (Marx 1975)' and 'unequal exchange of wages for labor power' (355) rather than an ahistorical mode of identity and 'cultural difference'" (cited in Hande, 2017, p. 24). To contribute to DHM approaches that are not particularly popular in disability studies, I utilize Marxist feminist methodology to explore and understand the concrete material reality that disabled people face in the global south on a daily basis. I argue throughout the book that a new DS perspective should be deployed that not only engages with disability but also takes into account its intersections with race, gender, ethnicity, class, history, and geographical location within the material context of post/neo-colonial, imperialist, and theocratic states. Such a perspective is radical and anti-ableist, because it is neither compliant to normative demands/standards,[4] nor is it complicit in the bourgeois democratic agenda. This is what I mean by "transnational": Engaging the local and global politics that render racialized/gendered/colonized/Othered bodies disabled by pure power imbalance and violence. I provide a comprehensive DHM analysis of all the case studies, organized in two parts: "processes" and "relations."

Unlike poststructuralists and postmodernists, for whom "experience" and "identity" are the ultimate destination around which they mobilize, I use the experiences of disabled survivors of violence throughout this project only as an entry point. I use the survivors' marginalized experiences as a point of departure, as opposed to a point of arrival, in order to understand the ruling relations that have organized those experiences in the first place. My intention here is to go beyond identity politics with the right and space to claim an identity to a more concrete theorization of a power structure that regulates our lives so as to change them. This entry point manifests how and why that particular experience has been socially and politically organized in the way it has and what needs to be done to change that. DHM helps to connect personal experience to a much bigger picture composed of the social organization of relations. Viewed from another angle, it also helps us understand how the bigger picture determines that specific experience in the first place. DHM grants us the necessary tools to draw the links between one story of wounding to the violent process that has facilitated it, and from there to the larger state and other ideological institutions that structure social relations that have caused that process in the first place.

For example, in the case of war injury, discussed in Chapter 2, the violent process that facilitates someone's injury is militarism, which is mediated by social relations of capitalism, imperialism, theocracy, nationalism, and patriarchy. Note that causing war does not mean just the particular action of initiating military hostilities; rather, I am referring to the entire process that predates every war, starts it, and prolongs it.

In Chapter 3, the violent processes of disabling the prisoners by torture and totalizing violence are shown as facilitated by incarceration, theocracy, and patriarchy. In Chapter 4, for instance, the violent processes that facilitate the victims' disability is Punitive Limb Amputation (PLA) mediated by the social relations of capitalism, theocracy, and kleptocracy. In Chapter 5, those violent practices include wounding, burning, and disfigurement, mediated by patriarchy, misogyny, toxic masculinity, ableism, theocracy, and the culture of impunity.

Ebert (1996, p. 7) describes historical materialism as:

> a mode of knowing that inquires into what is not said, into the silences and the suppressed or missing, in order to uncover the concealed operations of power and the socio-economic relations connecting the myriad details and representation of our lives . . . [historical materialism] . . . disrupts "what is" to explain how social differences—specifically gender, race, sexuality, and class [and to which Erevelles (2011) has added disability]—have been systematically produced and continue to operate within regimes of exploitation, so that we can change them. It is the means for producing transformative knowledge.

DHM theorists of disability argue that the social construction of the disabled body emerges from "the specific ways in which society organizes its basic material activities (work, transport, leisure, domestic activities)" (Gleeson, 1997, p. 194). Historical materialism presupposes that labor is the core organizing force in history; for humans through their relationship to labor and within historical contexts "produce" their lives versus just living their lives. The Marxist framework sheds light on the ways in which the capitalist economy survives the worst depressions and recessions through its enormous flexibility to accommodate various shapes and means of profitmaking. This happens through the "regeneration" of resources via the expansion of territory via theft (dispossession) from the global south, and the "redistribution" of resources through the preservation of class-hierarchies at home (Harvey, 2004; O'Connor, 1989). Relying on DHM, this project attempts to show that violent processes such as war are socially planned, organized, and carried out by people. For instance, in a war, disabilities created are the by-product of weapons made by people and purchased precisely to kill and maim. In addition to the necessity of war for capitalist economies and imperialist (religious or secular) states, there are other factors that have a bearing on who gets killed/wounded and who does not. Take, for example, the unsafe working conditions in the sweatshops of the global south in which most of the necessary products are manufactured for the consumption of people in the global north. Workers in these sweatshops become disabled as they try to survive and make a living. In this example, we can think about how the disability of global southern workers is produced and sustained with respect to their location in the social division of labor. It is their location in the social division of labor that has determined their disability, rather than the reverse. This means that we need to pay attention to preexisting conditions and social structures, which lead to inevitable results/forms. The world's economic system is a social structure that requires that workers from the global south labor in un(der)/paid jobs to survive. The inevitable result of working often for twelve hours a day, seven days a week with dangerous machinery, unsafe long walks to work, and extreme heat is wounding, disability, and/or trauma. Therefore, disability in this case is not an accident but a socially organized condition.

Theoretical Constructs

In this case, my transnational theorization of disability has several constructs, which I define in this chapter[5] as class, state, and ideology. According to DHM, the dialectical relationship between labor and capital leads to a relation called class. The state, on the other hand, is an organized structure composed of people that serves the interest of the ruling class, meaning the capitalist, nationalist, and imperialist powers. Althusser (2001, p. 109) states that "Ideology represents the imaginary relationship of individuals to their real conditions of existence." Following Althusser, I define ideology here as a concept or a set of beliefs rooted in a particular social order, held by a certain group of people, to serve the interest of the ruling class while concealing material conditions.

In this project, violence is examined through the DHM lens, meaning it is considered as a "relation" and a "process" rather than an event, a thing, or a phenomenon. It then makes the transition to the final result, which according to DHM is called "form." How violence creates disability is a "mediation" that leads to a form called "disability." To prevent violence, it is necessary to step back and first abolish the "preexisting conditions" that lead to violence. For instance, if poverty causes disability, then we must go beyond fighting poverty to understand what kind of a socioeconomic system requires poverty to sustain itself. This forces us to think about distributing wealth equally so as to ensure that one person's poverty does not lead to another's enrichment. The historical circumstances extended from the past should be changed, not just the apparent violence.

Marx invites us to pay attention to the preexisting attributes of different processes and relations in order to understand why and how they result in their eventual consequence. For example, for this project, there are two key preexisting attributes to consider: ideology and class. These two are the preexisting attributes for all three relations that we discuss in this project: theocratic nationalism, capitalism, and imperialism. All are embedded in class-based societies and ideological foundations. By class-based societies, I mean societies that are run on the lines of a capitalist economy, which is based on the internal contradiction between labor and capital. This relationship is not inevitable, meaning we can abolish it. Marx's conceptual tools to understand this argument are internal relations, dialectical contradiction/unity, form, and mediation.

Marx avoids categorical and linear thinking; instead, his unique paradigm of critical thought is based on internal relations. Categorical thinking is a popular way of thinking but not always sufficient, especially if we are dealing with complex phenomena. Categorical thinking is based on distinction(s) between different categories, such as different animals and plants, but is insufficient for studying a phenomenon in relation to another phenomenon. In such a case, we might have to invoke Marx's dialectical thinking, for it reminds us that social relations should be studied relationally as opposed to categorically. There are two ways of thinking relationally—one focuses on external relations, the other on internal relations. The first is the most common in natural sciences, such as chemistry, and helps to understand how two phenomena interact and what happens as a consequence. For instance, a specific combination of oxygen and hydrogen results in water, which can continue to exist without any connection with its constituents (hydrogen and oxygen).

Alternatively, internal relational thinking is much more complex, because in this case the result of the interaction between two internally related phenomena remains dependent on those phenomena and cannot exist independently of them. This is a core concept pertaining to Marx's dialectical thinking. Capitalism must be thought of as a relation. It is the unity of two contradictions that cannot live on its own, independent of its contradictory components. Labor and capital are opposed to one another, yet simultaneously united in the relation called capitalism; this unity of opposites is the essence of dialectics. One of these two components, capital, is perceived as "positive," as it wants the relationship to continue; it profits by exploiting the other. Labor, contrastingly, is perceived as "negative" because it can abolish this exploitative relationship at any moment (the "negation of the negation" in Marxist terminology). Human emancipation, then, depends on labor's decision to end this exploitation.

Returning to Marx's conceptual tools, he argued that relations are not neutral. For him, the state was not just a neutral entity that represents people; instead, the state is a "socially organized relation" that functions to serve the interest of a particular class. Marx called this the unity of contradictions, "form." Form is a result of an internal relation, and unlike the result of an external relation, it cannot exist separately from its constituents. Sometimes this form moves between the two contradictory components of the dialectical relation and gets them closer to each other. It might even move among its original constituent relation or other relations internally or externally, while always being connected to its two opposite sources. Analyzing and studying the movement of a form, according to Marx, is called "mediation."

Are processes that lead to disablement/wounding, such as poverty, war, and environmental destruction, unavoidable? Marx would argue that all three are inevitable results of a preexisting condition called capitalism. If we start to look at war, poverty, or environmental destruction as the results of preexisting conditions, namely capitalism, then we can prevent them if we change those preexisting conditions. Inspired by Marx, I argue that there are other forms of violence that are disabling that are also a form/result of preexisting relations, and therefore can change if we change the preexisting relations that lead to them. Using DHM can foreground the enabling conditions necessary for the transformation of exploitative social relations that create and support the oppression of subjects of difference.

Can We Afford to Dismiss the Medical Model and the Social Model?

The existing approaches to disability include the medical model, social model, postcolonial, cultural, posthumanist, materialist models, etc. The medical model is a method of approaching disability based on "curing" or "fixing" disabled people. Medical model proponents (mostly healthcare professionals) locate disabled people's limitations in their impairments, rather than in the barriers that are imposed on disabled people by the surrounding society. Another way of understanding disability is the social model. In the 1980s, the social model emerged as a radical move within conventional disability models of the day. Social model proponents argue that disability is a social construct generated by a society that utilizes research models such as the medical theory as a means of locating an impairment in the disabled individuals themselves, rather than detecting it somewhere in society (Oliver, 1990). DS scholars first emerged as critics of the medical model (and of essentialist biomedical theorists) and perceived it as deficient (see the works of Rosemarie Garland-Thomson and Simi Linton). Social model proponents believe that disability is a long-term social state that is incurable and that "medical intervention, at best, would be inappropriate, and at worst, oppressive" (Oliver, 1983, p. 56).

Russell and Malhotra (2002), both DS scholars of political economy, argue that the social model of disability is inadequate for several reasons. First and foremost, its proponents treat the environment surrounding the disabled person as "neutral," as if this environment has not been designed and created by human beings with individual, social, cultural, and political subjectivities. They perceive the source of the problem of oppression of disabled people as being rooted in the discriminatory attitudes of other people. They imply that if we change those attitudes, suddenly we will have a world with equality and social justice with no disability oppression. Russel and Malhotra argue that this model makes invisible the structural barriers and inequalities that are created by the concrete social relations and modes of production. Russel and Malhotra articulate their position as:

> the view that disability is a socially-created category derived from labor relations, a product of the exploitative economic structure of capitalist society: one which creates (and then oppresses) the so-called disabled body as one of the conditions that allow the capitalist class to accumulate wealth. Seen in this light, disability is an aspect of the central contradiction of capitalism, and disability politics that do not accept this are, at best, fundamentally flawed strategies of reform or, worse, forms of bourgeois ideology that prevent this from being seen. (2002, p. 2)

Theorizing from the perspective of TDM based on the DHM, I suggest that dismissing the medical model, or medicalization of disability completely, can create two theoretical and practical problems. One is shaming and problematizing a disabled person who decides to seek a "cure" or go through rehabilitation (e.g., physiotherapy, prosthesis). The second problem is being denied the right to access medical treatment and healthcare. This problem is particularly pronounced in countries with expensive or no healthcare. Most of the countries in the global north have a universal healthcare system. However, when we talk about the "third world," that is, "where 80% of the world's disabled population live" (Priestley, 2001), the problem of dismissing the medical model multiplies. In fact, the medical model is imperative in the "developing world," for there are many parts of it which lack doctors, nurses, healthcare, or medication—making the medical model the dominant one in considering disability. This urges us to think and theorize differently about "disability in the majority world."

Neither can we dismiss the social model of disability because it helps us understand that what disabled people demand from society is neither treatment nor cure but an acceptance of their condition (Barnes, 2019), a state of affairs in which "experts" do not try to restore them to what they "should" be. This is a very attractive view to uphold, however, we need to be wary of the poor and racialized people with little to no healthcare, especially in non-Western contexts. In the first case study that I analyze in the Chapter 2, the wounded Iranian veterans and civilians did not tell us that all they needed was "acceptance." Yes, they emphasized acceptance but, at the same time, they spoke out about the lack of medical support and a proper healthcare system in place. The disabled veterans and civilians do not locate the problem in themselves or in society but in the healthcare system (run by the state) that has ignored their existence completely. Therefore, it is important to think dialectically about disability and disablement in global contexts, and to avoid thinking linearly or universally, where we simply dismiss a view and embrace another.

Furthermore, DS emerged as a field to include bodies that are excluded, not as an oppressive field to cause more oppression against disabled people. Every time we "assume" what a disabled person needs, we fall into the trap of normalization, as we become complicit in the ableist assumptions of the normative world, such as insisting on the tragedy model, assuming that disabled people only survive and never thrive, or that "their" lives entail only gloom and doom. Besides, just because contemporary DS scholarship frowns upon approaching disability from a perspective of medical need, we cannot simply ignore the medical needs of a massive population of disabled people in certain parts of the world, such as the Middle East. We need to be aware of every disabled body's needs by simultaneously keeping in mind all approaches to disability. In *Brilliant Imperfections*, grappling with the Gordian knot of contradictions between cure and care, Eli Clare (2017) maintains that neither an anti-cure politics nor a pro-cure (merely biomedical) approach can account for the messy relationships we have with our bodyminds. Eli Clare reminds us that a cure is an ideology grounded in normalcy (itself another ideology), and that neither a fervent desire for a cure nor a zealous defense of avoiding medical apparatus can be helpful for disabled bodyminds.

On the other hand, the social model has been successful in taking over the global north and their institutions, such as the United Nations. The social model has even tried to globalize itself through the United Nations Convention on the Rights of Persons with Disabilities (UNCRPD), by advocating for disabled people's rights and benefits as an oppressed group of people (Meyer, 2014). However, the same logic has never applied to disabled people in the global south. They have rarely been approached by the rights and benefits discourses, as if their disabilities are part of the "natural" state of affairs there. This indicates that a universal idea of disablement has abysmally failed, because transnational, local, and international advocacy groups do not fight for equality for disabled people in the global south. Instead, they just fight for their survival. Even though good intentions likely motivate the globalization of DS, it is essential not to assume that we know the problems disabled people deal with everywhere in the world.

The social model is a good prescription but not for every disabled person and every context. I argue that the international disability movement is *not* a transnational movement because it is constrained behind and within (socially constructed) borders, and are therefore, dependent on the approval of states. Even though the UNCRPD is celebrated as an achievement, based on the social model, it has never been concerned with people who become disabled by violence. It has especially neglected to focus on disability caused by violence in the global south, which has been the focus of this project. Neither has it been alarmed with people disabled by shoddy environmental practices everywhere in the world.

The Transnational Aspect

Besides being rooted in the material world, the TDM I am developing here means (a) we can imagine a world with no borders and avoid trying to impose a universal disability identity upon all disabled people; (b) we can resist what mainstream DS has been teaching us, which centers "whiteness" and the "West" as its inseparable norms (Chen, 2012; Dossa, 2008; Erevelles, 2011; Meekosha, 2011; Bell, 2006; Gorman, 2016); and (c) we can start imagining an organized and diverse group of people with "no universal disability identity and no necessary ties to the states" (i.e., circumventing the international borders and nation-states, as local and global blocks of power or empires); (d) foregrounding the dialectic of disability—care as well as building the transnational infrastructures of care including solidarity and active witnessing; (e) reimagine disability justice as a global project and hold ourselves accountable for what transpires in transnational contexts (Kazemi & Karah, 2021c, 2023).

Building on the works of DS scholars, whose works have added the social and racial division of labor to our understanding and theorization of disability (such as Erevelles, 2011; Gorman, 2005; Russell & Malhotra, 2002) and drawing upon the case studies as well as my own embodied experiences, the new disability model that I am developing in this project dismisses neither the medical model nor the social model. In fact, a transnational theory of disability that I am articulating here is not replacing/negating other theories of disability but amending and transcending them, so that they are in turn enfolded into it. The TDM does not approach disability by locating it inside the disabled individual. Neither does it locate the problem only in the surrounding society. The TDM, instead, locates the problem in the violence of exploitive social relations (e.g., theocracy, patriarchy, capitalism, imperialism, ableism), the dialectics of global politics, historical infliction of pain upon the poor and marginalized body (e.g., PLA, colonialism, slavery, Indigenous genocide, indentured labor, war), and destruction of the planet by the ruling bourgeois class causing health issues for every species as well as the actual experiences of the disabled people in the global south as they encounter these violent practices.

The TDM acknowledges the materiality of disability/wounding and leaves it up to the disabled people to seek treatment/rehabilitation or not. The TDM resists the ideology of normalcy. At the same time, it refuses to treat disabled humans as docile objects with no power in perceiving and determining their conditions and potential treatments. The TDM remains respectful of human autonomy and decision-making power. The TDM, unlike other disability models, is not a bourgeois approach. It looks at disability and disablement in global contexts and not just the Western/global-north context, and unlike most existing models, it engages with transnational disability-production mechanisms such as war, capitalist markets, and theocratic impositions, to name just a few.

Transnational(ism) is a historical as well as political category of "social organization," which is composed of national and international relations (i.e., political-economic relations) (Mojab & Gorman, 2007). In their analysis of wars in the Middle East, Mojab and Gorman (2007) theorize that "labeling cultures and communities 'transnational' while conceptualizing the state as a de-stabilized, localized, and diminishing entity, encourages the perception that contemporary wars and crises are manufactured locally rather than geopolitically" (p. 60). Their argument is key in understanding the relationship between disability, nation-states, borders, and politics. Inspired by these conceptualizations and taking into account the model extracted from Marxist theory and geopolitics, I argue that disability, as well, should not be seen as a local phenomenon. This is because it is manufactured globally by geopolitical forces that start and sustain violent processes and relations that cause disability (e.g., armed conflicts, state terror, environmental destruction).

To transnationalize the context of DS in relation to (socially organized) violence, one should take into account disability oppression in relation to the transnational capitalist modes of production (Gorman, 2005). Using the TDM, we can attempt to transnationalize our approach to disability in relation to different cases of violence. However, without analyzing the nation-state, we would risk becoming entrapped in a mystical understanding of the ghost called capitalism, which constantly haunts our dematerialized understandings of disability. Gorman (2005) argues that "transnationalism" and "diaspora" must be understood as historical and political categories of social organization. Culture, as a dimension of both the nation and diaspora, must be understood in relation to consciousness and political struggle—both gendered and classed. Using a concept of "transnationalism" that has been separated from an analysis of the structure, organization, and social relations of the state has particular consequences for understanding disablement.

Transnational Forms of Political Consciousness

Contemporary mainstream DS scholarship expects us to celebrate acquiring a disability as a condition that every human at some point in their life experiences. The TDM asks us, however, what if my disability has been acquired under the oppressive conditions of poverty, economic exploitation, state terror, police brutality, GBV, imperialist expansion, war, inhumane working conditions, and lack of access to adequate healthcare and education? What if human variations (e.g., race, sex) are per se used in the construction of disabled identities for exploitative purposes (e.g., slavery, indentured labor, colonialism, immigration law, travel bans, etc.) (Erevelles, 2011)? And finally, how do we build solidarity across disabled bodies and communities while we negotiate the distances that simultaneously divide and damage us within the contemporary context of global capitalism-imperialism? Like the social model, the TDM recognizes the problem of ideological and institutional discrimination surrounding disability (Oliver, 1983). However, the TDM is not just a theoretical model; it is also a political project that places enormous emphasis on "political consciousness."

Reality and consciousness are internally related. Political consciousness, according to Gorman (2005), is "a quality related to a social group, rather than as a sum of individual ideas held by members of the group" (p. ii). Also, according to Marx, consciousness has a dialectical relationship with material reality, for it's not separate from social being (Marx, 1845/1976). Following Marx, I argue that we can both "make" what we know (i.e., knowledge production) and also "live" what we know. For example, when it comes to war, we, as war survivors, can refuse to mobilize only around our experiences, and instead, "live our consciousness arisen from that experience" to end the social organization that gave birth to our experience in the first place. According to Bannerji (1995), it is not enough to care only about expressing our experiences or having the space and right to do so. We should also organize ourselves in order to end the oppressive structures, which against our will, determine our experiences.

Furthermore, it's always important to ask, "Whose disability are we talking about?" Because we know that "[e]normous gaps . . . exist in evidence about disability, especially in low and medium resource countries of the world" (Bickenbach, 2011, p. 655 cited in Oliver & Barnes, 2012). Puar (2017) and Gorman (2016) have, similarly, argued that different disabled peoples' accessibility needs are often fought for as if disconnected from other disabled peoples' struggles. For instance, accessibility of buildings is often something that a middle-class, disabled, U.S. citizen expects to receive from the state, and sometimes they do receive it. However, the access they enjoy seems disconnected from hundreds of people who "become" disabled every week in wars and minefields globally. This is what I mean by global class relations of disability.

Furthermore, our system(s) of thought about disability are determined by the structures that rule over our consciousness. This means that we should approach "disability oppression" or "creation of disability" in conversation with consciousness and agency; otherwise, we will end up floating in an ahistorical empiricist void. I conceptualize the TDM as a political project that involves us consciously mobilizing around our experiences as a starting point and from there move on to the first expose and then end these exploitative relations that produce so much violence against disabled bodyminds.

Disablement Without Borders

Because it is accompanied by concepts such as survival, resistance, and struggle, "disablement without borders" could become an essential part of the emerging TDM and in the process critically engage interjections into two important arenas. One is the way in which DS as a discipline consistently depoliticizes and individualizes "disablement." Second is the material reality of militarization, environmental destruction, and poverty that harms (disabled) people every day everywhere, especially from the global south. It is helpful to use the survival/resistance/struggle framework through the TDM to approach "disablement without borders." I argue that the TDM can help us mobilize around these different dimensions of "becoming" disabled through exploitative social relations and being conscious of it, including individual survival, interpersonal solidarity, and resistance. All of this shapes the articulation of TDM praxis and consciousness in the broader struggle for disabled people's liberation from disability, race, class, and gender oppression, and that can organize us against disability-production mechanisms such as the proliferation of disabled bodies in wars and armed conflicts.

Despite enormous efforts by anti-war activists, civil society organizations, coalitions, individual-activism, and other organized efforts, we are still at war. We live in a world that can annihilate itself fifteen times over (Edwards, 2012). If our practical efforts are not getting anywhere, then according to Marx's consciousness theory, our thinking must be flawed. I suggest that we rethink the ways in which our consciousness of disability is organized given our geographical locations and the global politics that are assigned to those locations. If we narrate our stories as embodied experiences, "collapse narration into analysis" (Gorman, 2005), and share these narratives with our communities through technologies that facilitate transnational solidarity, then we can claim that we are moving toward transnationalism as a field of theorization (Mojab & Gorman, 2007). I further contend that a disability theory and praxis, based on transnationalism, has the potential to resist globalization in two ways. First, transnationalism through travel, television, social media, news, and electronic devices can help us form and maintain communities virtually. This means that we get a chance to document a life of oppression and abuse by telling our stories and transforming those stories into analyses, political consciousness, and political action. Second, transnationalism can become a way for us to organize around our narratives and keep them flowing, in opposition to globalization's strict policing of labor, media, and the flow of capital (like oil transportation). If we read the "stories of disablement" we encounter as "embodied experiences," then we can resist the social relations (such as the state as embodied oppressor) carried out by "actual people" that rule over our lives.

Transnationalism not only helps us mobilize around our experiences; it can also help us form a collective political consciousness to fight the violent structures that cause those experiences. Transnational communication and organizing can take us somewhere beyond solidarity. It can take us to a point where our collective struggle can cross borders without us actually traveling across them. I therefore argue that we can consider travel as not just the physical act of moving from one place to another but as a transnational technological act, because we live in a world where crossing borders without proper documentation is criminalized. Further, bio-surveillance technologies currently in use at borders make it even harder for people to mobilize physically (Gorman, 2016). Therefore, by mobilizing our transnational stories of disablement,[6] survival, and resilience across borders, we can resist the exploitative social relations that dominate our lives.

I chose to call my disability model/theory, "transnational," as a way of bypassing the international borders and nation-states, as local and global blocks of power (or empires). I further elaborate on the transnational aspect of my disability model, which is a form of transnationalizing disability justice, in each chapter (e.g., the "transnational infrastructures of care") (Kazemi & Karah, 2023) in Chapter 5, where I discuss the transnational care activism conducted by ordinary women helping the acid attack survivor, Masoumeh Ataei, to fundraise for her eye surgery, and the "transnational disability praxis" in the Conclusion, where I discuss the necessity of transnational- and "crip solidarity" (Kazemi & Karah, 2023), multilingual activism (Kazemi & Karah, 2021c), and collective accountability for any disability-rights advocacy project.

To acknowledge the inseparability of care and disability as a dialectic and to contribute to the formulation and recognition of "transnational disability justice" framed in transnational thought, praxis, care, and activism, in every chapter, I discuss what constitutes "infrastructures of individual and collective care" in and among the disabled/wounded survivors of violence.

Political Consciousness, Class Struggle, and Disability Oppression

One type of knowledge linked to political consciousness, as a way of thinking, being, and becoming, is what McLaren and Farahmandpur call "revolutionary pedagogy." They state: "The aim of such a pedagogy is to encourage the development of critical consciousness among students and teachers [and maybe disabled survivors of violence] in the interests of building working-class solidarity [along with solidarity among peace educators] and opposition to global capitalism [and imperialism perhaps which would then result in resisting wars such as Russian invasion of Ukraine]" (McLaren & Farahmandpur, 2001, p. 1). Inspired by their pedagogy, I argue that anti-war activists, organizations, collectives, and peace educators should join the struggle of the working class and should build solidarity with them at the international level, because we are fighting the same battle. The TDM can be used as a tool by disabled war survivors, non-disabled war survivors, disabled veterans, non-disabled veterans, critical educators, and anti-war activists to organize ourselves and join the working-class struggle transnationally. If peace educators and anti-war activists realize that a war-free world has never and will never be achieved under the capitalist system, they might reconsider their position regarding global capitalism. The solidarity between the working class and anti-war activists/educators can take our battle to a whole new level, where the prospect is not as chaotic as it is now and has been for centuries. Gorman (2005) insightfully observes that "without a concept of class consciousness, . . . an anti-ableist standpoint is simply a social subjectivity (or location) from which certain organized social relations are visible" (p. 175). As such, "class consciousness" is a fundamental requirement in any social movement, especially in this case, the anti-war movement, involving activists, peace educators, disabled veterans, and non-disabled veterans. For us to join the working-class struggle, first we should understand our position in the social division of labor.

Marxist theory teaches us that if social relations change, the experiences that they cause correspondingly change. The transformation of relations happens when we refuse to reproduce them. We, as transnational disability theorists and scholars, should organize around those experiences of disablement as political actors with a particular political consciousness. Our consciousness should result in concrete and sensuous activity; otherwise, we will not have understood Marx properly. He emphasized the unity of thought and action as a way forward to end ideological abstraction. Our political consciousness, rising from knowing those experiences, should result in political action. Otherwise, we will have produced a new ideological layer to be added on top of the abstraction that is already wrapped around people's experience of disablement in the global south.

This chapter brought into a single zone an assemblage of relations and processes that have their origins and consequences in the devastating wounds that social and economic forces can inflict on individuals and collective human experiences. People get wounded under/by political, social, and institutional power, and reciprocally by how these forms of power themselves bounce off the manifestations of social resistance that they must silence to sustain themselves. I introduced a new model for DS that I termed the transnational disability theory, based on the DHM, geopolitics, and the DS lens, to shift our current analysis of disability and, in particular, to grasp the reality of disabling conditions such as war, state terror, gendered violence, and their resultant wounds, especially in the global south. I demonstrated how this model can pave the way for a revolutionary understanding of disability and its relationship with the nation-state, contextualized within transnational social justice consciousness and activism. Additionally, I discussed the ways in which we can organize ourselves against violence as political actors and agents.

2

Gaping Wounds

Disablement in the Iran-Iraq War

> Water's silence can be drought
> or a howl of thirst,
> wheat's silence can be famine's
> triumphant growl, just as
> darkness is the sun silenced.
> But human silence is loss
> of the world and God.
>
> —Ahmad Shamlou[1] (Translated by Sholeh Wolpé)[2]

To understand the experience of becoming and remaining disabled among the veterans and civilians who were wounded in the Iran-Iraq War, I consulted all the available books, memoirs, blogs, visual arts, reports, documentaries, published interviews, and eyewitness accounts written or told by the veterans themselves. I also conducted a digital study of the Iranian veterans' online comments[3] on the state-sponsored or state-affiliated Iranian news agencies' websites, mainly because those sites were where veterans had an online presence and regularly commented on the disability benefits' policy updates, published by those new agencies. The online comments are actual complaints and concerns, coming especially from those who do not have or find a platform to voice their concerns in society. Since many of the veterans are immobile due to the physical restrictions/barriers of the outside world, including a lack of elevators, ramps, personal support workers, and curb cuts, they either stay home or remain locked up in institutions. This means that going online and expressing their concerns, only if they have access to an Internet connection, is sometimes the only way for their voices to be expressed. I also conducted a textual analysis[4] of several documents that indicate how the parties involved organized the war and why they did so (e.g., UN Security Council Resolutions) (United Nations, 1987) and a few documents from the U.S. National Security Archives that have recently become declassified (NSA Archives, 2015).

In this chapter, using the Transnational Disability Model (TDM) (Kazemi, 2017, 2018), which involves defetishizing disability (i.e., attending to the social relations behind the creation and perpetuation of disablement), I examine what constitutes the material reality of disablement for the veterans during and after the war. Using TDM, I examine the social relations that produce and perpetuate disability in the survivors, including capitalism, nationalism, theocracy, and imperialism, all of which operate based on class and ideology. The process of the production of disablement in this study consists of six categories: nation-building; initiating a military invasion; prolonging the war; using unconventional weapons; the global community's silence; and certain nations' support for Iraq. The process of the perpetuation of disablement includes poverty, institutionalization, unemployment, state corruption, fetishization of disability by the state through the ideological construction of "living martyr" and imposing it on veterans, inadequate medical care, "chemical incarceration,"[5] (Fabris, 2011) lack of disability accommodation, lack of physical and emotional accessibility, hierarchization and ranking of disabilities and their severity, and the dysfunctional system for the allocation of benefits to veterans based on the severity of their disability, which I call "soma-technologies of disability measurement" (Kazemi, 2024a). As a result of these processes, there is a high rate of suicide and addiction among the surviving veterans, with many of them experiencing survivor's guilt, extreme poverty, and post-traumatic stress. The perpetuation of their disability as a systemic abuse has pushed the disabled survivors to a point where they would sometimes rather be dead than alive in emotional and physical pain.

Iran-Iraq War: Ideology, Class, and Nation-Building

As the longest war of the twentieth century, the Iran-Iraq War stretched from September 1980 to August 1988. According to the *Encyclopedia Britannica* (2022),

> the number of casualties was enormous but equally uncertain. Estimates of total casualties range from 1,000,000 to twice that number. The number killed on both sides was perhaps 500,000, with Iran suffering the greatest losses. It is estimated that between 50,000 and 100,000 Kurds were killed by Iraqi forces during the series of campaigns code-named Anfāl (Arabic: "Spoils") that took place in 1988.

To understand how social relations such as nationalism (either secular or theocratic) are behind deadly wars, we first need to understand why nations, and in this case, Iran and Iraq, were interested in prolonging the war, even though this meant producing more disabled and dead bodies. In 1980,

Iran, as a newly established ideological state, was interested in spreading its Shia ideology everywhere in the Middle East (Abrahamian, 2008). Iraq, on the other hand, led by Saddam Hussein, was interested in establishing the League of Arab Nations, oppressing every dissident, Shias, and Kurds, and ruling over the Sunni-Islamic world (Al-Khalil, 1999). The United Nations Monitoring, Verification, and Inspection Commission issued a report about Iraq's unresolved disarmament issue, which stated that during the war, Iraq deployed tons of mustard gas, tabun, and sarin against Iranian soldiers and civilians [including Kurdish] (United Nations, 2003). There is substantial evidence suggesting that the United States provided Iraq with intelligence concerning Iranian soldiers' locations and numbers while being fully aware of Hussein's intentions with chemical weapons, including sarin (Harris & Aid, 2013; Hiltermann, 2007; McGovern, 2013; Robinson & Goldblat, 1984; Timmerman, 1991). Phythian (1997) argues that the United States and Britain seemingly remained "neutral." But, in reality, they supplied both the Iranian and Iraqi states with weapons, especially Iraq, not only in order to keep them in war but also to let Iraq have the upper hand. He demonstrates that the United States and Britain's ultimate goal was to keep the countries busy in war, so none of them would jeopardize the flow of the oil supply and trade in the Persian Gulf; as well as to protect the other Gulf States, who happened to have a lot of oil (Phythian, 1997). Note that the capitalist social relations behind the war are evident here. The United States and Britain did not intervene in the war to end it but to sell their weapons to both parties and police the flow of capital/oil from the Middle East.

Saddam and his supporters in the Ba'th party were determined to rule over the Sunni-Islamic world by becoming an undisputed military power. Iraq imported the most advanced weapons, as it was "the Soviet Union, France, China and Chile who sold Baghdad much of its off-the-shelf weaponry" (Frankel, 1990, p. 3). Meanwhile, "West Germany, France, Britain, the United States, Belgium, Austria, Switzerland, and Brazil all sold the components, machines, and tools—much of its material with civilian as well as military application" (Frankel, 1990, p. 3; Hooper & Goldenberg, 2002; Gordon & Engelberg, 1989). As is evident, the sources providing weaponry support for Iraq were diverse, although by 1982, the Soviet Union refused to help any longer. In 1983, Iraq regained the support of Moscow, however, with a contract valued at $230 million USD. At this time, unlike 1980, Iraq was producing simple equipment or purchasing it from non-Soviet sources. Now, using prospective trade agreements, Saddam appealed to China for more weaponry.

Iranians, on the other hand, depended on "nationalist sentiments, revolutionary zeal, and the *Shiite cult of martyrdom* to their utmost limits to compensate for their complete isolation" [emphasis mine] (Katouzian, 2010, p. 344). They believed in the famous slogan of "neither West, nor East: The

Islamic Republic." Therefore, not only did they not have a diplomatic relationship with the United States, but they also did not receive the Soviets warmly. Iran's military equipment, on the other hand, was managed with support from Libya, Syria, Pakistan, Israel, South Yemen, and North Korea. Declassified CIA documents show that from 1981, Iran purchased a massive number of weapons from its sworn enemy, Israel, with approval from the US (Walcott & Mayer, 1986). Interestingly enough, a former U.S. military colonel by the name of Oliver North also sold weapons to Iran illegally through intermediaries. This act was a part of the Iran-Contra controversy, with the profits directed to Contras (i.e., anti-communist U.S.-backed militia) in Nicaragua. All these global players who armed both sides of the conflict should be seen as aggressors and agents who knew what their weapons were going to do: kill and disable. Therefore, disability caused by war is produced and maintained transnationally by global class relations and geopolitics.

I defined imperialism, in the Introduction, as a form of indirect intervention by one nation or a group of nations in other nations' affairs, which affected the lives of its people (even in future generations) by disrupting their social, political, and economic relations. In this particular case, the violence of imperialism can be analyzed from two separate, but related, aspects. The first way that the violence of imperialism was delivered during the war was the military and intelligence support both countries received. The second way was the global community's silence and indifference concerning the humanitarian disaster affecting unarmed Iranians and Iraqi Kurds (multiple attacks between 1983 and 1988) caused by Iraq's use of chemical weapons against Iran and the Kurdish region of Iraq. "Iraq's use of chemical weapons was condemned—both in national statements, such as the U.S. condemnation of March 1984, and in UNSC Resolution 512 of 1986" (Littlewood, 2006, p. 17). However, in reality, the Iraqi state got away with using illegal Weapons of Mass Destruction on both the Kurds and Iranians. This silence is another indication that disability is produced and maintained transnationally by global politics, for silence is a political response. When disability is produced through the use of un/conventional weapons and the whole world chooses to remain silent, "[this] silence encourages the tormentor, never the tormented" (Wiesel, 2008, p. 118). I call this silence "disabling imperialism."

During the war, hundreds of thousands were injured and/or permanently disabled. Tens of thousands, including unarmed women and children, were exposed to chemical weapons and needed long-term treatment. Those disabled permanently were called *jānbāz*, in Farsi/Persian,[6] which means those who "are willing to sacrifice their lives" (Ghamari-Tabrizi, 2009, p. 109). As such, not only did the war produce more than half a million dead bodies, it also produced more than one million disabled people who were apparently "willing to die." According to the veterans' own words included in this chapter, the theocratic state of Iran has been brutal to its war veterans by neglecting them and not providing sufficient care for their injuries. It is evident that not only were their disabilities created as a result of the world powers' imperialist interventions, Iraqi nationalism, and Iran's desire to export its ideological revolution but also as a result of the Iranian state's sustaining those disabilities by not caring for the survivors.

Production of Disability by Secular and Theocratic Nationalism

Historically, nationalism and nation-building emerged in line with the rise of the middle class in the process of transition from feudalism to capitalism (Hassanpour, 2015). Hassanpour argues that Marx problematized both nationalism and theocracy as (political) ideological claims practiced in a class society. Additionally, Marx argued in favor of the process of nation-building but only if it is used to radically transform a society and replace class society with communism. His vision entailed a classless world not divided by borders, in other words, a transnational world (2015). Marx critiqued nationalism and national borders, for he understood attachments to nation and ethnicity along with language, tribe, gender, and territory, as "predicament[s] of class society, which he called 'prehistory'" (Marx, 1970, p. 22, cited in Hassanpour, 2015, p. 239). In other words, Marx believed that sharp differences in power relations are rooted in class relations; and these sharp differences are reproduced through the capitalist social relations. Marx, thus, problematized nationalism theoretically and ideologically. This, however, does not mean that Marxists have perceived national liberation movements unfavorable as a rule, because each and every one of them can be assessed separately under interrelated considerations. Ideology and class are the most crucial components of both the nation-building process and nationalism (Hassanpour, 2015). It is the nation-state, formed by the ruling class, which enforces the dominance of its ideology throughout society, and the fetishization of nationalism sometimes obscures the contentious class relations rendering them invisible. In this process, Marx thought, the ruling class/bourgeoisie uses cultural ideology (part of the "superstructure" in Marxian terms), such as religion to control/guard the economic "base" (natural resources) (Hassanpour, 2015).

In the case of Iran, the "ruling class" is the clerics and military personnel close to them (IRGC: Islamic Revolutionary Guard Corps) who uphold/promote their religious ideology (Shia nation-building) and control the entire gamut of natural resources (economy). If the ruling class feels threatened, they will use any potential ideology to destroy ideas of peace, transnationalism, or coexistence. These ideologies include patriotism, fascism, xenophobia, anti-Semitism, hatred, and war. The core capitalist logic, Hassanpour (2015) argues, is to "expand or die." Iran, Iraq, and the countries that helped them both were all engaged in the core capitalist dynamic of "expand or die." Behrooz Ghamari-Tabrizi (2009, p. 107) argues that the Iran-Iraq War "transformed into a vehicle for the consolidation of the Islamic Republic's power," and the Iranian state managed to "exploit it as a state-building tool." The ideological-theocratic regime of Iran, led by an extremist cleric, mobilized and armed the nation's men and boys as young as twelve (i.e., child soldiers), relying on religious jihadist sentiments, "the Shia cult of martyrdom" (Katouzian, 2010, p. 344), and the massive number of armaments inherited from the Shah. On the other hand, as Al-Khalil (1990) argues, in Iraq, Saddam Hussein's dream was always a Sunni pan-Arab nationalist Middle East—run by his Ba'th party. Although he appeared secular at the policy level, he was not actually running a secular state. His horrendous oppression of the Shia population who had been living in Iraq as second-class citizens, as well as his fear of Khomeini's Shia revolution just next door, indicate that his nationalism was Sunni-Islamic, and not secular.

Perpetuation of Disablement

After several decades, Iran is still haunted by the effects of chemical weapons (Wright, 2014). As per statistics, 221,682 Iranian people were killed during the war with Iraq, while 554,858 Iranians (including unarmed women and children) were rendered disabled (MehrNews, 2012). There are more than half a million disabled Iranian survivors of the war with visible burns, blindness, chronic fatigue, sexual dysfunction, mood disorders, and/or severe bleeding problems, who have received no acknowledgment from the international community whatsoever (Ahmadi et al., 2006; Bajoghli, 2015; Najafi Mehr et al., 2012; Wright, 2014). Today, after three decades, many veterans live with post-traumatic stress who then often "face marital maladjustment, which predisposes them to sexual disorders" (Ahmadi et al., 2006, p. 5). Moreover, the number of "mentally disabled" veterans (with acquired brain injury due to shrapnel shells or explosion shocks) and those who must deal with post-traumatic stress is increasing (Samimi, 2014). A phenomenological study conducted by Najafi Mehri, et al. (2012) suggested, "victims of mustard gas experience fatigue differently from patients with acute and chronic diseases" (p. 185). And poignantly, "due to the occurrence of late respiratory complications of mustard gas exposure, 20 years after this incident, the number of chemically injured victims has been reported to be at least 45,000 people" (Ghanei & Harandi, 2008, as cited in Najafi Mehri et al., 2012).

According to the Iranian veterans' own words, their immediate caregivers (usually their wives), and their children face financial hardships in accessing medication and adequate care every day (Samimi, 2014; Defapress, 2016; Katouzian, 2010; Fashnews, 2016; Quds Online, 2015). Disabled veterans who have inhaled or touched chemical agents need expensive and scarce[7] medications to survive the pain, breathing problems, and the restlessness that they experience on a daily basis (Fashnews 2016).

Survivors with physical injuries are mostly cared for at their homes and sometimes in nursing homes, which indicates the gendered basis of care.[8] The same thing applies to veterans with an acquired mental disability (brain injury) as a result of coming into contact with explosions, shrapnel shells, and high-pitched sounds. The mentally disabled veterans are the most vulnerable ones. For some, even their families sometimes refuse to deal with them at home. They are usually institutionalized in places that are nursing homes for disabled veterans, which are called sanatoriums (*āsāyeshgāh*). Even there, they mostly live in very poor conditions in terms of nutrition, sanitation, and welfare. The current long-term care, sponsored by the Iranian state for the disabled veterans and civilians, is very much inadequate and inefficient.

In a documentary, titled *Amnesia*, directed by Ahmad Soleiman Nia (2012), an anonymous group of mentally disabled veterans with brain injuries, who are institutionalized, along with the on-site psychologist, talk about their living conditions and the brutal treatment (e.g., physical beatings, arbitrary arrests, hours of cruel interrogation [IranPressNewsTube, 2012]) they receive from the state for speaking up against the inadequate services. The institutionalized veterans tell the cameraperson that the feeling of worthlessness hurts them. They say, "We are useless, and everyone has forgotten us." They say that their addresses change very frequently, or they go homeless, because their landlords kick them out of their homes. Their stress makes them very irritable, and they accelerate swiftly to the point of screaming and swearing for no apparent reason. In the footage, the on-site psychologist states that if people were only aware of their condition, then they wouldn't take it personally and would try to understand the veterans' trauma and stress and act accordingly. Some veterans, on the other hand, complain about being overmedicated in psychiatric wards and nursing homes in order to force them to remain silent or to fall asleep. In the documentary footage, they say that if they complained about the existing welfare system, they were given an injection or electric shock to remain silent. This was especially the case with the mentally disabled veterans who were institutionalized. However, as Burstow (2015) suggests, not only do psychiatric medications and treatment, such as electroshock (ECT), fail to heal people, but it has also been conclusively proven to cause disability, disease, and imbalance, such as cognitive impairment. Burstow (2015) posits that people who find themselves in psychiatric wards become prisoners of systemic abuse, such as being administered psychiatric drugs that "frequently" cause the condition [they are] alleged to address (p. 180). Therefore, what happened in the psychiatric and rehabilitation wards to the Iranian veterans was by no means a healing or treatment process. Instead, it was a disability-production mechanism that perpetuated their existing condition and caused more problems. I argue that the psychiatric apparatus in Iran, just like any other psychiatric apparatus in the world, is rooted in the medical model of disability, eugenics ideologies, and capitalist exploitation, within a context of social, political, and economic power imbalances.

In Iran, like many other societies, disability is associated with a sense of tragedy and shame. In other words, the disabled person and his/her family are expected by society to experience grief and shame (Goodrich, 2013). In the public's view, having acquired a disability through war is different from other kinds of disability that are acquired congenitally or through natural causes or accidents. This is largely due to ideological perceptions that people uphold, such as "patriotism" or "martyrdom," concerning the justness of the fight in which disablement occurred. Therefore, disabled veterans receive a certain amount of respect that non-veteran disabled people rarely do. Kashani-Sabet (2010) points out that the relationship between disability and the state can vary drastically based on possible causes of disability. This is definitely the case in Iran. However, this does not mean that all veterans necessarily receive special attention from the state. In fact, in the case of Iran, quite the opposite is true; most Iranian veterans with disabilities live in poverty and with inadequate care and, as mentioned earlier, are often institutionalized in psychiatric wards and nursing homes. Nevertheless, it's worth mentioning that there is a very small minority or caste of veterans who are considered "insiders" to the regime, known as "Noor-e-Cheshmi" in Persian, which literally translates to "apple of the eye," meaning that they are close and dear to the state. Although a very small circle, they enjoy certain economic advantages and social privileges that other veterans and ordinary disabled Iranians can only dream about.

Disabled Iranian veterans in particular, and disabled Iranians, in general, complain about inaccessible buildings, streets, curbs, and pavements (Hallajarani, 2014). They cannot go outside their homes because they cannot get around due to inaccessible buildings and the lack of ramps.[9] If there is a ramp, they often lead to a body of water without a bridge (Goodrich, 2013). Unfortunately, many disabled war veterans are afraid to voice their discontent with the economic and social conditions that they are forced to endure, because the Iranian state may immediately silence them by cutting their minimum social welfare benefits and often imprisoning them even before they voice their grievances publicly. There have been veterans or their family members who have committed suicide[10] or immolated themselves as a result of extreme poverty.

Soma-technologies of Disability Measurement

Iran's population is about 88 million. Although there are no accurate statistics, it is estimated that 11 to 14 percent of the population have a disability (Human Rights Watch, 2018, p. 2). The disabled veteran population in Iran is estimated to be between 400,000 and 560,000 (Alaedini, 2004, cited in Moore & Kornbelt, 2011). The reasons the exact number is not known can be traced back to the fact that many of the veterans never identified themselves to the Disabled Veterans and Martyrs' Foundation (DVMF) to receive benefits, or they might have died before getting a chance to be recognized by the DVMF. Traditionally, almost everywhere in the world, disabled war veterans receive special treatment (Moore & Kornblet, 2011). It is "special" in the sense that the rest of the disabled population typically does not receive the same "privileges" that veterans do. In the case of Iran, the DVMF is the organization in charge of providing this special treatment. According to a recent Human Rights Watch report on the rights of disabled people in Iran (2018, p. 27) as well as the disabled veterans' own words, the current long-term care sponsored by the Iranian state for them and for civilians is inadequate and inefficient.[11]

The DVMF, which veterans simply call "Foundation" (*Bonyād*) in short form, is known for corruption and scandal. Even domestic newspapers controlled[12] by the state's Ministry of Culture and Islamic Guidance have reported this corruption[13]. The Foundation is given preferential access to state contracts and by extension, like rich corporations, is a major player in Iran's construction and developmental industry projects, such as hotels and estates. This would suggest they have sufficient funds to invest in major residential and commercial projects. Disabled veterans, however, are usually told that the Foundation does not have enough funds to meet their needs, and therefore, they should just be "content" with what is given to them.

The DVMF[14] is the only authority that can determine the "severity" of survivors' injury or disability. Thus, if disabled survivors want to claim that they have been exposed to chemical weapons or explosions and get their "disability percentage" determined, they must provide extensive documentation and have their health examined by the medical commission of the Foundation. The medical commission needs proof to determine the percentage. For example, they require proof from civilians that they have been to the contaminated areas (polluted by chemical weapons), confirmation from the government of the municipality, and proof of medical examination.[15]

The DVMF has a Health Deputy Branch responsible for convening medical commissions and determining the "disability percentage" of injured veterans or what I call "soma-technologies of disability measurement." Since the Iranian state through the Foundation's medical commissions measures veterans' disability by a percentage system and allocates their social welfare accordingly, the percentage that the veterans receive remains very important to them. The percentage can determine whether they might get their medication for free, receive financial help every month, receive homecare (e.g., a personal support worker or nurse), or whether their children can get into university with special privileges through the quota system. As such, they mention that "percentage" as part of their identity, usually when they leave a comment online or when they are interviewed.[16] Essentially, the number/percentage defines almost every aspect of life. This is why, even when introducing themselves, veterans mention their percentage, almost as if it is a part of their identity. For example, they call themselves "a-certain-percentage" veteran (e.g., 40 percent veteran).

We know from Deborah Stone's (1984) extensive work on the ways in which societies seek to rationalize difficult distributive decisions vis-à-vis disability "benefits" that disability determination has been increasingly medicalized over time. According to Stone, disability is difficult to measure, and disability determinations are subject to much debate. Even in the presence of medical "approval" or certification of the disabled, the definitions of what constitutes disability vary among nations (1984). Historically, the assessment of veterans' needs has been assessed solely according to specifics directly related to their medical condition (WHO, 2011). Currently, attention is paid to whether the veterans' needs are presented in a more holistic manner and what can facilitate their rehabilitation process or improve their functioning process (WHO, 2011). The Iranian state requires that disabled veterans and civilians "prove" their disability in order to receive any financial help, medication, and/or treatment (Kasaiezadeh, 2015, 2016). The first item in the long list of supporting documents is proof that a particular recognizable explosion or attack caused their injury, which they call an accident memo/report (*soorat-e-sāneheh*) (Afkarnews, 2013). Every veteran is expected to carry their accident memo/report with them, since this document contains important information regarding the expenditure unit (revolutionary guards, army, and police force) to the frontline of combat, as well as the location and severity of a veteran's injury.

According to the survivors' own words and the information presented on the DVMF's website, this document contains two key components. The first is the record of a certain incident (shooting, explosion, bombing, etc.) that resulted in injury or disability. The second is the record of treatment received. Obtaining both parts can be a very difficult task for several reasons. First, the war happened before the advent of widespread computer use, which means that all record-keeping was done in hard copy. According to the survivors, many of the explosions and bombardments led to the destruction of such papers.[17] Therefore, it is not easy to find proof that a particular explosion happened at a certain time and place, thirty or more years earlier. Second, combat field hospitals, which kept proof of treatment provided for wounded veterans, were often hit by bombs themselves.

The same thing could also have happened to the paperwork or records stored in administrative offices on the battlefield. This has made it impossible for some veterans to prove what happened to them and to provide documentation of any treatment they received. It was also sometimes the case that veterans who acquired an injury in battle did not seek immediate treatment and continued to fight to help their fellow soldiers. Now after decades, they cannot prove that they had to decide between surviving, by receiving a timely intervention, or letting others die. Furthermore, there are many cases of veterans only beginning to experience health problems due to something that happened to them during the war many years later.[18] One veteran wrote in an online comment on a news website that when he sought help from the DVMF, he was told that he was lying and that maybe he was recently hit by a car and that he was not a veteran at all.[19] As such, veterans who do not possess the accident memo with full details face numerous obstacles in convincing the DVMF of their injury.

Many veterans believe that the "percentage system" is a discriminatory one, because it divides them into groups with drastically different benefits. I call them "soma-technologies," because they measure the veterans' disabilities by numerous biomedical tests, bureaucratic policies, and rules ratified by the state. The medical commissions at the DVMF assign a "disability percentage" to the injured veterans based on those technologies, mediated by political and ideological bureaucracies. Seyyed Hadi Kasaiezadeh, a veteran, wrote in his blogpost:

> I think the medical staff at the Foundation work like robots who have been brainwashed and just manage to make us feel worse. I myself never go to the hospital as long as I am conscious, unless I faint or have a seizure, then my children take me. How can they compare what we did [in the war] to a few numbers/digits [disability percentage]? I have given up on them in this life, but in the afterlife, I will make sure that justice is served.

Mohammad, a chemically injured, 15 percent-disabled veteran in Shishdar region, states:

> I got shell-shocked trying to rescue my fellow soldiers. On the same day, they took me to Shahid Salimi combat field hospital and after a while I felt troubled mentally. I went under treatment for mental disability. I went to the Ilam province's revolutionary guards station.

Now, they say we have no record for the Salimi hospital. When I go to the medical commission, they tell me that I have been injured in my lungs. Since you don't have your mental disability/injury incident memo (*soorat-e-sānehe ye asāb*)/[memo of a mental-disability causing accident], you don't get more than 3% disability percentage. (Afkarnews, 2013)

A veteran's brother said that he committed suicide due to his inability to work, economic pressure, and the stress caused by unemployment. He attempted to obtain a disability percentage. Even though the application was complete, the foundation refused to acknowledge his disability. The veteran (Akbar Ghaeini) burned himself alive before the eyes of the staff of the Foundation in city of Qom. The veteran killed himself because of the foundation's irresponsible and unaccountable response to his needs. Mehdi Ghaeini, the veteran's older brother, told everyone that his brother attended the war, as a sign of his faith; therefore, he never applied for his disability support/percentage as long as he could work, despite his serious chemical injuries. He applied for his disability support after he realized that being shell-shocked would prevent him from working. Not getting a response from the Foundation, his traumatized state finally led to his extreme action as he took his own life by burning himself alive (Tabnak.ir, 2009).

One problem evident from the veterans' accounts is that they are usually struggling to raise their designated percentage to get more or better care. For instance, veterans whose disability percentage has been determined as less than 25 percent usually complain because few of their needs are ever met. A percentage below 25 percent qualifies a veteran only for basic medical insurance.[20] According to their own words, veterans whose disability percentage is 49 percent or below can use the university entrance quota only once for their children, but the children of veterans with a percentage of 50 percent or above can use the quota as many times as they want with no restrictions. Those with 50 percent and above can also qualify to receive a car.[21]

As is evident in the veterans' own words, the percentage system is elusive, because it is not geared toward rehabilitation and healing. Instead, it incentivizes the exacerbation of veterans' health issues and is more based on a counter-rehabilitation protocol where the more disabled you are, the higher "percentage" you receive. The material reality under this system is that those who are given higher percentages receive slightly more services from the state, although the social welfare system for veterans is extremely corrupt and dysfunctional. As such, the system pushes veterans to believe that the worse their health is, the higher percentage they are granted and the better care they can obtain. The on-site psychologist in the nursing home depicted in the documentary *Amnesia*, mentioned earlier, tells the cameraman that, often, the idea of rehabilitation after trauma is about helping the person feel better and getting them closer to their state before the trauma (e.g., natural disaster, war, car accidents, etc.) (Soleiman Nia, 2012). However, the percentage system or the soma-technology of disability measurement functions as a counter-rehabilitation mechanism, "pushing veterans to never become rehabilitated or feel better. If they do, they risk losing the percentage they have already been given, which means losing already inadequate benefits" (Kazemi, 2019a, p. 10). In a veteran's battle with the state to be recognized as a disabled person in need of care, the complex dialectics of cure-pride or the "elimination" versus "production" of disability are present. On the one hand, veterans are expected to "get better," rehabilitate, and avoid becoming a "burden" on the state, while, to keep or increase their percentage, they are incentivized to "not get better" or even get worse. Unlike the notion of disability pride in the West, where disability identity and entitlement are negotiated with the state to ensure the individual's right to receive recognition and access services, here the impasse imposed on disabled veterans by the state is through the ideological justifications that getting disabled for the state and by the state is what constructs them as the "legitimate" disabled veteran who is allowed to survive. Here the disability identity is not a vehicle for constructing pride or assuring entitlement; rather, it is a relationship with the state, ensuring the state's survival and legitimacy, not the veterans' access to resources.

Somatechnics of "Cure" and the "Sacred" State

Discourses about rehabilitation or cure inspire uncomfortable conversations within Disability Studies (DS). Eunjung Kim (2017) claims that cure is a form of violence. "Curative Violence," according to Kim, "is when cure is what actually frames the presence of disability as a problem and ends up destroying the subject in the curative process . . . [becoming] at once remedy and poison" (p. 14). In *Curative Violence*, Kim does the important theoretical work of introducing us to the complications of cure. It argues against the dominant narrative of cure as a final journey with a clear destination. Kim conceptualizes cure as a "transaction" or "negotiation" of potential risks, benefits, and harms taken on by bodies seeking transformation (p. 10).

The Iranian society, both within and outside its geographical borders, very much holds ableist attitudes toward disability, perceives it as "lack," and craves cure at all costs. While working with the Iranian survivors of violence (e.g., survivors of war, genocide, displacement, political torture, and Punitive Limb Amputation [PLA], and acid attacks), I have stretched myself between their needs and my politics as a student of DS. This has not been an easy task. I have often asked myself whether I can avoid apologizing for "cure seeking," while narrating its violent excesses. Eunjung Kim (2017) examines and analyzes these tensions in Korean society, enabling us to imagine possibilities for disabled lives that are free from violence when care is seen "as a negotiation rather than a necessity."

On a personal level, I have lived most of my adult life in Canada, where universal healthcare, although of average quality as per "first world" standards, is available. My research, however, is situated in Iran where healthcare is expensive and unavailable to all, accompanied by an ableist and curative culture prevailing both inside the nation and among the Iranian diaspora. Kim (2017) argues for ways to rethink "cure" as "a set of political, moral, economic, emotional and ambivalent transactions that occur in social relations" (p. 41). This observation is accurate in many contexts including Iran. If the survivors lived in a society that didn't demand what McRuer (2010) calls, "compulsory able-bodiedness," they would not suffer as much, encountering the ableist violence that doesn't "approve" of their injuries, such as blindness, mental disability, or disfigurement.

The rationale behind the "percentage system," or soma-fetishization of disability, appears reminiscent of Puar's (2017) argument in *The Right to Maim*, that the Israeli Defense Forces (IDF) do not shoot the Palestinians to kill them; rather, they shoot to maim them. As such, their logic, as Puar (2017) argues, is "will not let die." There is certainly a resemblance between "the IDF's logic to keep Palestinians alive, but not let them live," and the Iranian state's logic to "keep the disabled veterans alive by often providing a minimum to keep them alive but not to let them get better." However, the IDF's logic is more comprehensible coming from a settler-colonial state who has illegally occupied the land, and its intention is to sustain itself at any cost, similar to other settler colonial states such as the United States, Australia, and Canada.

In contrast, the Iranian state is not a settler-colonial state by definition, although it commits despicable atrocities by indiscriminately oppressing its own people, imprisoning journalists and activists, public executions, torturing political dissidents, PLA for petty theft, running gender apartheid, and turning Iran into a huge prison for women, members of the queer communities, and religious minorities like Bahá'í, not to mention sustaining a corrupt economy that fosters extreme inequality between social classes. How do we explain this level of atrocities from a "legal" state? Usually, states need their masses to rule over them, to reign over their lives and properties, and to control them. Therefore, states usually need the masses to be there and be alive (although not necessarily living a quality life but to be there physically), so their labor can be tapped, and their taxes can be collected. However, with ideological or theocratic states, things could be different, in the sense that the state could even benefit from its citizens' deaths, if it fits with their ideological agenda, and if they could frame it as "martyrdom" in order to guarantee their own survival as a "legitimate" power.

The ideological state needs to cultivate the culture of "sacrificing" for the divine state, as a way to justify its legitimacy. It is in this context that veterans' deaths become as valuable as their lives, if not more, because the state can take advantage of their dead bodies on the front line, or after the war, to show that the masses are ready to die for survival of the state. Once someone goes to "jihad" to fight for God against the "sacred state's enemies," whether the person comes back alive or with/out injury, the state's interest has been served, since there is an extra soldier fighting the enemy. As such, the person's life or death is immaterial to the state, which can be read as ultimate indifference. It is in this set of circumstances that the veterans' life and death should be read juxtaposed with the ideological state's apparatus and its intricacies, which remain in power as long as someone goes to war for it.

Furthermore, reading the veterans' accounts, I have come to realize that the percentage system has been effective in disuniting the veterans and reducing them to "percentage" categories who often envy each other's supposed disability benefits. Therefore, instead of perceiving themselves as one community with similar needs who can get organized and fight for their rights that should be the heart of every disability-rights project, they have been pushed by the state's dividing policies to perceive each other as competing rivals. The collective disability consciousness discussed in Chapter 1, as a key component of the transnational disability theory I proposed, comes in handy here. The Iranian state's ideological and bureaucratic policies have hindered the disabled veterans from developing a collective disability consciousness that could have mobilized their organizing and activism despite state repression.

Soma-fetishization of the Disabled War Veterans through the Ideological Construction of "Living Martyrs"

During and after every war, states are left with the crucial job of narrating and remembering violence in such a way that the ideological legitimacy of the state and the now-concluded war are not questioned.[22] The Iranian state has been selling an "official public narrative of the war" since it started (Haghgou, 2014), and the disabled survivors are a major part of it. Haghgou argues that to legitimize the war and the state's necessary existence according to Shia ideology, the Iranian state has been involved in the project of "cultural nationalism" since the war started (2014). This project of cultural nationalism is anchored in the process of "memorizing" and "remembering" the war, using it as a powerful tool to legitimize the theocratic regime's rule through its ideological cultural constructs, such as the notion of the *jānbāz*, strategically invented and added to the Persian vocabulary by the state in accordance to its ideologies of "jihad" and "martyrdom." After signing the ceasefire, the war did not end for either the state or the people who had fought it. After thirty-six years, the state still uses "memorialization" or "commemoration of the war" in creating a culture of imaginary "struggle" against an invisible "enemy." This happens amid a strategic public amnesia about the dissidents who were imprisoned, tortured, and killed by the state during the 1980s when the war with Iraq was being fought, and a large group who were hanged after the ceasefire with Iraq was signed. This public amnesia was forced upon the nation, as nobody was allowed to ask a question or even talk about the political prisoners, executed and buried in anonymous mass graves on the outskirts of Tehran and other cities (Abrahamian, 1999). As such, the state has used "forgetting" certain things and "remembering" others as a tactic to (re)establish itself in the past forty-five years after the revolution.

The Iranian state has strategically deployed the concept of "resisting" against "forgetting" the eight years of "sacred defense" to sustain its dominance and control over the nation. Haghgou (2014) argues that the Iranian state keeps the memory of the war alive "as a mechanism for 'modelling' of the past in the present moment" (p. 75).

As elementary school children, we were supposed to visit disabled veterans (of the Iran-Iraq War) in nursing homes and pay respect to the martyrs in cemeteries on a regular basis. When I was twelve, we participated in one of those school trips to an institution that was home to several war veterans who had become disabled because of Iraqi chemical weapons used during the war. The institution was a three-story complex, with each level accommodating twenty to thirty veterans. Each of them had been living there for ten to seventeen years at the time. We were a group of twenty-five students holding gifts we had brought for them. Each veteran received a shirt and a set of nail-clippers because our principal thought that this was what they "needed the most." One of the staff gave us a tour around the facility. He described the building as having three levels, from which the first level was home for those who have up to approximately 25 percent disability; the second level housed disabled veterans of approximately 25 percent to 45 percent disability; and the third level encompassed veterans with approximately 45 percent disability and above. Those on the third level did not receive visitors because the level of chemical burns/injuries on their bodies was so severe that it prevented them from tolerating any clothing, and they lay naked on their beds all day. Being a twelve-year-old, I was curious to visit all the veterans and was confused about why these people were being taken care of in an institution, or why they were living in such difficult circumstances. What had caused those horrible chemical burns? Wasn't the Iraqi army prohibited from using chemical weapons according to the Geneva Convention?

As I entered the cold, hospital-like nursing home, I saw three beds next to each other in the first level. Patients were lying on each bed, covered by white sheets with only their heads out. It was a depressing and gloomy place, an institution thick with the smell of cleaning chemicals. I looked around and walked toward the bed which was positioned next to the window, the farthest to the door. I said "hello" in a shaky and timid voice, perhaps because I felt shy as a twelve-year-old. The veteran lying on that bed moved his eyes slowly toward me to capture the owner of the tiny voice. He looked up and said to me, "Do you know how it feels to be forgotten for seventeen years? Do you know how it feels not to have any visitors for seventeen years?" I did not know what to say. Was he happy to see a visitor? Was he upset for not having had any visitors so far? Was he missing his family? Was he missing his friends with whom he had gone to war but without whom he had come back? I felt ashamed, helpless, ignorant, and powerless. I felt bad that he was lonely and abandoned, both by the society and the state that was responsible for providing care for him. For more than two decades since then, I am still searching for an answer to that veteran's question.

Haghgou (2014) reveals that the Iranian state's project of cultural nationalism is carried out through texts, memoirs, photography, museums, street art, memorial sites, cinema, theater, and commemoration events. Oddly, to this long list of cultural production sites, I add both martyrs' cemeteries, which the Iranian state calls the *Golzār e Shohadā* or Rose Garden of Martyrs, and the nursing homes for disabled veterans, which the state calls *Āsāyeshgāh* or Asylum. This seems like a bizarre addition, but if we think about why the staff in my secondary school would take us for mandatory visits to these sites, we start to see the same project in effect here. Schools were not supposed to take us to nursing homes and cemeteries to make the veterans feel cared for and loved. This was also part of the cultural nationalism project to prepare the next generation for the same "sacrifice" and "defense" against internal and external "enemies," both present and future. The main agenda was the regime's survival at any cost and the social relations of capital within the nation-state. This Shia-nationalist acculturation process was done by inculcating the idea of martyrdom in the younger generation, preparing them to accept the legitimacy of the past wars, and grooming them to fight the future wars.

Bannerji (2005) argues that it is a mistake to think that cultural production sites, such as religion, text, art, or language, can exist in isolation from power relations embedded in the social. In fact, considering them as independent categories that can function outside the relations of power is an ideological construct itself. Therefore, it is important to take a holistic approach when thinking about cultural production, in relation with the material world, mediated by social relations. In other words, perceiving culture, theocracy, or religion as neutral and harmless "ideas," conceals the oppression and exploitation that could be happening within them as routine practices. Along with Haghgou (2014), I contend that the Iranian state's survival, achieved partially through the project of cultural nationalism, occurs at the price of silencing a myriad of war stories. This concealing of truth and concrete evidence once again reminds us that we are dealing with an ideological regime, because the very function of ideology is to conceal the reality in favor of the ruling class.

The state accounts and narratives of the war are deeply shadowed by invalid facts and untruths, based on manufactured, ideological knowledge. The proliferation of state-sponsored content on disabled veterans and the Iran-Iraq War "is a well engrained component of the same ideological machinery in 'protecting' the status and sanctity of the [1979] revolution" (Haghgou, 2015, p. 35). The construction of "living martyrs" as a social category is not the only ideological category within the Iranian state's cultural production projects. Educating future generations with ideological, and therefore fragmented, knowledge is an insurance policy for the state to sustain itself without having to worry about potential dissidents. According to Marx (1845/1976), ideology and ideological knowledge production operate as a process that separates the individual from material reality. This is why the Iranian state uses ideological knowledge as its public war story to indoctrinate the new generation of Iranians. If the younger generation ever could discover the real experiences of those who fought in the war and have come back, they might start questioning its legitimacy. The war's legitimacy is the foundation upon which the Iranian state has established itself. The state cannot afford any questioning; any kind of query invariably means questioning the legitimacy of the state.

In this context, consider this parallel example from India. India's Hindu Nationalism, according to Bannerji (2005), is a political and cultural project that equates "national" with Hindu, aiming at homogenizing the entire Indian polity. Hindu nationalism is a Hindu-nation-building project carried out through mobilization of discourses such as essentialized Hinduism (*Hindutva*) and proliferation of ideological cultural productions such as state-run TV shows. Bannerji (2005) demonstrates that the process of cultivating "Hindu Nationalism" with a significant increase in Hindu right-wing movement in India is partly carried out via reference to manufactured evidence from imaginary glory days of the nation, a romanticized past, authenticity, and "true" Hinduism.

The same logic applies to the Iranian state as it fights to legitimize itself every day, as it has done since the 1979 revolution. This is an ongoing process in which the Islamic state struggles to cultivate its national narrative, deeply rooted in the manufactured glory days of the nation (not Iran as a country but the Shia *umma*) at the dawn of Shi'ism some 1,400 years ago (Haghgou, 2014). For instance, the ubiquitous referral and comparison of disabled veterans to a prominent historical Shia figure, Imam Hussein's brother, Abolfazl, who was mutilated during the highly grieved, yet celebrated, incident of Ashura,[23] is framed in a way to indicate that the Iran-Iraq War resembles previous wars fought in defense of and for the integrity of Shia Islam.

The cultural nationalism project is not easy to carry out though, because it needs a constant struggle on behalf of the state to exploit the nation and oppress people's individual and social liberties through a sophisticated and corrupt judiciary system. To make the process easier, the state manufactures the truth to decrease the space between consent and coercion. Manufacturing the truth usually involves a missing link between what has actually taken place in the material world and what is being narrated in the here and now (Bannerji, 2005; Shahidian, 2002). Finally, this ideological concealment between material reality and ideology facilitates the fetishization process that I discussed thoroughly in the Introduction. The concept of "living martyr" becomes a fetish, an ideological construction that produces disability as a fetishized category of body, meaning, and being. This also involves the fetishization of social, political, and economic relations, as well as the fetishization of ways of being and becoming disabled.

Free Labor of Dying

Given the elaborate lengths the state goes to in its construction and maintenance of the memory of the war, it is ironic that it does not actually care about the "real/material" remnants of the war, the disabled bodies of the wounded, both soldiers and civilians. What the state considers as a remnant is a "memory," which it has been manipulating since the war ended. The Iranian state has assigned a special role, a form of free labor, to disabled veterans who have survived the war. The idea of "living martyrs" is an assignment or a form of free labor that disabled veterans are supposed to carry out and perform. This construction has been propagated through popular culture, poems, films, museums, and myriad events. This works as a form of fetishization that masks the reality of disablement in wounded soldiers. The Islamic Republic is an assemblage of class society, kleptocracy, carceral statehood, and Shia militarism, which uses disabled and dead bodies as a resource for cheap labor. This is what I mean by fetishization of the dead and disabled bodies as sacrificial commodities for the state. The disabled bodies of "living martyrs" are used to ensure the survival of the state by performing crucial, free, and ideological labor for the state, while "remaining" disabled in the meantime by the state.

The "living martyrs" (read disabled veterans) and the way the state deploys their bodies is a remarkable fusion of the social and medical approaches to disability. They have medical conditions that allow society to understand them as disabled, and the state uses medical institutions and a lack of care in order to keep them unwell. This proves that the state has a political stake in keeping them unwell, to ensure that they can perform their ideological role/function. This is another layer of fetishization that the state adds to their multilayered processes of producing and maintaining disabled bodies, as part of their capitalist-theocratic approach in which bodies of the masses are human shields during war and ideological objects in the aftermath of war.

The "living martyr" essentially exists as the "living dead," fulfilling the obligatory, ideological role of the state but not existing as a living disabled human who wishes to live with adequate care and support. This contradiction is a traumatic experience, an extra layer of psychological pressure on the disabled veterans who are expected to occupy an impossible position of being and not being at the same time. Muhyi al- Din Ibn ʿArabi (d. AH 638/ 1240 CE) had defined *barzakh* as "an imaginal border that joins by separating, such as an isthmus or a bridge, and that is the site of a passage for bodies and spirits; a partition, a screen, between two modalities of being, spiritual and corporeal, widening and delimiting, this world and the other; the site where the impossible can manifest itself in concrete form" (cited in Pandolfo, 2018, p. 156). In this context, this *barzakh* is a space, an image, the eclipse of human presence, a fetish, a purgatory that a "living martyr" is expected to occupy. This framed "image" is an imaginary status that rests at once in the material world of the experience of wound, trauma, and "almost dying," in its historical reality, and on the autonomous ontological status of the "image" itself as the state views it. This fetishization process produces a "living dead" with no affect but ideology, and a "dead living" whose disability is stigmatized, glorified, and erased all at once.

This contradiction, once internalized by the veteran, becomes a commodity fetish, a part of reality concealing all of reality. Once the commodity fetish takes over the real person who is behind it, the exploitation process begins, and sustains itself as long as the veteran does not resist it. In other words, the fetishization process relies on the veteran's silence to suppress his agency behind the ideological role of a "living dead" in order to survive and receive the bare minimum services to scarcely live, or to remain living. Therefore, the theocratic-capitalist state produces disability as a problem in need of erasure (read solution), by suppressing the veterans' humanity and agency as disabled persons, discriminating against them, and commodifying their wounds.

Toward Nonideological Forms of Knowledge

Growing up in Iran, my classmates and I were taught that the war was about defending our nation, Islam, and the revolution against Saddam Hussein and the West. The Islamic Republic claims that it was defending its borders with Iraq for the entire eight years of the war, and even calls the war the "sacred defense." This has been challenged by numerous scholars and historians, demonstrating through historical evidence that the state was only defending its borders for three years (1980–1983) and was actually on the offensive for the following five years until 1988 (Abrahamin, 2008; Ghamari-Tabrizi, 2009; Katouzian, 2010). Commanders often ordered veterans to run in front of the enemy tanks and form a "human shield."[24] However, the official state narrative completely denies this, with many surviving veterans claiming otherwise. The reality is that the Iranian state has only fought one actual war, but it is always in the process of "defense and resistance" against imaginary wars waged upon its "revolutionary values." The state calls this process "promoting the culture of martyrdom," because it argues that the "enemy" is attacking us on every possible front. Therefore, the whole society is in need of protection.

If veterans, researchers, historians, and scholars, who have studied the war, would have the space and security to tell us what actually happened, the public would have access to what I call the "nonideological" knowledge of the war, a knowledge that is based on truth and not manufactured narratives. We know that if people have access to the truth their view of the state changes, which ultimately poses a threat to the state that rules by justifying its existence based on manufactured narratives of the war. This nonideological knowledge and consciousness may also lead people to oppose the state in the form of protests, demonstrations, and possibly resulting in an overthrow of the authoritarian state.

Haghgou (2014, p. 72) discloses that the official public war story is used "as an educational repository, where the experiences of those men and women are to be used as models for the current and future of state building." Therefore, all this effort, on behalf of the state, is for producing ideological knowledge around the war as a process of "culturalization." The archival materials of the Iranian state consist of several sources, such as the *Foundation for the Preservation and Publication of Values of the Sacred Defense* (Sāzmān hifẓ āsār nashr arzeshhai defā' moqaddas), the *Foundation of Martyrs and Veterans Affairs* (Bonyād shahīd va omūr īsārgarān), and Tehran Peace Museum, among others. In these sources, produced by the state, the category of "living martyr" is not limited to what it means literally but what it means in relation to the "sacred" state's futurity. The Iranian state sustains itself by funding and empowering organizations like the Veterans' Foundation that overlook the production of cultural content on the Iran-Iraq War and uses disability as a token, tool, or propaganda technology, to construct that content.

Disabled veterans, or "living martyrs," are constructed as part of the state ideology, in the forms of "embodied cultural icons," rather than disabled persons in need of care. What is reflected in the cultural materials produced by different institutions is, in fact, a direct implementation and concretization of how "living martyrs" should behave.[25] This is an indirect way of ensuring how they make sense of their disability and wounds, or how they behave as being more than ordinary human beings. "Living martyrs" are constructed as extremely gracious and patient people who are supposed to be "content," if not euphoric, with what has happened to them. Note that "content," in this instance, means apolitical, because claiming a disability identity inevitably constitutes a political relationship between the individual and the state, in which the state is expected to provide support and access for the disabled. The disabled veterans, however, are expected to perceive their disability as a "blessing" from Allah, who has been kind enough to have given them an opportunity to "give" something for their faith, country, and revolution. Sadly, we rarely hear their actual voices.

Wounded veterans, who returned from the war, have a particular form of consciousness arising from their concrete experience, which should serve as an entry point to produce a nonideological form of knowledge. I say nonideological because it does not conceal the connection between the individual subjects and the material world. One example includes memoirs, or any other cultural production, written/produced by veterans. However, the veterans must be allowed the freedom of expression to narrate what actually happened in the battlefield and not repeat what the state wants them to. Although a veteran challenging the "state's official narrative" (Radstone & Schwarz, 2010, p. 133; Haghgou, 2014, p. 53), while inside Iran, could face arrest, torture, imprisonment, and deprivation of their small monthly disability support allowance, some may subtly challenge the official version of events and get away with it. For instance, when Bajoghli (2014), a researcher, had attempted to interview the veterans, one of them had said to her: "Miss, do you want the official version that we have to tell the television crews every year?" (p. 42).

Defetishizing the Body

Bannerji defines cultural nationalism as a nation-building project often rooted in tensions and conflicts propagated by sexism, racism, casteism, ethnicity, religion, imagined "enemies" of the nation, and a historical prototype (i.e., good old days of the nation). Through the project of cultural nationalism,

Bannerji argues, the state is in a constant oscillation between consent and coercion. One way to manage this steady struggle is the invention of ideological categories such as "woman," "the glorious past," and "culture." To this list, I add the category of "living martyr." These categories are disconnected from the historical and material context in which they exist. When we look at the "Living Martyr" category within the official war story of the Iranian state and analyze it through Bannerji's (2005) cultural nationalist lens, we can start to defetishize this concept.

The process of defetishization is necessary if we aim at seeing a real person with a disability behind the ideological construct of the "living martyr." Haghgou (2014) points out that the ideological content of the constructed categories can tell us a lot about those who created them and why they did so. As such, if we can carry out a thorough analysis of these categories, we will be able to unveil the social relations behind them. This unveiling process is equivalent to a defetishizing process, which I defined in the Introduction as a component of the TDM and has the revolutionary capacity to produce nonideological knowledge and praxis.

One way in which the process of defetishization can take place is by listening to what the veterans have to say about the war and by refusing to believe the "official narrative" (Radstone & Schwarz, 2010, p. 133) that the nation-state imposes on us and on those who die and become disabled through wars. If we aim at producing a form of knowledge based on the material reality under which disabled people live, we need to shift our analysis and pave the way for a revolutionary understanding of disability and its relationship with the nation-state, capitalist economy, and class society, contextualized within transnational political consciousness and activism. It is as important to organize ourselves as disability-rights activists as it is to organize ourselves against disabling wars, and resist becoming ahistorical and apolitical selves existing outside relations of power.

3

Rotten Wounds

Madness and Disability in Prison

I am sitting here haunted by those Shahla Talebi (2011) calls "Ghosts of Revolution," the Iranian dissidents who participated in the 1979 revolution, overthrew the Pahlavi monarchy, were suppressed, arrested, and tortured, and eventually went "mad" under torture in the new Islamic regime's prisons. As I did in the previous chapters of this book, I strive to defetishize the disabilities created under the violence of exploitative social relations, in this case, political suppression, imprisonment, torture, and withholding care. The task here is to attend to the material reality that the Iranian political prisoners in the 1980s went through, and the ways in which their bodymind acquired disabilities/wounds throughout this process, and how their bodyminds responded to that violence. I also discuss the disability-care dialectic in and among political prisoners so as to understand what constituted the infrastructures of collective care, access, and interdependence among them in response to the imposed disablement and madness.

I use the Transnational Disability Model (TDM), developed in Chapter 1, to resist objectification of disabled prisoners in the hands of the state apparatus and to foreground the possibility and necessity of people's participation in making their own history. The TDM approach does not end at the exercise of power on the prisoners' bodymind but extends to the politically conscious human beings who can analyze their own roles in their history, and according to Sakhi (2014), "respond" to that power. As such, using a TDM lens rooted in the Dialectical and Historical Materialism (DHM), I argue that it's not just the state that used the prisoners' bodymind to exercise its power but also the prisoners who utilized their bodyminds to respond to and resist the state apparatus.

This chapter stems from resistance, hauntings, transgenerational political struggle, agony, pain, and, in the words of Primo Levi (1989), "proxy witnessing." Levi, a Holocaust survivor, defined the term as a way of accessing someone's testimony who has ceased to speak through other people who continue to speak for that person. This is not a testimony that usually stems from a place of memory but consciousness, because I have accessed the data in this chapter via proxy witnessing not firsthand experience. In other words, as Marianne Hirsch (2012) claims, we can come to remember other people's memories through a process she terms "postmemory." Hirsch defines this metaphor "as the relationship that 'the generation after' bears to the personal, collective, and cultural trauma of those who came before—to experiences, they 'remember' only by means of the stories, images, and behaviors with which they grew up. But these experiences were [nonetheless] transmitted to them so deeply and affectively as to seem to constitute memories in their own right" (p. 5). This is also similar to Octavia Butler's concept of hyperempathy, created in the *Parable* series, which leads people to experience the perceived pain or pleasure of others in their own body. However, Couser (2012) has argued that memory is "a notoriously unreliable and highly selective faculty" (p. 19). Relating personal experience, the legendary and resistant survivor of Iran's prisons, Shokoufeh Sakhi, contends with Couser's claim that even one's own memory is not a camcorder with absolute accuracy, never mind a memory accessed years later via different layers of proxy witnessing (personal communication, 2019). This means that there will be inconsistencies in this chapter's narratives, and I acknowledge the holes and fragmented information that characterize what is presented in this chapter. The accounts are not meant to present as absolute truths, but as memories—lived, experienced, and communicated both directly and indirectly.

Part of this impossible story is the story of those who were tortured to the point where their bodymind couldn't take the pain and agony anymore in the realm of rationality, so they resorted to irrationality/madness as an alternative way of being in the world. The Islamic regime's goal was to turn dissidents into supporters, Marxists into Muslims, comrades to enemies, revolutionaries into torturers, university students to interrogators, and nonbelievers to believers. Afterall, "this revolution—like others—had devoured its own children." (Abrahamian, 2008, p. 181). Many dissidents resisted, some gave in, broke[1] and participated in the harming of their mates, and some went mad. Madness in the 1980s' context in Iran's political prisons cannot be interpreted as a neutral biomedical or health issue but a sophisticated mechanism and reaction from the bodymind to the ideological prison apparatus and suffering. In that context, madness meant "no" to the conversion process, where all other means had already been exhausted and all other roads paved. The mad prisoners managed to deprive the Islamic regime of having an extra cog in their torture machine. Torture is about isolating the victim (Bernstein, 2015) and taking the body away from the person who lives in it. By going mad, the mad prisoners reclaimed their bodyminds which had been taken away from them by the torturer and the entire disciplinary apparatus and made it their own. They wandered into the world of madness and left the prison while still in prison.

Methodology

Over the past twelve years in exile, I have been engaged in an ongoing investigation of incarceration and torture in post-revolution Iran, through conversations, ethnographic fieldwork, and formal interviews with diasporic intellectuals, political dissidents, journalists, survivors of state violence, and community organizers. I have also continued to work alongside exiled survivors of the Iranian regime's atrocities, organizing with families of the executed political prisoners as part of two transnational movements, *Justice-Seeking* and *Justice 88*. These movements are being fought by survivors and family members who have refused to remain silent, following the extermination of their relatives throughout the 1980s and in the massacre of summer 1988 ordered by Ruhollah Khomeini.

Although the observations and interactions described here took place over several years in different settings from the 1988 prisoners' massacre's commemoration events in Canada to hiking trips in the United States to Skype calls from Germany, Sweden, Switzerland, Netherlands, the U.K., and Australia, for this project, I interviewed thirty former political prisoners who survived torture and imprisonment in the 1980s in Iran. They now live in exile, as part of the Iranian diaspora. I conducted the interviews in Farsi/Persian and later translated them into English.

My interviewees from a wide range of political affiliations reported that they, their family members, and their acquaintances were persecuted primarily for their political beliefs and opposition to the new Islamic Regime. Political groups persecuted by the regime included: the People's Mujahideen Organization of Iran (MKO); the Organization of Iranian People's Fedai Guerrillas (OIPFG) and its offshoots, the OIPFG (Minority [Aghaliat] and sixteen Azar); the Union of Iranian Communists; the Union of Combatant Communists; the Organization of Revolutionary Workers of Iran (Rah-e Kargar); the Iranian Organization of Sahand; the Forghan Organization; the

Organization of Razmandegan for the Freedom of the Working Class; and the Organization of Paykar for the Emancipation of the Working Class.

I conducted interviews with them in person and/or using online technology. All my participants have escaped Iran after release and sought asylum in Europe, the United States, Canada, or Australia. For their security, I use pseudonyms to refer to them or those to whom they refer. The names of the former political prisoners who have written their memoirs are cited as is. Wherever they have written a memoir using an alias, I have also mentioned the alias in citing their works. If they have used their own names, I too have cited them using their real names.

My technique was convenience and snowball sampling. As the survivors' communities are tight-knit and most people know each other closely, they immediately informed each other about my research. Shahla Talebi, the author of *Ghosts of Revolution: Rekindled Memories of Imprisonment in Iran* (2011), who is a survivor of both the Shah's Regime and Islamic Republic, helped me enormously with locating participants and building trust between us. If it were not for her vast network of survivors, I would not have accessed the communities I did. Shahla stayed in my home for more than twenty days to talk about my project and identify people I should approach for interviewing.

Prison Memories, Memoirs, and Incommunicable Pain

What we know about the atrocities committed against dissidents is what witnesses have shared. Some survivors of the tarnished Islamic Republic of Iran's prisons in the 1980s, who managed to stay alive, have written a memoir, revealing what happened to them and their fellow prisoners. Some have been organizing with family members of executed prisoners in exile as part of several *jonbesh-e-edalatkhahi,* or the "justice-seeking movements," to hold the Islamic Republic leaders accountable. This resulted in the establishment of public platforms, such as Iranian People's Tribunal[2] in The Hague.[3] Some, on the other hand, have not spoken at all, perhaps due to the impossibility of re-telling what they witnessed. As Agamben (2002), inspired by Levi, reveals: The true witnesses of extreme atrocities are often those who have lost their capacity to speak.

Few names kept repeating themselves in their heartbreaking stories discussed multiple times by multiple survivors, in my perusal of Iranian prison literature from the post-revolutionary era as much in conversations with prison survivors. Many were just names, meaning, I could not for sure match a name against a living evidence, such as a memoir. Some were executed, some were hospitalized or institutionalized in a psychiatric ward, or ended their own lives after dealing with severe physical and mental health concerns.

Besides, the Iranian People's Tribunal's Truth Commission (2012) found that "Some people went mad in prison; everybody suffered either physical or psychological damage. In Evin and Ghezelhesar prisons, it was possible to hear people being tortured and their bones broken at night; the witness's jaw was broken during torture" (p. 188). These people had entered the Islamic Republic's prisons with a non-disabled bodymind and exited it (if at all) with shattered ones. What had happened to them? Who were they? I call them "mad" prisoners.

I use the word "mad" to refer to wounded political prisoners whose behaviors and actions were considered different from what others around them perceived as "normal"[4] in the existing context. Nonnormative behavior included remaining quiet and not speaking with anyone for long periods, going nude in public, staying under really cold or hot showers with their clothes on for a long time, becoming incontinent, not caring about personal hygiene, going periodically catatonic and not moving for long periods, refusing to eat for days and then suddenly devouring everything they could get their hands on, hoarding food and other things, masturbating in public, cursing guards and Regime officials, imitating animals, going against the ward's regulations, being delusional, and being actively suicidal. These behaviors are ones often described by the fellow prisoners I have spoken with, and in rare cases by family members. However, madness played out in many shapes and forms. For instance, prisoners would perceive their cellmate as mad if s/he gazed into oblivion and remained silent for a long time, or one who was engaged in washing her/himself too much or obsessed with cleaning was perceived as someone with obsessive compulsive "disorder." If someone refused to use the bathroom, and therefore, became malodorous and unbearable, s/he was perceived as mad. Finally, one with unrealistic hopes would come across as delusional.

Shokoufeh Sakhi, a former leftist political prisoner who spent eight years in three different notorious prisons in post-revolutionary Iran (nine months of which was in the "coffins-cell"[5]), was the executive director of the Iranian People's Tribunal. Sakhi (2017) problematized a purely legal approach to justice-seeking by indicating that the survivors should not be reduced to helpless victims, bearers of the perpetrators' power inscribed on their bodyminds. Instead, she argued, people who have resisted the Islamic Republic's power in one way or another should be allowed to say how they responded to power. The point, as Sakhi (2014) argues, is to acknowledge the "response-ability" of the survivors, however tormented their sense of agency, subjectivity, and autonomy may be. This shift of focus from the perpetrator's power to survivor's response to power is what distinguishes a legal approach to "justice-seeking from an ethical approach" (Sakhi, 2017).

Inspired by Sakhi, I partially conceptualize mad behavior on the part of mad prisoners as a response, response-ability, or ability to respond to the forms of power, exercised in political prison (Kazemi & Karah, 2022).[6] By "response," I mean resistance, submission, breaking, collaboration, silence, etc. I also refrain from pathologizing those behaviors from a bio-medical perspective, which usually disregards the historical and socio-cultural context in which the behavior occurs. Instead, I strive to unpack those "non-normative" actions and expressions as ways to comprehend them, not to diagnose, label, or judge them. Furthermore, I foreground the materiality of the flesh and the mind as they get tortured, disciplined, and wounded and inevitably acquire a disability but manage to resist and reclaim their dissident selves embedded in the bodymind from the brutal state apparatus that sought to break and alter them into collaborators.

The first step toward destigmatizing and understanding madness is to contextualize it within a clear social and historic trajectory. Before interpreting one's behavior as madness, we need to ask under what circumstances the behavior emerged.

Annihilation of the Other

> I have lived on the lip of insanity, wanting to know reasons,
> knocking on a door. It opens. I've been knocking from the inside.
>
> —RUMI

The Iranian People's Tribunal, a grassroots justice-seeking movement, conducted a thorough investigation using the Truth Commissions run by several judges and reached this conclusion: "It is believed that around 20,000 dissidents were executed and disappeared between 1981 and 1988. The victims' bodies were buried in undisclosed mass graves. To this day, many families do not know where their loved ones are buried. The Islamic Republic of Iran refuses to give any information about where the graves are located, but a number of graves have been discovered by the families. This difficulty is symptomatic of the effects this atrocity had on the families of those directly victimized by the massacre. Wives, mothers, sisters, husbands, brothers, daughters, and sons of victims have suffered extended psychological and emotional damage" (Iranian People's Tribunal, 2012, p. 6). The hallmark of these atrocities was the 1988[7] massacre, where approximately 4000–5,000 leftist political dissidents were executed, most of whom had already served their prison sentences and should have technically been released (Abrahamian, 2008; Akhavan, 2017).

Shahrnoush Parsipour—a prominent writer, arrested for having "banned" literature in her car trunk and incarcerated for four and a half years—estimates that in late 1981, the average age of her ward mates was nineteen and a half (1995). According to numerous accounts, prison memoirs,[8] witness testimonies, interviews, and the findings of the Iranian People's Tribunal's Truth Commissions, prisoners were held under extremely inhuman conditions, and the torture methods comprised beatings, sleep deprivation,[9] standing still for up to seventy-two hours,[10] *bastinado* (beating the sole of a victim's feet with electric cables),[11] flagellation, and *ghapani*.[12] "Other forms of torture included squeezing of testicles, infliction of burns with lighters, cigarettes, or hot irons, deliberate mutilation, tying of prisoners to gallows for long durations in winter and summer, and the violent thrusting of a ballpoint pen up a prisoner's nose" (Iranian People's Tribunal, 2012, p. 21).

In the year 2000, a letter was published from the memoirs of Ayatollah Montazeri (2000), former designated successor to Ruhollah Khomeini, after he had been removed from power and placed under house arrest.[13] He wrote:

> Do you know that a large number of people have died under torture by interrogators? Do you know that in Mashhad prison, due to a lack of medical care and attention for young girls, they were forced to excise the ovaries and uterus of around 25 of those young girls and in that manner, *nāqes kardand* [mutilated/disabled] their bodies and reproductive organs?! ... Do you know that they took [sexually assaulted or raped] young girls by force in some of the prisons of the Islamic Republic? Do you know that when young women are interrogated, usage of vulgar and *nāmoosi* [sexual] related terminology is commonplace?

In addition to that, according to numerous published memoirs and the Iranian People's Tribunal's Truth Commission, during the 1980s "political prisoners in Iran, besides getting beaten and abused on a regular basis, were also kept in grossly unhygienic conditions. They were denied soap and the right to showers. The prisons were overcrowded, leading to cases of skin disease. Showers were cold, where provided, even when families offered to pay for water heaters. Cells were teeming with rats, clothes, with lice. One survivor reported that a clergyman came to inspect her cell but would not enter because the smell was so ghastly" (2013, p. 24).

In Ghezelhessar prison, for instance, between 1982 and 1984, many prisoners developed various health problems, such as kidney failure due to the extremely poor quality of drinking water, constant pain, infected feet caused by bastinado, headaches, skin disease, toothaches,[14] mental disorders, vaginal infections, urinary tract infections, and sleep terrors. Sinus infection devastated Siavash, one of my interviewees, in Ghezelhessar prison. Skin fungus was prevalent. Lice was everywhere. At all hours, there were long queues and long waiting periods before using the bathroom. There was little to no sunshine. Also, extreme humidity caused breathing issues. The air quality led to respiratory disease among the prisoners due to very little air circulation. One of the survivors, Nastaran, whom I spoke with, developed chronic bronchitis as well as claustrophobia as a result of being stuck in small spaces with many people over long periods.

While in solitary confinement in Gohardasht prison, Siavash heard people screaming and almost howling at night. Perhaps, they were using their voice to resist the maddening silence and declare themselves alive. Siavash stated: "One person howled, and that caused a chain reaction. The ward trembled when they screamed at night. In 1986 [after three years in solitary], I screamed, too." Based on my conversations with many survivors, I learned that these chain reactions were common among many groups, such as those with epilepsy, who would scream or howl at night. This could have been seen as a sign of collective resistance. In Nastaran's ward in Ghezelhessar, she remembered three inmates with epilepsy would have a chain/contagious reaction to each other's seizures. Other prisoners had learned that once this happened, they needed to put a spoon in the epileptic prisoners' mouth to prevent choking.

One form of torture that produced many mad people was the so-called "resurrection"/"boxes"/"graves"/"machines"/"the human-making factory" or (*kārkhāneh-ye-ādam sāzi*), "the human-making machine," or (*dastgah-e-ādam sāzi*), that was tested in Ghezelhessar prison from the fall of 1983 to the summer of 1984. "Prisoners were forced to squat for hours in boxes in the form of coffins, with Quranic incantations sometimes blared loudly at them, during which time they were intermittently beaten and whipped on their heads and faces" (Iranian People's Tribunal, 2012, p. 34). On one occasion, when Nastaran was kept in the "coffins" in Ghezelhessar, she was beaten so badly by the warden, Rahmani, that she temporarily lost her sight in the right eye. The cable's tail in the warden's hand landed exactly on Nastaran's eye. She regained her sight but only after a few months. Another survivor, Taban, said that she was subjected to flogging on three different occasions. The floggings were so brutal that they caused internal bleeding in one of her kidneys. On another occasion, they beat her so badly that her body turned black from bruises, and she became incontinent for a while. Nastaran said, "Another prisoner, [H.] had been operated on. An extra piece of flesh had grown between her breasts. It was scary."

One woman lost both ears to infection as a result of being beaten so severely. By the time she was allowed medical treatment outside the prison facility, at the insistence of her family, the infection had already caused severe hearing loss. Over the years, even after her release, in spite of multiple procedures and operations, she eventually lost hearing in both ears. This is an example of how violence causes disability, a scar that remains on the bodymind forever.

Furthermore, bastinado destroyed many prisoners' feet. One prisoner, Hassan, mentioned another prisoner whose feet were flogged with an electric cord or cable to the degree that they had turned black, which led to double amputation of his legs. The little toe was gone in some cases. Beatings with electric cables caused many brain injuries in prisoners as their head was hit frequently. Hassan told me about a prisoner who had suffered a concussion after being hit by an electric cable in the head repeatedly during his interrogation. After that incident, the prisoner showed signs of madness, although only in the wintertime. Kidney failure as a result of bastinado was prevalent. Sir Geoffrey Nice, who investigated the 1988 massacre of political prisoners in Iran, states, "dialysis was provided for prisoners with kidney failure, not to save them but to give them more time to be tortured" (Nice, 2013). A survivor, Iraj Mesdaghi (2012), in his testimony before the Iranian People's Tribunal, also talked about the process of "not letting die so they can torture you more."

Similarly, here is how Siavash described his experience with bastinado and the logic of "not letting die" right after his arrest in June 1982:

> It [Evin] was a slaughterhouse. I knew it would be. We were told about the torture. The [bastinado] cable had three braided strands. They shoved a dirty cloth in my mouth, so I couldn't breathe. Two or even three people flogged at the same time. Once it [the cable] hit my feet, the pain was so enormous that it caused me to involuntarily jump up in the air and lift the bed with the guards sitting on me. My teeth broke. I couldn't even crawl. There was a room reserved for people who had been physically destroyed. Only three non-disabled were able to carry others to the bathroom. There were foams of blood everywhere on the floor. The volume of floggings was so much that many died under it. Many people's kidneys stopped working, and they had to go through dialysis. The Regime would force them to go through dialysis, so they could torture them more.

Even more than thirty years after their release, some survivors continue to have nightmares and sleep terrors. Some developed phobias they never had before. Nastaran mentioned that she developed a fear of heights, which she never had before going to prison. Some became claustrophobic. Others still sit on the edge of their seat more than thirty years later, since in prison they had to live in extremely overcrowded cells like sardines. Many developed irreversible physical conditions and permanent damage, such as spider veins, varicocele, backache, extreme pain in the legs and feet, and seizures after enduring mandatory standing for up to seventy-two, or more, hours at a time. The psychological effects were also devastating. Some started hallucinating after remaining sleepless for days at a time. As is self-evident from these accounts, "becoming mad" is a historical materialist process and category—not just a pathology. Madness is also a locally created human condition as much as an alternative state of existence, so as to handle extreme forms of dehumanizing torture and prolonged incarceration.

The Right to Wound: Neither Life, Nor Death

Zohreh was one of the names that kept appearing in other former prisoners' memoirs. She was referred to as a bright university student majoring in pure sciences at a top university at the time she was arrested. I interviewed a few prisoners who had had a chance to either see Zohreh or share their cell with her. Sousan, one of former prisoners I interviewed, remembered that one day, while she, Zohreh, and a few other inmates were in their cell, Zohreh knocked on the door and asked the guard to open it so she could go to the bathroom. Extreme restriction on going to the bathroom was another level of physical and psychological torture the Islamic Republic of Iran (IRI) imposed on the bodyminds of the prisoners. The guards had the power to delay or deny the prisoners any access to the toilet, the most basic physiological need.[15] Making the prisoners beg to go to the bathroom by ignoring their cries, not opening the door, giving them three minutes or less to relieve themselves, and ignoring the resultant health complications that the prisoners had to deal with (e.g., digestive problems, chronic constipation, urinary tract and vaginal infections, hemorrhoid, kidney issues, etc.) was standard practice in certain periods in the 1980s. Zohreh continued to knock on the door for a while, asking the guard to open it. At times like this, sometimes the door would never open, and so the prisoners had to use the plastic cups they got for drinking water and tea to empty their bladders and more. This was a conscious effort on the regime's part to humiliate the prisoners before each other's eyes and force them to respond to their most basic needs without privacy and dignity.

Zohreh got so frustrated and, while knocking on the door, screamed, "Fascists, open the door!" The door opened immediately, and a guard said, "Whoever wanted to go to the bathroom, come out now." According to many accounts, instead of taking her to the bathroom, they took her away for weeks and put her in a solitary cell to punish her. At this point, Zohreh's psychological status worsened by the day. Shahla Talebi (2011) writes in her memoir, "She [Zohreh] was constantly beaten and chained to the heater in her cell. She was left in the dark for days and nights without food and medication" (p. 141). At the same time, Zohreh had a thyroid gland problem, for which she was supposed to receive medication. The prison officials prevented her from accessing her medication. At some point, they resumed her medication but then stopped it again. This prevented her from sleeping properly for almost two months. That is when her hallucinations started. This sleeplessness, coupled with the horrible living conditions, made her life unbearable. Sousan told me that she was not sure what exactly they did to Zohreh, but she heard from fellow prisoners that while in the solitary cell, Zohreh was crying, screaming, and calling the name of her ex-husband.

As soon as Zohreh was brought back to the ward, she started walking fast, asking her mates why they could not hear the masses who had come and gathered behind the prison gate to free them. In most of the prisoners' memoirs that mentioned this incident, it was presented as a sign of her delusion. However, one could argue that Zohreh was just dreaming out loud, or perhaps she expected people to show up at the prison gate and do something about the horrors going on in there. Zohreh's expectation of accountability from the masses, for whose freedom and prosperity she had been incarcerated and tortured, seems neither demanding, nor delusional. Zohreh, perhaps, wanted people to come and put an end to that horrific suffering her and her mates were living. What could be better than imagining a revitalized revolution behind the prison gates? What could be better than the masses again exercising their power to open the gates and free everyone, just like they did in 1979? When the revolutionaries overthrew the Pahlavi monarchy in 1979, people ran into the prisons and freed all political prisoners. Zohreh had also been a prisoner of the former regime, so it was not odd to hope for something that had actually happened before. Why was she perceived as delusional, when she was just imagining a dream coming true?

After years of imprisonment, Zohreh was eventually released but hospitalized intermittently in a psychiatric ward until she ended her own life in 1998.

No "Special" Treatment

Prisoners who already had a disability at the time of their arrest did not receive any accommodations for their conditions. For instance, one prisoner who spent fourteen years in prison already had eye problems, mobility issues in his hands and legs, a hunchback, and a speech impediment. He neither received accommodation for his needs nor any relief from torture. Hassan, for instance, witnessed prisoners whose buttocks had been permanently damaged due to the extent of beatings. Ghapani caused permanent damage to shoulder and/or hands and legs in several prisoners. In some cases, they didn't stop there and went on to execute the prisoner who had been severely disabled as a result of this form of punishment. A physically disabled prisoner, Mohsen Mohammad Bagher, who starred in the prominent Iranian filmmaker Bahram Beyzayee's film, *Stranger and Fog*, was executed in 1988. Two mad prisoners, M. R. and A. A., were executed in the 1988 massacre. The regime either murdered the mad and disabled prisoners in the infamous 1988 Prison Massacre or kept them several years after 1988, and eventually released them, sometimes into a psychiatric institution. I know of two mad prisoners who were moved to a psychiatric institution from prison. There was a case of another prisoner with severe mental health concerns, someone who prison officials were well aware of but refused to release. They kept him in prison without treatment for two to three years until he reached a severe level of delusion.

Prisoner P. S., who had polio, was executed in the summer of 1988. N. M., who had a spinal cord injury as a result of a failed suicide attempt, was hanged in the 1988 massacre even though he was disabled from below the neck. This wasn't the only time they took disabled and injured prisoners before the firing squad or sent them to the gallows. Hassan remembered that an epileptic prisoner with a physical disability, who had even served his prison sentence and should have technically been released, was killed in the 1988 massacre. In some ways they were harder on disabled prisoners. These harsh institutional spaces tend to be "macho" spaces that think of disability as weak, so disabled people were particularly targeted, as they were in the Holocaust.

One prisoner who had an ovarian cyst underwent surgery, but they also removed her uterus and ovaries without her permission. She wrote many letters to state officials and complained about it, but they didn't do anything in response. It is still unclear if this was done deliberately to sterilize her or if it was done as a result of neglect or malpractice.

These accounts support the mountain of existing evidence that health has social determinants and is not just a physiological and biomedical category. These examples show how systemic state violence causes short and long-term health problems for the prisoners whose only crime was desiring justice, freedom, and prosperity for all.

Silent in Flames

Ervand Abrahamian writes in his book, *Torture and Confession: Prisons and Public Recantation in Modern Iran*,

> The [Peykar organization's] leader, Mohsen Fazel, ... was arrested in January 1981 ... [and] placed in solitary in Evin for 139 days—most of the time in complete silence without reading materials. *He preserved his sanity by exercising, tapping Morse code messages to the neighboring cells, composing poetry in his mind, and keeping a diary on orange peels* [my emphasis] and smuggled-in papers. (1999, p. 128)

Although staying silent is expected (though not always exercised) in solitary confinement, in the public ward, not speaking with others was viewed as a nonnormative behavior. There were people in prison who had behaved completely normally but eventually and sometimes abruptly, ceased to speak with others. In some cases, if they were close with one person, they would speak to that particular person alone. There was a prisoner who suddenly started stuttering with no previous history of doing so. The prisoner had been threatened with death by some unspecified means, horrifying enough apparently to have caused him a speech impediment.[16]

Nastaran spoke of a child in prison who could not hear her own voice in the public ward during the day because of the chaotic noise there (sometimes 100 to 130 people would be talking to each other all day). At night, she laughed so much, enjoying her own voice, and finding it so interesting. She stayed up at night laughing and talking to herself. "Kids were the hope inside the horrors of prison," Nastaran said.

Shahrnoosh Parsipour, who was imprisoned before and after the 1979 revolution under both regimes, writes in her memoir that while in Ghezehesar prison, after serving three years of imprisonment with no apparent charge, trial, or conviction, the prison's warden, Haj Davoud Rahmani, ordered others to "boycott" her. This meant not talking to her under any circumstances and pretending she didn't exist. In her memoir, Parsipour (1995) meticulously maps out her experience of almost absolute seclusion. She was not physically taken out of the ward to the solitary, but she experienced what I call "de-socializing"—still surrounded by others but not allowed any human interaction except with her mother who was imprisoned too. Parsipour writes that only people who do not speak for a while understand what the process of literal silencing is like.

According to her, after not speaking with others for a while, one's brain starts to adapt to that condition by talking to oneself, as if there is another person inside you with whom you speak. What she describes is beyond the typical self-talk everyone has. This is an intensified situation where you can only interact with yourself, as self and as the other at the same time. As such, Parsipour explains that, at this point, you might start moving your lips and literally speak with and to yourself. Others around you may find this a strange pathological behavior—a sign of madness. However, you are engaged in talking to yourself precisely as a way to survive and to, perhaps, avoid madness, giving up or submitting to the regime. This paradox came up in many prisoners' accounts, where the prisoner tried to survive severe isolation and seclusion by hanging on to "self" as the self and as the other. At this point, she decided to escape other people's judgmental gazes by covering her mouth with her headscarf, which was mandatory to wear when walking in the yard and in the presence of male officials anyway. While her lips were covered, she moved her lips freely without fear of being judged. Thus, she continued to cover her mouth with the corner of her scarf and easily talk to herself. Interestingly, another prisoner who had just been brought from solitary to the ward was doing the same thing, covering her mouth with her scarf. It was only after seeing her do the same that Parsipour realized why others were staring at her with a puzzled and concerned look. In her memoir, she further adds that when she was not allowed to talk to anyone, she started talking to herself and even laughing with herself, at herself. Later, when this particular punishment was ended, she found out that several others had gone to her mother and expressed concern over her "strange" behavior.

Guita: The Sound of Hush

> We had all the words in the world / yet did not speak what mattered / because one word was missing: / Freedom!
>
> —AHMAD SHAMLOU (TRANSLATED BY SHOLEH WOLPÉ)[17]

Guita, one of the prisoners whose story I was told by her mates, was alive and aware of what was going on around her, but she refused to speak to others, use the toilet, and to bathe. Her behavior was deemed "madness." She started this behavior after she got out of the "coffins." Was Guita mad? Did her reluctance to participate in social activities, such as conversing with others, mean she had lost "it"? And if yes, what had she lost? Madness could have been her way of staying alive while having the least amount of engagement with the world that had harmed her so badly. Guita had stopped communicating with the outside world in familiar, known, "normal," and conventional ways. She would sit next to the door in a fixed spot and stare into oblivion. Did Guita stop being in the world in social conventional terms, which involved talking, giving eye contact to others, eating, using the toilet, etc.? What had stopped in Guita? Was she experiencing a huge flow of emotions, the intensity and enormity of which, her bodymind could not bear? I believe that Guita's decision of not to speak should be interpreted as a form of resilience and survival to overcome the horrors of captivity and torture. When a person encounters something impossible to tolerate, they must either fight, flight, or go numb, according to the most basic human reaction to danger (Rothschild, 2000). Perhaps, Guita had left her body (going catatonic) in order to survive. Not speaking does not mean not communicating; but even if it did, that could be interpreted as a decision not to take any risks. Remember, in certain periods throughout the 1980s, even the simplest exchange of words between two inmates could bring horrible punishments upon them.

Furthermore, Guita's condition could be described as catastrophic psychic trauma, the metapsychology of psychogenic death, or (Maurice) Blanchot's paradox, "something which never takes place happens nonetheless"

(1986, p. 14, as cited in Tarantelli, 2003, p. 919). Tarantelli (2003) reveals that since psychogenic death is virtually impossible to observe on a phenomenological level; we can only illustrate it with descriptions from survivors of horrible atrocities, such as the Nazi extermination camps, where it occurred on a massive scale. Tarantelli, like Bettelheim, Primo Levi, and Giorgio Agamben, uses the figure of the "non-human human," the Muselmann, to explain this phenomenon.

Over and above those who were immediately selected for the gas chambers, a large percentage of inmates gave up and died within days of their arrival at the camps. Those ghostly figures were called the Muselmann or "walking corpses." The Muselmann were crumbling (Levi, 1959, p. 101), and their state "signaled the approach of definitive indifference" (1989, p. 79), after which physical death was inevitable. Because the Muslemann had lost the capacity to speak, the narration of their state from within was impossible, and the surviving witnesses, like Primo Levi, could only describe it because they had not lived it. Levi wrote (1989, pp. 83–84),

> When the destruction was complete, what had been accomplished was not recounted by anyone, just as no one ever returned to tell the tale of his own death. Even if they had paper and pen, the drowned would not have testified because their death had begun before that of their body. Weeks and months before being snuffed out, they had already lost the ability to observe, to remember, to compare and express themselves. We speak in their stead, by proxy.

It is worth mentioning that this notion has been contested by some Holocaust scholars such as Sharon B. Oster (2014). After reviewing countless Holocaust memoirs, Oster (2014) argues that unlike the popular belief, the Muselmann was not an ontological category based on a "difference" between those who were near death and those who were farther from it. The other, shadowy self of each prisoner was a Muselmann whose death was so close. Oster (2014, p. 317) suggests that the literary Muselmann is an "impossible Holocaust metaphor." She warns us that "we should not confuse metaphor with denotation: what is a figurative 'self-that-died' for some was a *temporary experience* [just like disability/madness] for others" [italics are my emphasis]. Why did survivors distinguish between themselves and the Muselmann, even though they might have temporarily "become" the Muselmann? Similar to the prison survivors distinguishing between themselves and the mad prisoner, could this have been, as Oster suggests, a way of separating the self from the shadowy non-surviving self that one might have become? This difference, this wall, this distinction, I argue, is also what we, as an ableist society, strive to actively build, to overcome our ableist anxiety through cultural and practical (re)production that there "must" be a difference between us and them, between the disabled and the temporary-able-bodied, and between the sane and the "insane."

> This [madness] happened to all of us
> —Morteza

Kupers, a prison psychiatrist and an astute critic of solitary confinement (2006, p. 2), states, "Consider as an example the scenario where the disturbed/disruptive prisoner winds up in some form of punitive segregation, typically in a super maximum-security unit where he remains isolated and idle in his cell nearly twenty-four hours per day. In the context of near-total isolation and idleness, psychiatric symptoms emerge,[18] even in previously healthy prisoners." Keeping in mind Kupers' argument, I asked every participant, including Morteza,[19] whether they have witnessed any prisoner(s) who entered the prison with a relatively non-disabled bodymind and then developed "mental illness" or madness in prison. I also offered them a chance to talk about themselves, if they felt comfortable doing so. His immediate and blunt answer was that "this [mental health issues] happened to all of us." He specified further that the period between 1981 and 1984 was the most horrific period to have experienced political imprisonment in Iran's entire history of dissent and political resistance.

Darius Rejali (2007, p. 2) writes in *Torture and Democracy* that "Victims without [visible] scars do not have much to authorize their complaints to a skeptical public." This becomes especially relevant here as we discuss the invisible scars on the bodyminds of prisoners. According to Mesdaghi (2006), mad/disabled people inside the IRI's prisons were living proof of the violence that was committed against prisoners. The IRI regime, as a young state in the modern era, is an amalgamation of a hardliner religious-fundamentalist ideology, carceral statehood, and a commitment to corporal punishment. This regime arrested its political dissidents on a massive scale in the 1980s and incarcerated and tortured them for years. However, once prisoners showed nonnormative behavior or psychological distress, the regime didn't commit them to psychiatric treatment (not at least until years later). Nor did it provide for them any kind of psychological therapy. Instead, it kept them either in solitary confinement or near other prisoners for two reasons: (1) to use those prisoners' bodymind as a "mirror" to frighten and threaten the others that this is what they could "become"; (2) and to objectify the distressed prisoners' bodymind and turn them into "scary objects" to exert extreme psychological pressure on others to recant, repent, submit, and write letters condemning their past political activity (read everything they ever stood for). This process of "sustaining" one's wounds is what they not only did in the case of the captive dissidents but also in the case of their own supporters, including disabled veterans who were injured in the Iran-Iraq War. Therefore, being denied treatment or support after one acquires a wound is a political process, as it involves active annihilation and systemic neglect. Additionally, this process shows the deeply embedded ableism in the minds of regime officials. The assumption that a mad prisoner is scary, undesirable, or dangerous stems from ableist and sanist attitudes, and simply false assumptions that mad people are to be avoided, while research shows that people who identify or are labeled as mad are no more violent than the rest of society (Burstow, 2015).

I asked my participants whether they thought madness happened at once or gradually. Hassan said, "It started slowly, gradually, the way they [the mad prisoners] would speak, we'd signal to each other that we'd need to take care of the person a little more closely. Sometimes, though, it would start suddenly. Even in the sudden ones, there were little signs of change in their words or behaviors." He gave an example when I asked for further clarification. "N., for instance, one day devoured a huge piece of cheese in one shot." In prison, where most of the time prisoners were given little food, devouring a big piece was not "expected" behavior from a prisoner. Another example that I was told constituted a nonnormative behavior was when someone would take off their clothes in solitary cells or in a public ward. That would indicate to others that something was going on with that person. Another indication was swearing at the guards with no fear, not caring about the regulations, walking outside the cell or ward if the door was open, and performing past scenes or past episodes of their lives for others like an actor on the stage, which would actually reveal to others what might have been done to them by the prison officials. In other words, they used art and their bodies as a medium to communicate their pain with their mates where language would inevitably fail them. For example, if a mad prisoner performed a rape-like scene then the other prisoners might have guessed that she had been sexually abused.

Access to Space, Hygiene, and Medicine

> Not for the sake of forests / or for the sea but for a leaf, / for a drop brighter than your eyes. / For your sake, / for the sake of everything small and everything pure / they fell to the ground. / Remember them.
>
> —Ahmad Shamlou (Translated by Sholeh Wolpé)[20]

According to many accounts, no one knows what medication prisoners were given when ill. In response to my question of whether prisoners who needed medicine were provided any, Siavash said, "You ask about medication? The system was about annihilation not healing." Nevertheless, prisoners at certain periods in the 1980s were provided some medicines, such as painkillers. One woman prisoner, F. S., said her head would spin suddenly. It could have been a movement disorder or the side effect of a medication they gave her. They gave her a medication that made her like a zombie, which she hated. I asked all my participants if the regime provided any psychological or psychiatric help for the mad prisoners, and the answer was always "no." Sometimes, if the mad prisoners screamed ceaselessly and their behavior was out of hand, they would be injected with a tranquilizer. F.A. was one of those who were injected. In some cases, they mentioned that the regime would provide the prisoner with lots of sleeping medication or something similar, which would turn them into a zombie. S.T. told me about when she couldn't sleep for more than a week after her arrest and yet she refused to take Valium, a medicine that prison officials offered. She took some medication twice or thrice throughout her eight-year-long imprisonment, but usually she was scared to accept the medication they offered, as she didn't trust them.

In the early 1980s, prisoners had to sleep like "packed sardines"[21] or "books in a shelf"—unable to even turn around in their sleep. If one person wanted to sit up and cough, someone would take his/her spot in a fraction of a second. That person would have to sit up until morning when the guards would wake them up for a mandatory Islamic prayer before sunrise. One prisoner told me to imagine a plant in a pot. "If you change the plant's spot to a cold place with no sun, the plant will react to that," he said. "We couldn't sleep in those conditions." Under these overcrowded and unsanitary living conditions, there were plenty of lice everywhere, which caused various health issues. In addition to that, the prisoners dealt with severe scabies and fungus.[22] In the fall of 1981 and winter of 1982, during the peak of both state violence against dissidents and unimaginable living conditions in overcrowded prisons, people with severe rashes caused by scabies and fungus needed to take cold showers for relief. Under these conditions, some prisoners had a mental breakdown—meaning they would suddenly lose "it" and show "nonnormative" behavior. Some would get infuriated. Some would laugh intermittently, and others would cry endlessly. Morteza told me about one prisoner, a former member of the military, who had been arrested and imprisoned by the IRI. While in prison, he suffered from a chronic headache. The cell/room's handler/representative, who was usually an elected member of the mates in the room, asked the guard a few times to take the man to the prison's infirmary. A couple of times, they agreed and took him to the infirmary where he was given morphine. The headache was with him for another week, until one day he fell asleep. When he woke up, his one eyelid wouldn't open, but the headache was gone. He almost lost his sight in one eye, because one of his eyelids wouldn't open anymore.

Morteza remembered another poignant case of a prisoner, a former factory worker, who started laughing uncontrollably one day and then cried. Others tried calming him down by talking to him. He then got up, went to the bathroom, ate his own feces, and came back to the cell/room. He opened his mouth, and that's how everyone knew what he had done. Morteza thought that during those days the piercing fear of endless interrogation haunted every prisoner at all times, even in their sleep. Another haunting dread was the imminent threat of execution. "This man [the factory worker] wasn't the only one. Many experienced this unbelievable psychological pressure. Many laughed and cried endlessly during the day or in their sleep," Morteza said.

Who "Cares"?

Another maddening factor was the regime's false claims telling prisoners they had been "forgotten" and that "nobody cares and looks for you." Many prisoners' families were kept in the dark about their whereabouts during the 1980s. Many were forcibly made to disappear, and their families were not told where their bodies were buried. One prisoner told me that the only hope inside prison for him was that his family and friends still cared about him. The internalization of the belief that "no one cares about me" could totally break people.

In solitary confinements like Gohardasht, the silence was excruciating. Silence, a non-ending oblivion, a wall that never crumbles down, a deep valley of no human connection, of solitude that was beyond overwhelming and maddening. I interviewed a survivor who tolerated the solitary for three years and didn't submit to the regime. He told me that sometimes in the solitary cell, he would dance all by himself as if there was nice music playing just for him. He loved life. He said, "In a battle, you pay a price. It takes a toll on you. That's what a struggle is all about."

Another ongoing form of abuse was verbal abuse, using extremely inappropriate language given the society's already-existing patriarchal culture, taboos, and norms. Punishments were to be anticipated for everything that went against orders and ward "regulations" enforced by the guards and tavvabs (i.e., prisoners who collaborated with the guards in running the wards and hurting other prisoners), including the smallest things that showed you were still a human. In the so-called coffins even sneezing was punishable. At certain periods, passing an object to your mate was seen as political behavior, some sort of uplifting cooperation, a sign of solidarity, your belief in commun(ism), or something to show the other person that there is still hope.

"Saning" and "Saming"

Sakhi (2017) defines *tavvab* as "a prisoner who has converted religiously and politically to Islam and the Islamic state" (p. 158). The tavvab/repentant/covert/collaborators' presence, who had become part of the ideological-punitive system, exerted intense psychological pressure on other mates. For obvious reasons, it's next to impossible to carry out a proper quantitative analysis to find out how many prisoners had become a tavvab in certain periods in the 1980s in the IRI's prisons. Nevertheless, according to many survivors, "repenting" was neither the exception nor the rule in the 1980s but a minority issue. One survivor, Morteza, estimated only by observation that a small minority, perhaps 10 to 15 percent, of the prisoners had "repented" and were actively collaborating with the IRI. The majority, though, were trying to observe the regulations, not collaborate, avoid interaction with tavvabs, and not appear as a radical resistant prisoner. Agah, Mehr, and Parsi (2007) describe the largest groups of prisoners as those "who had decided to do their time in a dignified manner and leave the prison alive" (p. 82). Besides this majority and the minority collaborators, there was a group made of those who "were unrelenting in their beliefs, uncompromising in their attitudes, and openly intolerant of the harsh rules and regulations imposed by prison officials" (ibid.). In other words, they remained resistant and never submitted to the regime. They were called *sar-emoze'-i*.

Former prisoner and prison scholar Iraj Mesdaghi (2006) makes a distinction between "giving in" to the torturers (i.e., providing sensitive information endangering your comrades while under torture) and "collaborating" with them (e.g., becoming part of the repressive machine, identifying dissident activists, and participating in their arrest, torture, and execution) (p. 297). Collaboration should be seen as an essential part of the panopticon[23] system under the IRI's disciplinary apparatus (i.e., political prisons), to the extent that the tavvabs became the eyes and ears of the prison system, which benefitted the regime in profound ways. In the Nazi-era concentration camps, the prisoners who collaborated with the Nazis were called "Kapos" (Goss, 2019). The same were called "prisoner officials" in China (Lifton, 1989).

From a political economy perspective, it is important to note that the tavvabs provided free labor for the regime, which is profitable in a class society like Iran. Tavvabs provided the regime with invaluable information; they watched the prisoners' behavior, interpersonal relationships, and every single thing about them. The level of detail about the prisoners that the tavvabs collected and shared with prison officials is unimaginable. They would watch every move of the prisoners, such as what the prisoners read, at what parts of a book they paused (and possible analysis of that), what they ordered from the prison market, how they spent their moments, and whom they talked to about their emotions, their well-being, and their feelings about their visitors and their family.

The second factor that made the tavvabs essential for the prison system was "sharing the blame" logic, which meant sharing the crime with your victims so they could be blamed for your crimes, too. This is how fascism operates, as it did in the concentration camps under the Nazis. Kapos were just like tavvabs, and their function in the camps was just as important as the tavvabs were to the IR's clerical-fascist (Kalantari, 2016) rule. For a little comfort, or a promise of an earlier release, they would do anything. At some point, the collaborators could actually become worse than the guards. They had turned into a minority group with their own "culture"—a certain behavior—a way of being in prison for survival. Many of my participants insisted that at times the tavvabs would harm them in profound ways, much more than the guards did.

Sakhi (2014, p. 5) calls the tavvab-making process after Emanuel Levinas, the "*saming* process." I call it "Muslimization," a process intended to destroy any opposition to Shia theocratic rule by either killing the dissidents or destroying their political selves through "saming." The Muslimization, or "saming," process included forcing people (i.e., "the others-of-the-Islamic state") to confess[24] verbally that they are Muslims and to pray five times a day as Muslims are required to do. Many of the survivors informed me that the IRI did this in order to break one as a person. The regime did not actually care about one's sincere beliefs in Islam as a religion. Their goal was to hollow out prisoners, turning them into what Foucault (1975) called "docile bodies," to ensure obedience and submission.

In 1988, after the infamous prison massacre, they flogged some secular-leftist women until they agreed to pray, whether or not they were faking it or out of real belief. Then the guards would suddenly open their cell doors at certain times when Muslims were supposed to pray to make sure that they were performing the prayer (see Talebi, 2011). The point was not about a real conversion; it was about breaking you as a person. They did not care if the person really believed in Islam. Instead, they wanted them to be "Muslimized" or the "same" as them, obeying the Islamic Republic in its existing form. This example is about "giving in" to the torturer in order for the pain to stop, rather than "collaborating" with them.

Mesdaghi (2006) indicates that the IRI experimented on political prisoners in order to learn new techniques for breaking people and turning them into what Sakhi (2014), calls "Survival ego" or an object of survival (p. 219). In the IRI's political prisons in the 1980s, especially between 1982 and 1984, everything was forbidden, especially the display of any kind of empathy. Even if you claimed you were a true tavvab/convert, the slightest sign of "caring for the other" was equal to never being believed by the regime as a "true" convert. The responses they received were quite different. The IRI's political prisons were a machine of torture, madness, massacre, and forced repentances, but the responses it received from the prisoners were not just submission and repentance. It also received heroic resistance, or what Sakhi, who actually resisted the regime for eight years and never repented, calls "effective resistance," which means refusing to assimilate to the IRI and become what I call, "Muslimized."

Sanism (Birnbaum, 1960; Chamberlin, 1990; Perlin, 1993) is a form of oppression (like racism and sexism), often leading to negative stereotyping, pathologizing, labeling, exclusion, and dismissal of people with mental health histories. I am using the word "saning" in this section to emphasize the sanist tendencies of the prison system in Iran that did not believe that prisoners could develop mental health issues as a result of the trauma they were enduring. They assumed that the mad prisoners were "acting" mad, and to "sane" and normalize them, all they needed to do was to beat them. The regime engaged in what I call the "saning" process, beating the mad prisoners until they stopped "pretending" that they were mad. Particularly during the years between 1981 to 1984, as well as the summer of 1988, many prisoners were in so much distress, having to deal with enormous psychological pressure. I was told by his mates about a male prisoner who went mad after getting sexually assaulted by a guard. To make sure the mad prisoners were "really" mad, Ghezelhessar's warden, Davood Rahmani, would beat them severely. He would put enormous pressure on them, to the point where they would break (i.e., submit to IRI and collaborate with it) or just continue to be mad. His logic was to beat someone until they became "sane." I call this the "saning" process. Evin's warden, Assadollah Lajevardi, didn't believe in madness among dissidents either. He believed that beating enough would "sane" the insane who had gone "crazy" under torture. Haj Davood said, "Everyone is sane. If you're insane, you're playing games. We will beat you until you become sane" (Mesdaghi, 2019, personal communication).

Muselmannization vs. Muslimization

> Ahh, captive voice, / will your despair's splendor / never plow a passage to light / through the thick of this detested night? / Captive voice, / last of the last voices . . .
>
> —Forugh Farrokhzad[25] (Translated by Sholeh Wolpé[26])

Torture is an ontological crime, argues Simona Forti (2017), because in the twentieth century, unimaginable forms of dehumanization and depersonalization brought about a "new form of life," as witness testimonies from the Nazi death camps demonstrated. The testimonies indicate the prisoners experienced and witnessed something unthinkable, as if they were discovering a new type of life that was not a given in the world they thought they already knew. Bernstein (2015) argues that torture reduces the voluntary body to an involuntary one. Primo Levi's (1959) depiction of Muselmann for instance, as a living dead or an almost-dead living, Forti (2015) argues, is the precise manifestation of the involuntary body taking over the person's existence, where the voluntary body ceases to exist, and the body reacts extemporaneously to certain stimuli. In Levi's testimony, many argue, lies one of the most important, not just literal but also philosophical, pieces of testimony about this new form of life, the Muselmann, brought about by torture and annihilation in the death camps. Because we do not just live in the world, we are also of the world, Forti emphasizes (2015), and we are open to others. We have a lot of habits that repair us from injuries, but the kind of life that arose in the death camps was a sort of denaturation of victims without any kind of possibility to appeal to something else that is different from their own pain. This form of life was possible due to the destruction of uniqueness, as integrity, some could argue. Forti (2015) argues that we can call torture an ontological crime, because the victim became a thing in total possession of another force to which they could not respond (Forti, 2015). Thinking in line with Forti, I argue that being reduced to the involuntary body *is* a response to the crude power the victim is forced to experience. The Muselmann's condition is the bodymind's response to annihilation. The Muselmann's reduction to being an involuntary body manifested itself in their unwitting reactions inscribed to their flesh, but this is not a given in the existing world, or the world we already know. This form of life is perceived as new because suffering is also assessed by the ideology of normalcy. We have normative suffering, a type of what we see around the world and get used to, versus nonnormative suffering, a type that has never or rarely happened before or happened in places we didn't expect it to happen. Auschwitz is a symbol of nonnormative suffering: something above and beyond anything anyone could ever imagine. What happened in the IRI's prisons in the early 1980s was also a process of staring into the Gorgon's eyes. Many who survived emphasize that no matter how hard they try, it's impossible to convey what they witnessed.

Giorgio Agamben (2002) perceives the Nazi concentration camps as primary spaces of biopower, where power confronts its victims without any mediation and with the greatest intensity. Drawing on Agamben, I argue that the political prisons of the IRI are also where fascist power confronted dissidents without any mediation, with the greatest force. If the concentration camps were designed to produce "bare life," as Agamben argues (1998), the fascist-theocratic political prisons were designed to produce "bare life" in the form of humans with no humanity left inside them, the *tavvabs*. In fact, the tavvabs were the product of a process that, Sakhi calls "capitulation-assimilation." I do not consider the mad prisoners as illustration of "bare life"; instead, it is the tavvab who has become empty of subjectivity and has turned into what Sakhi calls "the survival ego" who lives in itself for itself. The clerical fascism of the IRI, uncannily resembling Nazi fascism, is essentially another version of the sovereign exception that Agamben talked about, which functions by producing "sacred life" in every one of its subjects. Drawing on Agamben's "sovereign power" that has the power to decide which lives are valuable and politically relevant, Bargu (2016) defines the concept of "biosovereignty" as the ways or processes in which state sovereignty is established, practiced, and sustained on the body (and the minds) of the subjects on whose lives the state rules. This ruling, as Foucault has told us, is not just about life and death, but also ruling "over life," which involves disciplining bodyminds, as well as controlling and punishing them in state institutions such as prisons and psychiatric hospitals (Foucault, 1975). Tavvabism, Muslimization, or Saming, therefore, was also a process of exercising biosovereignty by which political dissidents were turned into empty living beings. In other words, the "Other-of-the-Islamic-state" was turned into the "Same-as-the-Islamic-state" (Sakhi, 2014). Resistant prisoners and mad prisoners refused to let the state take over their bodyminds. They claimed their own bodymind sovereignty by resisting becoming "samed" and "saned" by the state.

Interpretations, Enigmas, and Aporias of Madness

> We had tolls. Many developed stomach problems. Many went mad.
> It's a war. You fight, you resist, but the implications are there.
>
> —SIAVASH

One of the survivors, Hassan, believed that when different people receive a shock (such as unexpected arrest, the imposition of torture, extreme pain, imminent threat of death, etc.), their reaction is not necessarily the same as one another. According to Hassan, "Some people can overcome it, and some people are *weaker* [my emphasis] so they get hurt." He told me about a few cases he witnessed after the 1988 massacre.[27] He said, "People lost their loved ones overnight. There was a man named Abbas whose two sisters were executed, but he *remained himself* [my emphasis], up until the last day of his life; he accepted what had happened." It seems to me that by "remaining himself," Hassan meant "remaining strong," in opposition to going mad, meaning "being weak." I do not subscribe to the notion that "going mad" is a result of "being weak," and I am confident that this view is as much a product of ableist culture as it is of misogynist and patriarchal politics. Although I didn't hear it directly from my participants, some implied that if you're "strong enough," you don't fall into madness after severe torture. The process is complex and does not lend itself to an easy quantification of one's "strength" in relation to madness, tolerance, and endurance. We can never really know or predict who this will happen to—a key failing of psychiatry as a field is its inability to live up to claims of being able to predict who is "susceptible" to so-called mental illness (Burstow, 2015). More studies need to be conducted of prisoners' experiences to determine what pushes people toward, or prevents them from, crossing the line to the world of madness. Notions and qualities such as "strength" are historically and socially constructed in response to societal norms. Therefore, "strength" should be examined critically in each context, and not reduced to a quantifiable characteristic, especially in a highly politicized institution, such as prison.

What does "strength" constitute in the context of a political prison? Is possessing strength a means to resist going mad? Can you consciously control when and how you go mad? Can we separate the body from the mind and say that the body obeys the mind, for consciousness is an attribute of the mind? Where are sanism and ableism located in this example? Are we reproducing the existing ableist and sanist discourses by perceiving and locating madness as an "adverse" condition that is inherently in the weak person's bodymind, rather than a response from the person who is struggling against the most horrific circumstances and psychological pain? If we perceived madness as resistance in the context of totalizing institutions, are we glorifying and romanticizing broken bodyminds and bludgeoned souls?

Many participants believed that people reacted differently to the harsh realities of prison based on their different "capacities." This leads to questions such as: What is capacity, and what affects it? Perhaps capacity has to do with having a support system in place? For example, some who went mad lacked a support system (e.g., family outside who cared about them, a partner/spouse/lover who supported their cause and valued their resistance, acceptable living conditions after release, a job that doesn't require no "criminal" record). Does "capacity" also have to do with the people who wait for you in the outside world? Does capacity involve nature, nurture, or both? Sakhi (2017) argues it is unethical at worst, and naive at best, to conclude that those who somehow submit to the totalizing system are,

> The *"lesser" political prisoners* [my emphasis] who fail in their efforts to resist, explaining that failure is due to an absence of adequate quantities of will, faith, loyalty, and so on. To pretend to explain or even understand—let alone to assume a competence to judge—the intricate complexities of the soul of an individual prisoner is to remain trapped in the enclosure of one's being. It is not only to fail to respect the otherness of the other but also to participate in the very hubris of the totalizing system. It is, in short, completely to miss the point. (p. 8)

The same is true about mad prisoners. There is no way to quantify their resistance versus submission levels and conclude how much "capacity" or "strength" they possessed to resist the regime. Sakhi (2014) defines resistance as an indication of a prisoner's ability to respond to power, or response-ability. She says resistance is "a process, an event, aroused as a response on the part of human beings to something and for something. In this sense, resistance as a response evoked by a human condition, a response to and for, is the manifestation of human's response-ability, a human capacity to respond" (p. 2). Therefore, as long as the prisoner does not allow the totalizing system to replace their identity with a "system-compatible identity of the given system," they have resisted that totalizing system. It is at this crucial moment that "madness" must be interpreted as dissent and resistance, because it, in and of itself, prevents the totalizing system from metamorphosizing the prisoner from Other-of-the-state to Same-as-the-state.

No Mirror Here

> Siavash is one of my interviewees who served for 7 years in multiple prisons in and around Tehran, 3 years of which was in solitary. Once, Siavash overheard a conversation in the prison yard between a woman prisoner and her toddler son who had been born in the prison and never seen a tree or a sparrow in his life. The child had only known the world through her mother's drawings.

The IRI's prisons are a context in which dissidents enter with mostly nondisabled bodyminds but leave wounded. The fascist-theocratic social relations exerted on their bodyminds are what has wounded them (in some cases) beyond "repair," beyond an opportunity to feel, reflect, and fear. I asked all my participants about prisoners with physical and psychological wounds and why and how those wounds were acquired. They provided many reasons. Right after people are arrested, they are afraid of breaking under torture. The fear can pierce through their bodymind and become so immense that it would interfere with their natural physiological and psychological functioning. Fear of breaking under torture is sometimes worse than tolerating the actual torture, according to many accounts.

Additionally, this fear could make people susceptible to being reduced to a tavvab, rather than someone with an "ethical responsibility toward the Other" (Sakhi, 2014). The psychological pressure caused by these imposed contradictions, jigsawing between resistance and submission, sanity and madness, and self and "Other," was tremendous. Many could not put up with this pressure and gave in to the regime's demands, accepted the conditions, sometimes even collaborated with their own oppressors in apprehending those who were once called comrades. Some responded to this pressure by going "mad." Ceasing to exist in a certain form and metamorphosing into something else was a "response" to the nonnormative conditions they encountered.

One survivor, Nasrin Parvaz (2002), wrote in her memoir that imagining your future self who has submitted to the regime's demands, "repented," and "converted" to Islam, was immensely devastating and unbearable for the leftist/communist/Marxist prisoners. Some started harming themselves to death so as to prevent that nightmare from ever becoming reality. This self-injuring[28] behavior might have been perceived as "madness" or "irrational." Is wanting to preserve your dignity and remain human with agency madness? This was not used to just end their lives but to resist the regime's torture, which could result in betraying their friends. Using their bodyminds and lives as a shield to resist state violence was a deliberate political act and not necessarily a symptom of frustration and depression. Because the regime was determined to crush people with torture and break them at any cost, many political activists were prepared to die but not break. Self-injuring behavior, such as self-cutting, was not aimed at just ending one's life, although sometimes that was the inevitable consequence, but to deprive the panopticon machine of converting you to someone you are not (the "samed" as the state [Sakhi, 2014, p. 223]).

The prisoners who engaged in self-injuring behavior, in some cases, were already prepared to take the body away from the torturer and control the situation by what Banu Bargu (2016) calls "weaponizing their lives against the state" (p. 65). Fledman (1991) argues that objectification of the body is a method of resistance, since "the body as the terminal locus of power also defines the place for the redirection and reversal of power" (p. 178). As such, it is not just the state that uses the prisoners' body to exercise its power but also the prisoner who utilizes her body to resist the state apparatus. Fledman (1991) calls this "bifurcation of the self," where the prisoner consciously separates herself/himself from the body to objectify the body into an instrument against the panoptic machine. "The possibility of this transformation, through the mimetic reversal of the use of force on the body, according to Fledman, constitutes the basis of prison resistance" (Bargu, 2016, p. 59).

Finally, some neither went mad, nor submitted to the regime. It is unclear how we can quantify the trauma they have sustained. One thing is clear though: Their humanity was preserved because of their resistance. They actively kept their bodyminds from dwindling into a screw for the IRI machine.

Prison Inside Prison: Cell 38

One survivor, Morteza, believed that one reason for which mad prisoners often got worse was their segregated living conditions. He witnessed them being taken and held in one or more designated cells (i.e., for the "mentally ill" prisoners) with each other—people with similar mental health concerns. Morteza believed that their separation from others contributed to their further alienation and estrangement. Iraj Mesdaghi, who served ten years in various prisons in and around Tehran, said that he remembers a designated area for the mad prisoners in Evin prison, named Room 38. It was located between Ward One and Two (2006, p. 290). The space was set up like a room with no windows and was not a properly constructed cell like others. They used a stairs' landing connecting two salons and put up four walls and two doors as a designated cell. Ten to fifteen people who were all "mentally ill," according to him, were kept there. The room was filthy, foul-smelling, and full of dirt, as some of the mad prisoners soiled themselves and didn't take showers. The room's condition had become unbearable. The prison system's logic behind this segregation was not only isolating and further hurting the mad prisoners but also harming other prisoners by threatening them that they "could" end up like the people inside that room if they didn't submit to the regime. Passing by the cell you could smell the feces and urine, (Mesdaghi, personal communication, 2019). The guards would actively and constantly humiliate and insult the mad prisoners. They would move some of them to a solitary cell with another prisoner who was not mad in order to scare that prisoner—perhaps relying on what I call the ableist and sanist culture that existed in the outside world as well as in the prison. Not only was Cell 38 a segregated space, it was also an isolated space without others who could have cared for (i.e., taken them to the bathroom, showered, and cleaned them) and protected the mad prisoners from the guards' never-ending insults and humiliations. In other words, not only was disability actively created but care was hindered.

Interdependence

Mia Mingus (2010) defines "interdependence" among disabled people as follows:

> It is from being disabled that I have learned about the dangerous and privileged "myth of independence" and embraced the power of interdependence. The myth of independence being of course, that somehow, we can and should be able to do everything on our own without any help from anyone. This requires such a high level of privilege and even then, it is still a myth.

Working with disabled, mad, and traumatized survivors, I have come to learn that "interdependence" is often at the core of their interpersonal relationship, and a way of collective survival, especially in degenerative public spaces like prison and psychiatric ward. Conducting ethnographic research with prison survivors, I asked one participant why he thought people went mad in prison. Interestingly, he did not answer the question the first time, but went and talked to other former mates before returning to me with an answer. I think his response further supports the existence of "interdependence" and how prisoners have learned to think together and survive together, to share, and to decide collectively. He told me the reasons behind "enduring the circumstances" depended on the prisoners' 'motivation' for resisting, capitulation, fighting, or letting go of their agency as dissidents.

Many times, this motivation was composed of the prisoners' family situation outside prison: Are they waiting for him/her? Is there a child or a parent counting the seconds to see the prisoner once more? Being separated from your loved one and undergoing horrific torture were among the most significant factors in pushing the prisoners toward the edge of madness. Even physical proximity to mates in prison could be a factor that counted as an indicator of one's proximity to madness. For instance, if you were starting to avoid others and just be with yourself most of the time, that was an indication "you were on your way to the other side" (the world of madness) (H.K., personal communication, 2019). H.K. said the regime knew prisoners were much more psychologically and politically vulnerable alone than together. That is why they preferred to lock prisoners in solitary confinement rather than in public wards. He believed the regime would lock up every prisoner in the solitary if they could, but logistics didn't allow them to.

H.K. added that it was not just physical proximity that indicated the broken and/or mad prisoner's "departure." Other kinds of behavior, such as separating food, utensils, clothes, blanket, and money, also indicated the prisoner's tendency to disunite. In the 1980s, prisons were overpopulated, and the prisoners needed to learn to live collectively and not individually. This togetherness happened in different forms, such as eating together, reading a book together, listening to a book memorized by a person who had had access to that book, learning together as one person would volunteer to teach others what they knew such as English or French, walking together and analyzing the present conditions of inside and outside prison in order to take the best possible action against the regime. Leaving one's political group, clique, or commune, thus had a meaning. According to one of the participants who spent nine years in three different prisons, it was usually an indication of your tendency to break, become closer to the regime, or go toward a psychological problem. This factor became more complex at times, particularly if a prisoner belonged to a family whose politics were aligned with the regime. The prisoner might have received extreme psychological pressure from his/her family to "repent."

Access and Accommodation

It's impossible to talk about disability without talking about care—how people provide it, how those who need it receive it, and its availability. This is what I call the "disability-care dialectic," a unity of seemingly contradictory elements. This is to say that disability is a social relation, not a biomedical "problem" or an individual "tragedy," especially in carceral spaces like prison, which has its own internal contradictions, such as group/communal living arrangements, solitary confinement, or simply one's individuality. Sometimes, solitude is imposed on a prisoner like in the solitary, while simultaneously, being deprived of individual privacy can transpire when one is imprisoned in an institution. The type of care provided in Iranian prisons in the 1980s, according to many memoirs, such as in Mesdaghi's (2006) and Talebi's (2011), included performing rotating suicide watches on a distressed mate, striving to make sure someone didn't hurt themselves by checking on them constantly, lifting and moving the physically disabled prisoners who couldn't move on their own due to injury, kidney failure, pain, or infected feet, and bathing disabled prisoners who wouldn't do it on their own as well as caring for children collectively.

Another survivor, Afshar, told me about a few cases of prisoners with acquired wounds to the bodymind. A. A. was one that Afshar remembered who was dealing with psychological problems as a result of extreme torture. A. A. was a former university student, and therefore, a target of harsher treatment by the guards, as the regime resented them for their intellect, knowledge, and modern thinking. Their education and capacity to politically organize were considered imminent threats to the ideological regime, which operated based on 1,400-year-old religious ideologies. A. A. was executed in the summer of 1988, although he had already been struggling with mental health problems, and the regime was well aware of his condition. Afshar gave me an example of how A. A. would request access and accommodation for himself.

For example, he would leave his towel in a certain place if he wanted to let his mates know that he was not feeling talkative that day, or that he would hang his towel in a different orientation if he wanted to connect with others verbally on some other occasion.[29] It is interesting to note that "access intimacy" as care infrastructure can become a tool of disability consciousness to help communities living under unimaginable circumstances in order to accommodate each other without necessarily identifying as such. Mia Mingus (2011) defines access intimacy as "that elusive, hard to describe feeling when someone else 'gets' your access needs."

As a method of self-care (which constitutes another element of care infrastructure), A. A. told his mates that he viewed himself as a small sedan and others in the ward as big trucks, so he needed to protect himself against everyone else. This might seem a nonnormative method of communicating one's needs with others. Some would call it childish or "unmasculine." I call it illuminating and accessible, as it demonstrates the person's perception of himself in a relatable example, such as comparing car sizes.

In the summer of 1988, when the regime was engaged in purging the remaining prison population and massacring them, according to Afshar, many prisoners had figured out that the safest way to avoid being slaughtered was to be out of sight (therefore out of mind), and to pretend that they didn't exist. Otherwise, exposing yourself meant reminding the guards, who were looking for more prey to kill that you existed. For instance, if prisoners were in the solitary, they would usually kick the door and demand the guards to let them out. However, at this time they didn't make a sound. A. A., uncaring about this survival strategy, was screaming the whole time he was in the solitary cell, asking guards to give him his medication. Other prisoners in the nearby cells, using Morse code, advised him to remain quiet and not remind the guards of his existence. As soon as the bloodthirsty guards heard him, without losing time, they took him and executed him.

I asked Afshar what had caused A. A.'s psychological problems. He told me that they didn't talk about it much, but according to what he remembered, A. A. had a breakdown under interrogation, which involved hitting the prisoners' feet with a cable (bastinado), letting the feet get more swollen with every blow, and then forcing the prisoner to walk on their injured bloody feet so they could hit them more, causing the swelling to blow and bleed. After coming back to the ward from the interrogation room, A. A.'s behavior changed. He would, for instance, pull the blanket over his head the entire time so his mates wouldn't try to talk to him. This is an example of "access intimacy" (Mingus, 2011). According to what Afshar remembered, A. A. had told one of the mates about what kind of accommodation he needed. He told only that person how he liked to be treated, and that one person, like a liaison, communicated A. A.'s access needs to everyone else.

Although some participants would not confirm this was the case all the time, Afshar told me that most mates went above and beyond to make sure they accommodated disabled or sick prisoners. When the hot water was running for the first few minutes of the ward's bathing time, children, the elderly, and the sick/disabled would be prioritized over others. This shows a very important consciousness around access needs, which is a pillar for infrastructures of collective care. Those who disagreed said that the disabled/mad prisoners were not always cared for by their mates. They took a more ambivalent position, revealing that inmates didn't always provide care for each other; there was no absolute but only a relative attending to other people's needs.

However, Afshar claimed that even though the IRI's political prisoners in the 1980s were mostly teenagers or in their twenties who hadn't had the opportunity to grow intellectually or receive an education, they somehow organically knew how to care for those who were the most vulnerable on the grassroots level. He said that their rationale was that "these guys [the disabled prisoners] have been harmed on this path [dissidence], and that they are ours." In other words, as Afshar clarified, the prisoners wanted to "own" the harmed ones by caring for them as allies who had struggled on the same path fighting the same enemy. According to H.K., there was one condition, however. The collective care for the disabled prisoners would go on as long as those prisoners were against the regime. If they slipped to the other side, becoming collaborators, then the situation would change. Nevertheless, another survivor, S.T. (personal communication, 2019), told me that a "small" ideological difference didn't prevent the prisoners from helping the ones in need. For example, if a prisoner was too old and weak to bend down and wash himself properly under shower or shave his private parts to avoid getting infected with lice in the unsanitary prison environment, the younger prisoners would help him out. Even an alternative political identity or affiliation wouldn't prevent the younger ones from helping that person in need. But direct collaboration with the regime was beyond the pale.

Usually, my participants started talking to me about their own physical and psychological challenges in prison "after" talking about their mates' problems. There were often psychological or emotional reasons for this. One reason could be the nature of their particular prison-experience and how they managed to live, feel, and heal collectively. Again, this point brings me back to the matter of how care and access are socially organized between bodyminds in disciplinary public spaces such as a political prison.

Just as with everyone else I spoke to, Afshar believed no one came back from those days intact. No one was the same person after having been in the prisons. Many former prisoners now live in exile as asylum seekers, refugees, and immigrants. Therefore, they struggle with migration problems, such as integration, employment, and accessing treatment for mental health concerns. Having to work in a new country with a new language and culture while struggling with depression, post-traumatic stress, or extreme anxiety is an obstacle that participants often must grapple with. In many European countries, as well as in North America, where most of my participants live, the social welfare system has disability benefits, that is an insignificant amount of money allocated to disabled people who are not able to work. These benefits are not easy to access, however, especially for asylum seekers and refugees. In addition, people who cannot work need to provide medical documentation to the social security or welfare system of the host country in order to qualify or even apply for a disability status. If they get approved, they receive a small allowance for as long as their injury lasts. If their disability is permanent, they can receive a certain amount for as long as they live. For temporary conditions, such as certain physical and psychological disabilities, the applicant might need to regularly prove that they are "still" disabled, and that they haven't been "cured." This means that the social welfare system assigns a social worker to that person's case who monitors the person's dis/ability and bodymind to make sure they still qualify for an allowance. Afshar expressed enormous frustration with having to constantly deal with the social welfare system to prove that he is not able to work due to the injury his bodymind endured.

Conclusion

> Ah if freedom could sing a song / small / as the throat of a bird, / nowhere would a wall remain crumbled. / It would not take many years / to comprehend / that ruins are a sign / of human absence, / that human presence / creates life.
> —Ahmad Shamlou (Translated by Sholeh Wolpé)[30]

Hannah Arendt (2018) told us that after Auschwitz, we must learn to think without banisters. In other words, we need to destroy our previously held thought patterns around ethics and politics, unlearn, and relearn. After Auschwitz, the ways in which we think about what it means to be human and inhuman should be unsettled and re-contemplated. Thinking with Arendt, I argue that after bearing witness to the stories of Zohreh, Guita, and others whose names we do not even know, the ways in which we understand madness should be revised. We should not pretend we already know what madness is/means after bearing witness to what happened to the Iranian dissidents who were forced to stare at Gorgon (Agamben, 2002), lost their capacity to speak, and ended their own lives or otherwise died.

Stemming from twelve years of research with the former political prisoners who survived the notorious prisons of the Islamic Republic in the 1980s Iran, this chapter was an intervention to move us away from disability historiographies in which disability appears as a self-evident social identity (Borsay, 2002) and to write disabled people back into their own histories as they made it. As an heir to the past generation who resisted the theocratic state with their lives and bodyminds, I sought to reactivate those histories and let them enlighten the path for the present and futurity of revolutionary struggle against that same theocracy. In addition to discussing the political prisoners' treatment and living conditions in the 1980s Iran and the ways in which they responded to those conditions, I attended to the disability-care dialectic in and among political prisoners so as to understand what constituted the infrastructures of care and interdependence in response to imposed disablement and madness. Documenting dissidence by foregrounding the materiality of madness may come in handy for providing an intersectional locus for expanding the notion of experience within the fields of Transnational Disability Studies and Mad Studies. I intended to push the onto-epistemological boundaries of the humanities and social sciences to understand political violence as it grapples with the bodymind, as it leaves rotten wounds on the bodymind, and as the bodymind responds to this power by dissent. Furthermore, drawing on the DHM, I defetishized the dissidents' disability/madness by demonstrating how disability/madness is socially organized and imposed by the violence of exploitative power relations (e.g., theocracy and patriarchy). I also theorized disability/madness as a historical materialist category and provided a dialectical reading of how the bodymind of political prisoners is rendered disabled by the state even as the disabled bodymind serves as an act of resistance against state power.

4

Bleeding Wounds

Punitive Limb Amputation, Disability as Punishment for Poverty

Those that make war against God and His apostle and
spread disorder in the land shall be put to death or crucified
or have their hands and feet cut off on alternate sides.

—Quran, 5, 32

As to the thief, male or female, cut off his or her hands: a
punishment by way of example, from Allah, for their crime:
and Allah is Exalted in power.

—Quran, 5, 38

Please don't take away my hand! My daughter is very young,
and my elderly mother has been diagnosed with cancer.
I stole because these things were weighing down on me.
(the words to a judge from a man facing a punitive limb
amputation for theft)

—Interview with a punitive amputation
survivor accessed by Abdorrahman
Boroumand Center, 2017

I am not a scholar of religion, nor am I interested in the debates and disputes between the Islamicist jurists about hundreds of hadiths that the prophet may or may not have said 1,400 years ago. In this chapter, I focus on the materiality and implications of those words as they, taken up and enacted by the state apparatus, turn into bleeding wounds, bone fractures in stumps, blind eyes, and stoned bodies and a life with stigma and poverty. I care about the disabilities and woundings that are created as a result of interpreting, following, and enacting those texts. In this chapter, I discuss the religious logic behind disablement as punishment for poverty, how an ideology fetishizes and masks the existing inequalities (read poverty) in a society by creating more inequality (disability), and the meanings behind the public spectacle of performing the disabling act. In addition, I challenge Islam's contradictory claims of upholding the "wholeness" of the body while ordering the state to disable the body of the poor.

Class and (Imposed) Disability

One of the greatest achievements of the Enlightenment period was that its intellectual movement shifted the corporal criminal code to a humanistic one, which demanded dignity for the human body (Bernstein, 2015). Respect for the body was incorporated into social and cultural practices and a stop to punitive limb amputation (PLA) was demanded. The movement eventually led to the abolition of PLA and the death penalty in several European nations but not everywhere in the world. The apologists in the countries in which PLA is still practiced claim that PLA's goal is to "deter" people from stealing (Souryal, Potts, & Alobied, 1994). Furthermore, Kirkup (2007) writes that Yakuza crime syndicate members in Japan inflicted amputation on persons they found "guilty" of some offense in order to make them "stand out" in society, which indicated the reliance of the amputation logic on society's stigmatization of and already-existing ableist attitudes toward the disabled. In other words, the only reason that amputated people "stand out" is due to the ableist culture and "normative" logic that rules over society's collective consciousness. The logic would not be useful if normativity and ableism were not lived, expected, and enacted in society.

PLA has been a method of punishment since at least 1750 BCE. The Babylonian Code of King Hammurabi (circa 1750 BCE), which is considered the first known collection of laws, included amputation as a method of punishment (Mavroforou et al., 2014). The basic principle of the Code was equal retaliation, similar to *qisas* (the Islamic law of retaliation in kind, eye for an eye, retributive justice). The penalty of amputation was imposed on slaves who used force on citizens or physicians of that time whose operations blinded or killed nobles, which shows the classist, elitist, and oppressive nature of this law. Mavroforou et al. (2014), who conducted an extensive electronic search of the limb amputation literature, found that punitive amputation was used as early as the fourth century BCE in ancient Peru, based on the ancient artifacts found there. They also found that PLA was used in Peru, "where the *theocratic* [emphasis is mine] regime was based on three laws only, which prohibited false witness, theft, and laziness." It is interesting to note that to this day, the logic of "laziness" is mobilized where inequality against several social groups is justified as an individual problem rather than due to socioeconomic or class structure (Dorey, 2010). In *Crip Times*, Robert McRuer explains how austerity measures have literally wounded bodies and minds and then metaphorically intensified that woundedness by pointing to the faded scars and insisting that they merit austerity, as they have no value and supposedly generate no value (2018).

We also know from Friedmann (1972), who studied amputations and prostheses in primitive cultures, that the socioeconomic status or class of the criminal had a lot to do with the punishment s/he received, since "it was assumed that the upper, more educated classes were more responsible for their acts" (p. 117). An astonishing exception to this law was that if the thief could prove that hunger was the motivation for their unlawful action, "he was released and the village chieftain was punished in his stead, since it was the chieftain's duty to assure that no one in his care went hungry." In Islamic law, there is also an exception, according to some *fiqh* (Islamic jurisprudence) sources, that if a thief steals because he is hungry, he should not face amputation.[1] However, the Peruvian law is radically different, as it tries to hold officials accountable for people's hunger. Although this doesn't mean the law is less violent, it somehow tries to hold low-level state officials accountable, since they represent the system, whereas sharia law does not hold anyone accountable but the poor (read the "criminal").

PLA was used to punish enslaved people and the poor in Europe through the Roman and Byzantine periods up to the seventeenth century. There is historical evidence that the Iroquois and Seneca peoples in what is now North America used partial amputation of lower limbs as punishment around the fifteenth century or earlier (Lawson, 1951; Packard, 1963). Furthermore, around 272–337 CE, new legislation allowing amputation as punishment was introduced by a Roman emperor; it demanded that "slaves caught trying to escape imprisonment either were killed, sentenced to hard labor in the mines, or subjected to the amputation of a leg" (Mavroforou et al., 2014, p. 3104). Byzantine Emperor, Constantius Flavius Valerius Aurelius, introduced and applied particularly cruel methods of torture and punishment, including forced blindness, rhinotomy, castration, and amputation (Rautman, 2006). PLA remained prevalent throughout the Middle Ages, as torture of the body was seen as the only way to achieve justice (Mavroforou et al., 2014). At the time of European colonization of Africa (1884–1904), many slaves went through PLA and became disabled. In this twenty-year period, as European powers competed to exploit the wealth of Africa, between five and eight million Africans died from colonial violence, including systemic amputation and torture. Besides Africa, PLA was also practiced in Asia. An example from Asia is the Indian context, where in 1980, "[Indian] police blinded more than 30 prisoners by pouring acid into their eyes and poking at their eyeballs with needles and bicycle spokes" (Jack, 2017). This unimaginable act of cruelty came as a shock to the world, especially for a modern-day democracy like India. "The blindings had gone on, intermittently, for several months and there had been little attempt to keep them secret: the victims were low caste and often small-time criminals, and the town, when it came to hear of their barbarous punishment, largely applauded" (Jack, 2017, n.p.). It took the criminal justice system twenty years to hold two low-ranking police personnel accountable for the disaster that had transpired. Not to mention that the event became popular and "inspired" similar incidents as a form of punishment.

As is evident from the foregoing historical overview, PLA has always been practiced, from ancient times up to the present day, to punish the poor, slaves, and those who belong to the lower classes. The modern-day use of PLA still carries the same logic it did in Hammurabi's Code or the ancient Peruvian laws: punishing the poor for wanting more. Even in the modern-day Western world, the criminal justice system discriminates against the poor and punishes them by imposing probation fees, demanding high bail that only the rich can afford (Wacquant, 2009; Dorey, 2010).

Somalia, Nigeria, Afghanistan, Pakistan, Saudi Arabia, and Iran, where the religion of the state is Islam, are among the countries that still practice judicial limb amputation (i.e., right hand for first-time offenders; left foot for second offenders). PLA is a form of punishment, one among the intricate and labyrinthine machine of the Islamic judicial apparatus (*Hodud*), such as stoning, flogging, and eye gouging. These punitive measures lead to disabilities in their victims, intentionally imposed by legal authorities on a person as part of administering criminal justice (*Hodud, qisas*).[2] The Islamic Republic of Iran (IRI) as a clerical-fascist dictatorship (Kalantari, 2007, 2016) that has presided over a deteriorating economy and an increasingly corrupt establishment for four decades (Khoshnood, 2019) engages in public forms of corporal punishment, such as PLA as a punishment for robbery. Poverty under the IRI is criminalized just like in many other parts of the world. However, the IRI doesn't stop at sending small-time crooks, who shoplift or steal out of poverty and hunger, to jail. Instead, it cuts off their fingers, hands, or legs in public. This happens while those convicted of huge embezzlements just go to jail with weekend furloughs.

Rispel-Chaim claims that "the result of these bodily punishments [PLA] is that a healthy criminal becomes a handicapped[3] person. Paradoxically, the mutilation of organs in his or her body is believed to be a *healing* [my emphasis] measure for the criminal and the society to which he or she belongs" (2007, p. 76). Rispler-Chaim calls this phenomenon "Disability Caused by Human." Note that this is different from what Deborah Stone describes in *Disabled State*, as the punitive treatment of the "truly" disabled by the liberal democratic states (Stone, 1984). By performing the PLA, the Islamic state actively punishes the poor by disabling a non-disabled person or further disabling a disabled person.

I call PLA "disability caused by ideology enacted by humans." To apply the Dialectical and Historical Materialism (DHM) lens, in my distinction, I am striving to emphasize the role ideology plays (i.e., the historical materialist realization of ideology) in disabling people as it provides the necessary justification to convince people to wound their fellow humans. Additionally, PLA is imposed publicly in order to set an example, make a point, frighten potential thieves, and give a "lesson" to the person who has been convicted of robbery. Rispler-Chaim (2007) foregrounds this contradiction and describes it as follows:

> The general Islamic ethics of life as it emerges from the Quran and the Sunna, and the spirit of Islamic law, emphasize the importance of the preservation of the *wholeness and dignity of the human body* [my emphasis]. The Islamic prohibitions against suicide and self-mutilation stem from this same awareness that a trust must never be destroyed or damaged by its keeper. (p. 75)

She further adds,

> It is astonishing, therefore, that in certain legal scenarios Islamic law prescribes, contrary to the above perception and to the general ethics of life, the deliberate violation of the wholeness and dignity of the human body as means of physical punishment. This implies that the law not only tolerates but indeed *requires the creation of disabilities* in certain people who were born healthy, and thus punishes them for deeds which society abhors. [italics are my emphasis]

Since the rise of global capitalism, the very logic of which requires exploitation and keeping certain classes perpetually impoverished, poverty has been criminalized and frowned upon by the upper-middle class, elites, and the ruling class. The capitalist states serve the interests of the gigantic corporations and transnational oligarchies, as opposed to that of the masses. Therefore, nation-states whose very function is to serve the capitalist class also despise the poor and the homeless. Taking austerity measures, crushing unions, criminalizing poverty, pathologizing homelessness, cutting social welfare programs, such as disability support, and stooping so low as to insert spikes into park benches to prevent homeless persons from sleeping on them—all are among the cruel strategies states use to eliminate the poor (Wacquant, 2009) and the homeless (Rankin, 2019).

What is the connection between robbery and poverty? Survival Crime Theory suggests that marginalized and disenfranchised people in every society commit property crimes and low-level infractions in order to secure their basic survival. In other words, the theory puts forward that people usually do not steal unless they live in a capitalist society where there is inequality and private ownership. People do not steal unless they must, due to a pressing need such as hunger or extreme poverty and "social insecurity spawned by the fragmentation of wage labor and the shakeup of the ethno-racial hierarchy" (Wacquant, 2009, p. xxiii). As such, there is a direct relationship between the economic system in those societies and judicial limb amputation, which results in disability. In other words, people become and remain disabled because of poverty. Disability is used as a punishment for poverty. Various societies have applied punitive amputation as a punishment, based on the belief that crime can be "curbed" by spreading fear. Why is disability viewed as a form of punishment? And why is poverty punished with a wound/disablement?

Listening to Electric Saw in the Town Square

Like a wound that drips blood, / life-long; Like a wound beating with pain / all one's life; Opening eyes / to the world to a howl, / disappearing from it with hatred. / The great absence was this. / The story of ruin was this.

—AHMAD SHAMLOU (TRANSLATED BY SHOLEH WOLPÉ)[4]

Going to school under a strictly theocratic state is an indoctrination process. Louis Althusser argues that any educational system operates under an ideological apparatus and is therefore ideological itself (1968). An ideological educational system is acutely necessary for a state that has little legitimacy among the people. The young generation becomes an imminent threat to a state like that and compels it to keep them on a tight leash altogether. What's better than brainwashing the young generation and manufacturing consent for their survival? I went to school and attended higher education in Iran under the IRI. Growing up in Iran, I realized that some days, very early in the morning, a group of people gathered in the town square, while holding their children's hands, and later, a smart phone, watching and filming a PLA with an electric machine or an execution on the top of a crane. These horrific spectacles were real.

Contrary to its pronounced hatred for cultural modernity, capitalism-imperialism, and the Western world, the IRI enjoys modernity's products, such as advanced military technology, nuclear centrifuges, ballistic missiles, or even electric saws to amputate the poor. Since its inception, the Islamic state in Iran has engaged in public forms of corporal punishment, from murdering people on the roof of Refah School four days after the revolution to stoning women convicted of adultery, to placing dissidents before a firing squad in the deserts of Turkman Sahra and the Kurdistan mountains. Not only did such practices not end as time went by, as one might expect, they were actually developed to more horrific levels, such as hauling "criminals" on the back of a pickup truck in public while beating and verbally insulting them (Tamim News, 2020).

According to Islamic hodud for both crimes of theft (*sariqa*) and highway robbery (*qat' al-tariq*), "the criminal must be punished with measures such as amputations of hands, or the palms of hands, and/or legs. Forms of administering this justice are the amputation of the thief's hand, and the robber's hand and opposite leg. For highway robbery other punishments may be applied, including killing and crucifying, depending on the nature and severity of the offense" (Rispler-Chaim, 2007, p. 76). In Iran, PLA is likely to only happen to people convicted of "petty" theft. Ruling class or members of the state apparatus and their relatives, along with elites, who steal public resources, rarely get caught, never mind receiving a punishment other than a monetary fine.

To indicate the familial nepotism and corruption, even a new term has been created to refer to these untouchable elites in Iran: *Aghazadeh*, which literally means born to *Agha* or "noble-born" (Samii, 2005). This term has entered colloquial use in Iran over the past thirty years to describe the children of elite, "insiders," or men (rarely women) close to the state who have power and influence (Maloney, 2015). In 2017, a new term, *Zhen-e Khoob*, which means "good genes," has become synonymous with *Aghazadeh*s (Esfandiari, 2017). These people enjoy several privileges that are completely inaccessible to ordinary citizens, such as positions within the social and political hierarchy that facilitates their access to "inside" information, preferential treatment, and access to wealth and power across generations (Maloney, 2015). Therefore "fewer top positions are available to talented people without family connections" (Khalaji, 2014). For example, Shahram Jazayeri, an *Aghazadeh*, was the central defendant in a major corruption case involving fifty defendants, many of them sons of prominent clerics (also *Aghazadeh*). Charges against him included: "bribery totaling 38 billion rials ($4.75 million USD at the time), fraud to obtain loans amounting to 811 billion rials ($101 million USD at the time) and setting up bogus companies" (Corruption Watch, 2002). "In September 2004, his 27-year prison sentence was partially overturned, and he was occasionally released from prison on leave" (Samii, 2005, n.p.). This is while Amnesty International (2018) reported that between 2007 and 2017, the Iranian state "issued at least 215 amputation sentences and carried out 125 amputations, including at least six amputations in public" (n.p.).

Islamic Corporal Punishment: Hodud and Qisās

Qisās means retaliation, which also stands for retributive justice in legal terms. When a person intentionally kills another, sharia permits the victim's family to ask for an execution of the murderer. Or, if a person intentionally damages another's bodily organs or faculties, the perpetrator should be punished by becoming disabled similarly to his or her victim, to the extent that it is possible and feasible to achieve this symmetry. When the symmetry cannot be reached, a financial compensation can be ordered.[5]

Similar to Judeo-Christian traditions before it, Islam orders an extension of the biblical lex talionis, "an eye for an eye and a tooth for a tooth," and the Quranic instruction in 5, 45: "the life for the life, and the eye for the eye, and the nose for the nose, and the ear for the ear, and the tooth for the tooth, and for wounds retaliation" (Bengtsson, 2018; Rispler-Chaim, 2007; Souryal, Potts, & Alobied, 1994). Sharia prohibits many activities, such as alcohol or pork consumption, public displays of non-Islamic religious symbols or text, affection between members of the opposite sex outside of marriage, "indecent" artwork or media images, sorcery, homosexuality, cross-dressing, and fornication, or adultery. There are five crimes listed in the fiqh literature under Hudud: "fornication (*zina*), slandering a woman for [an allegedly] immoral sexual conduct (*qadhf*), alcohol consumption (*shurb al-khamr*), *sariqa*, and armed or highway robbery (*haraba* or *qat al-tariq*). The general Muslim public may sometimes count among the hudud eight groups of crimes rather than the five traditionally mentioned by the fiqh. The three additional crimes are political insurrection (*baghy*), apostasy (*ridda*), and intentional killing (*al-qatl al-'amad*), which requires a *qisas*" (Rispler-Chaim, 2007, p. 76). It's important to note that political insurrection requires a *qisas* under sharia, which basically closes any doors to dissent, social discontent, protest, demonstration, or any political movement to demand change.

Scholars like Kirkup (2007), Friedman (1972), and Mavroforou et al. (2014) have demonstrated that removal of limbs, organs, or parts of them has happened throughout history for ritualistic, legal/punitive, or medical purposes. In the Middle East, the punitive amputation of limbs has been the most prevalent cause of amputation to follow Islamic jurisprudence that granted "theological sanction" to corporal punishment (Haj, 1970). The prophet himself, Mohammed, personally ordered amputation as punishment for people. Haj states that the Quran explicitly requires amputation for robbery, as was the case for a long time before the emergence of Islam in the region. The Islamic holy book, the Quran, states "if a man or, woman steals, cut off 'their' hand in retribution for that which they committed" (v. 5, 33). Haj states that amputation at the wrist was usual, but that at least one case is known to him of bilateral elbow amputations for theft. Multiple amputations were done for people who continued to steal, as was ordered by the prophet himself (Haj, 1970; Kirkup, 2007).

Another verse states, "Those that make war against God and His apostle and spread disorder in the land shall be put to death or crucified or have their hands and feet cut off on alternate sides" (v. 5, 32). However, moderate Muslim and non-Muslim scholars believed that those verses should be interpreted in accordance to the historical period and social context as opposed to a vacuum in which everything is interpreted literally (Kirkup, 2007).[6] Nevertheless, as allowed by the Islamic jurisprudence and sanctioned by sharia, hand and finger amputations for theft have been legally conducted in the twenty-first century and remain routine legal penalties in some Muslim countries (Kirkup, 2007). As contradictory as it may sound, the same Islamic states sometimes do not approve of necessary medical amputation for war-related or minefield injuries or in cases of illness. Their rationale is that it may prevent the body's ascent to heaven if it is "imperfect" (read disabled) (Friedmann, 1972).

This violence of inflicting disability on lower-class criminals occurs in Iran as a "divine punishment," according to the ideology that the state imposes on its citizens in the form of sharia law. Can the existing models in Disability Studies (DS) help us understand what happens in such a scenario? Probably not. However, DHM can, if equipped with a DS lens and global politics. Moreover, we know that disability is usually associated with discrimination, lower incomes, and unemployment (Oliver, 1983), for the capitalist logic of making profit by exploiting labor power is always an ableist barrier for disabled people to access proper employment. There is also a cultural taboo that accompanies a disfigured limb, as it signals past criminal activity. DHM can help us understand how theocracy, class, and capitalist social relations cause a poor person to become disabled and remain so due to poverty (read getting dumped at the bottom of the social division of labor).

The IRI is an ideological and capitalist state for whom democracy and collective decision-making are alien concepts. In this political context, such a state only serves the interests of the ruling class and not society more broadly, meaning the working class or poor people always remain poor. The judicial system also serves the interests of ruling classes, who are often corrupt and dishonest. It is under this set of circumstances that the state engages in "following sharia law" and imposing punitive amputation on the poor who steal as a means of coping with poverty. Ironically, nothing happens to those who are close to the state and steal millions (e.g., the clerical caste, Islamic Revolutionary Guards Corps members [IRGC], and their relatives). So far, we can detect the role of class and ideology in this example and see the social relations of capitalism, theocracy, nepotism, and economic and social corruption behind imposed disablement. Here, the poor person who has been perhaps forced to steal becomes even poorer because s/he acquires a disability that will likely make it harder to find proper employment. The disabled poor often end up begging on the street or die of drug overdoses. The World Health Organization estimates that there are 1.3 billion people living with some type of disability in the world, of whom 200 million have difficulty functioning (WHO, 2011). It is predicted that disability will be even more prevalent in the future. There is extensive data demonstrating that disabled people face discrimination all over the word. Additionally, there are other factors that marginalize the survivors of PLA, such as cultural taboos around disfigurement, the shame surrounding a lost limb that could signal past criminal activity, as well as the social stigma attached to disability and criminality.

Souryal, Potts, and Alobied (1994) argue that the reason PLA is perceived as a cruel and outdated punishment for theft is due to the assumption that the penalty for such an "insignificant crime" should not be that harsh. They argue in favor of sharia law, reasoning that "rape and murder [for which the punishment is execution under sharia] are so rare in Muslim communities precisely because of the imposition of severe punishments for seemingly less heinous crimes such as theft." Besides this unsubstantiated claim, they argue that theft is a great sin in Islam because "thievery atomizes society by laying personal property prey to indiscriminate violation, thus keeping its members in fear for their freedom to own, trade, and worship" (p. 2). This argument seems to be more in favor of following the capitalist logic, liberal law, normative use value and exchange value, as well as other components of the capitalist economy, such as labor power and surplus extraction, rather than precepts about human dignity. They claim that the low crime rate in Islamic countries indicates the deterring effect of PLA (ibid.). This could be the case of one or more countries, if we decide to trust the provided statistics. However, Islamic countries display dramatic disparities when plotted on a crime index graph, with lower incidences of crime in Saudi Arabia, very high crime rates in Afghanistan, and Iran falling in the middle (World Population Review, 2024).

Disabling Theocracy: Rich Thief Disables the Poor Thief

"The corruption in Iran has become systemic; that is, corruption [read stealing] is deeply embedded in political and administrative systems and can no longer be attributed only to the rogue behavior of a limited number of bureaucrats" (Azadi, 2020, p. 1). Even if they get caught for financial crimes such as corruption, they can either pay a fine and get off, or stay in prison with exceptional amenities, such as Persian carpets, a private shower, and a private kitchen (not available to ordinary or political prisoners) (Tehran News, 2019). This happens while political prisoners live under dire conditions in notorious prisons. It is not a secret that "Iran is controlled by a few Islamic clerics, their relatives, and cronies who came to power following the Iranian revolution in 1979" (Torbat, 2013). Since 2008, Iran has entered a new phase of kleptocracy, with an uncountable number of corruption cases that are rarely prosecuted. Pooya Azadi (2020), who studies the structure of corruption in Iran, has classified corrupt actions into the following major clusters: (1) political corruption (e.g., lack of meritocratic standards for public appointments); (2) administrative corruption (e.g., bribery); (3) corruption involving parties from the nongovernmental sector; (4) favoritism; and (5) coercive corruption. Azadi informs us that there could be an overlap between these groups, although the most substantial in Iran currently is political corruption—which some refer to as "grand corruption" or "state capture."[7]

Currently, political corruption in Iran comprises a wide spectrum, such as clientelism, patronage appointments (Azadi, 2020; Behravesh, 2020), corruption in elections, smuggling and money laundering by the state, manipulation of statistics, recruitment of rank-and-file bureaucrats without regard to merit, patronage appointments (usually by the supreme leaders), rent seeking (Azadi, 2020), smuggling of goods from IRGC's exclusive ports (Kermani & Tale'i, 2011) and government involvement in drug trafficking (Azadi, 2020), and refusing to join the global money laundering and terrorist financing watchdog, the Financial Action Task Force (FATF), among others. "According to the Basel AML index [i.e., Basel AML Index 2017, Basel Ins. for Gov., Switzerland], Iran's financial system tops the world in terms of money-laundering risk. In fact, Iran has committed to addressing its antimoney-laundering regulatory deficiencies since 2016 but has not done anything till the time this chapter was being written (FATF, 2020). Considering the insurmountable consequences of FATF counter-measures on Iran's already troubled economy, there is good reason to believe that high officials have significant interest in keeping the status quo and deferring regulatory reforms that can make the financial system more transparent" (Azadi, 2020, p. 2).

In 2013, Reuters revealed that the supreme leader, Ali Khamenei, oversees an economic cartel, an organization called "Headquarters for Executing the Order of the Imam" (HEOI), called *Setād* in Farsi, that possesses assets estimated at about $95 billion USD (Stecklow, Dehghanpisheh, & Torbati, 2013). A six-month investigation by the news agency found that the HEOI "built its empire on the systemic seizure [read stealing] of thousands of properties belonging to ordinary Iranians: members of religious minorities like Vahdat-e-Hagh, who is Baha'i, as well as Shi'ite Muslims, business people and Iranians living abroad" (Stecklow, Dehghanpisheh, & Torbati, 2013). The name of this gigantic organization comes from an edict signed by the founder of the IRI, Ruhollah Khomeini. During the years after the 1979 revolution, many people realized that the new state wasn't going to yield them a sunny life. Therefore, they left the country. Simultaneously, in the years following the revolution, many upper-middle-class members of the former regime, such as high-ranking military personnel, were banned from any financial exchanges, such as selling their properties. Khomeini's order spawned a new entity to confiscate, manage, and sell those properties that people had been forced to abandon. Since 1979, the HEOI has become one of the most powerful organizations in Iran, though many Iranians, and the wider world, know very little about it (Stecklow, Dehghanpisheh, & Torbati, 2013).

Under the supreme leader's supervision, the organization began attaining property for itself and used the funds to accumulate more wealth for Khamenei. With those revenues, the organization also helps to fund the ultimate seat of power in Iran, the supreme leader's office. There is no way to obtain a complete picture of this organization's spending and income. Reuters revealed its books are "off limits even to Iran's legislative branch." It reported that in 2008 "the Iranian Parliament voted to prohibit itself from monitoring organizations that the supreme leader controls, except with his permission" (Stecklow, Dehghanpisheh, & Torbat, 2013).

The elites close to him or to his position within other powerful state organizations, such as the IRGC (Iran Wire, 2019) and *Bonyāds*/foundations (Sibley, 2022), are either corrupt or untouchable.[8] As such, the corrupt members of the state never get caught, and even if they are, they end up paying small bail fees and walk free. Between 2005 and 2013, "Out of the $700 billion earned during the presidency of Ahmadinejad for the sale of oil, $150 billion dollars have disappeared" (Milani, 2018). Furthermore, Akbar Torbat writes: "On February 3, 2013, President Mahmoud Ahmadinejad played a video tape in the Iranian parliament that tied the heads of two branches of the government, the legislative and judiciary, to a documented financial corruption case related to the Larijani brothers" (Torbat, 2013). It is hypocritical and poignant that none of these people (e.g., Ahmadinejad's administration, the Larijani brothers) who are suspected or even convicted of astronomical amounts of corruption get their limbs amputated. It's only the poor who steal a sheep or some small item that end up disabled. It's amid this corrupt sociopolitical landscape of the Islamic state that petty thefts transpire, and limbs get cut off, but this is true for only the limbs of the deprived.

"At least half of Iran lives below the poverty line as the government fails to solve the economic crisis," a leading economist, Hassan Raghfar warned (2023). Khoshnood (2019) writes, "The main cause of poverty in Iran, in the end, is its political system" (p. 69). It is important to note that rich thieves are immune from the PLA, but "poor thieves" are not. Even members of the state apparatus, such as the president, confess that poverty is ravaging the country (Tehran Times, 2016). This is despite the fact that Iran possesses abundant natural resources and is not a poor country. However, the clerical state's regional-imperialistic politics has brought upon the Iranian people the economic sanctions aimed at preventing the state from funding its proxy militias in Yemen, Iraq, Syria, and Lebanon by selling the country's oil (Sadjadpour, 2019).

Most recently, due to the skyrocketing price of housing in Tehran, many people have reportedly started to sleep in graveyards in Tehran's slums and even on the transit buses, since they have nowhere else to go (Tehran Times, 2016). Others have been renting building roofs to have a place to sleep at night. This misery and destitution are so ironic considering that Iran is the world's seventh-largest oil producer. The ever-widening gap between the elites (i.e., the clerical cast and those close to them) and the ordinary people has given birth to a contradiction. On one hand, the reality in Iran, which is reflected in the lives of millions, is the existence of a gender-apartheid system, extreme poverty, human rights violations under incarceration, political repression, drug abuse, children joining the sex work industry as young as twelve, child labor, illiteracy, grave-dwellers, and a vast market of people selling their vital body organs to make ends meet. On the other hand, the Instagram page *Rich Kids of Tehran* depicts a very different reality, a class of ruling elites and their pampered children, living a life of luxury earned by looting national wealth and the meager earnings of poorer classes.

In Their Own Words

In an educational video published by a reputable human rights organization, the *Abdorrahman Boroumand Foundation*, it is asked whether PLA, as form of corporal punishment, is a necessity in an Islamic society governed by sharia law. It's worthwhile to cite some of the topics explored in the video. The producers quoted a man facing a punitive hand amputation for theft charges saying to his judge, "Please don't take away my hand! My daughter is very young, and my elderly mother has been diagnosed with cancer. I stole because these things were weighing down on me" (Abdorrahman Boroumand Center, 2017). This is the same survivor with whose words I began this chapter. Unfortunately, he is just one of thousands of cases of Iranians driven to steal due to poverty. Despite the fact that hand amputation is handed down as a punishment for crimes like theft in the IRI not all Muslim jurists believe that PLA is necessary in an Islamic society. In fact, there is a diversity of opinions on whether or not hodud punishments can be legitimately carried out before the return of the Infallible Imam, a messianic figure in the Ja'fari school of Shi'ism, which is Iran's official state religion. For example, Seyyed Ahmad Khansari and Mohaqeq Helli, considered two of the three most prominent Shia jurists and sources of emulation, both clearly opposed the implementation of hodud. Ayatollah Khansari writes: "Just as jihad against the infidels is one of the exclusive duties of the Infallible Imam, carrying out hodud punishments is his prerogative. No one but this Imam shall in any case be authorized to do such things" (Abdorrahman Boroumand Center, 2017). Others note that punishments like amputation, lashing, and stoning are nowhere to be found in Iran's 1925 code of criminal sanctions, which renowned religious authority Ayatollah Seyed Hassan Modares certified as compatible with religious law.

In shocking interview footage that the Abdorrahman Boroumand Foundation (2017) managed to access, Mohsen Sabzichi from the city of Arak, a victim of PLA, appeared, one of his hands having only one finger left, with four already cut off. This exposure is a rare occasion because the IRI tries to prevent these cruel cases from being publicized, as they shatter its "facade," which it tries to construct on the world stage as a rational actor. I explain this phenomenon in more detail in the next chapter. In the interview, Sabzichi states: "They took us out of the solitary confinement handcuffed. From there, they took us to the prison yard where they had gathered all the prisoners, so they could 'watch.' I was looking under the blindfold and I saw a bloody machine. Nothing, there was no sanitation. It was a steel cutter. The warden, as if they were slaughtering an animal, said: 'It's nothing, it's just cutting off four fingers. As if it's something'" (Abdorrahman Boroumand Center, 2017). His amputation took place in the city of Aarak on May 18, 2011, as documented by the Boroumand Foundation. He described the moment: "They [the prison guard] tied my hand to the machine. And then, they pushed the knob. As I was watching, my fingers fell on the floor, and they were moving. [He closed his eyes at this point in the interview as if deeply sighing.] They cut my fingers off, bandaged my hand, and put me in an ambulance." After describing that moment, Sabzichi stated, "There were many people who didn't get a hand amputation sentence, though they'd stolen hundreds of times. For me, I got an amputation the first time. Therefore, I am upset and complaining. Why have they sentenced me to hand amputation, even though it was my first time [stealing]?" (Abdorrahman Boroumand Center, 2017).

Mohsen Sabzichi's words are consistent with many accounts of amputation having been carried out on poor people but not on the elites—those close to the regime who, with impunity, steal millions of dollars, evade tax, launder money for the state, or withhold billions from the national treasury owned by the ministry of petroleum in an attempt to facilitate Iran's oil revenue, which is hindered by the economic sanctions. The list is long, including Shahram Jazayeri, Babak Zanjani, Reza Zarrab, Akbar Tabari, and others. This demonstrates a correlation between poverty and PLA under sharia law in Iran, while the Quran proclaims that members of the community should "stand out firmly for justice" (4: 135). Neither any member of the elite, nor a person close to the ruling class accused and convicted of stealing money, has ever faced PLA, showing the selective and discriminatory nature of this cruel and irreversible punishment. Mohsen Sabzichi rightfully asks in the video, "If someone changes his ways after this [PLA], how is he supposed to make a living? Have they [the regime] thought this through?" He expresses further frustration, saying, "I cannot do anything. I can't even eat properly; even eating is difficult. Holding utensils is difficult. I cannot do anything [he repeats three times]. My life has become very hard; it has become hell. I can't button my shirt. I can't tie my own shoes; someone has to do it for me" (Abdorrahman Boroumand Center, 2017).

A certified lawyer who works in Iran stated, "As a lawyer, I can tell you, Iran's Islamic criminal code does include this type of punishment, and it is indeed carried out more or less." Additionally, Mohsen assures us that his case is not an isolated one and that there are many people who await this punishment in agony. Sabzichi continues as follows:

> There are 11 people in prison right now who have been sentenced to hand amputation. Their sentence has not been carried out yet. But they have carried it out on the three of us. One guy got [an amputation sentence for] his hand and foot. The other is me and then Hossein Shariat. There are still 11 people whom the judge has sentenced to hand amputation, but they have not yet carried it out. It's not clear: it might get carried out tomorrow, in two, or five years. My life fell apart because of hand amputation. I returned to my parents' home. I'm living in my father's home. I don't usually go out of the house because of what people say [he's probably referring to people's whispers, stares, and attitude that other disabled folks, burn survivors, and basically anyone with a visible difference, experiences]. We live in a very small and closed environment, and everybody has something to say. So, I hide my hand; I put it in my pocket,[9] or cover it with a bandage. (Abdorrahman Boroumand Center, 2017)

The most tragic part of the video comes when Sabzichi states, "Alright, I've made a mistake. Should I be humiliated this much?" The question that arises is what he saw as the source of his humiliation. Was it the act of rendering him disabled for theft? The disability itself? Or becoming disabled by the state?

Unfortunately, these cases are not isolated, neither in Iran nor beyond. For instance, since the (re)rise of the Taliban and ISIS, the world has witnessed more abhorrent and unapologetic performances of the "self-announced" hodud on innocent ordinary citizens who are ruled by the Muslim extremists. In 1999, in a packed sports stadium, an Afghan man's limbs were amputated while he was conscious, supervised by mullahs. It is both poignant and interesting to know that, according to his own words, he had been chosen to take the place of a rich Pashtun who, having committed a crime, paid a sum of money to the mullahs so that a prisoner of war received his punishment instead (Kirkup, 2007, p. 39). The victim described the gruesome scene as follows:

> Seven doctors approached me. They wore grey uniforms, surgical masks, and gloves. I could see one was crying. They injected me. After five minutes, my body was numb, though I was still conscious. Then they put clamps on my hand and foot and began to cut them off with special saws. There was no pain, but I could see what they were doing . . . I was transfixed by the sight of my foot being removed. There was a sigh and murmur from the crowd when they finished. It had taken about five minutes. (Kirkup, 2007, p. 39)

Claiming to be following sharia law, the ISIS also committed unimaginable atrocities, including PLA, against Yazidis as well as Iraqi prisoners who were captured (Sly & Ramadan, 2014).

"Curing" Poverty by Inflicting Disability

These corporal punishments are administered when sharia licenses a person to create a disability in another person's body and leave them disabled for the rest of their life. This rule, as many have argued, including Rispler-Chaim (2007), "stands in contradiction to the theological principle that the human body is no one's private property, and that one may not abuse or cause damage to one's own body, still less to the body of another person. The sanctity deriving from the creation of the human in God's image is purposely violated, and under religious license" (p. 77). However, there are many justifications that sharia apologists present, which I discuss in the following paragraphs.

Sharia apologists claim that physical punishment is not an end in itself, but an event serving "to reinforce in the conscience of believers the deterrent[10] consequences and the horrible cost of betraying community standards" (Souryal, Potts, & Alobied, 1994, p. 7). It is rather the last effort at "curing" and reforming the conduct of an individual after all previously tried measures, such as education and admonition, have failed.[11] Also, they claim that corporal punishments are more effective than nonphysical ones in deterring the potential sinner from even plotting a crime (Souryal, Potts, & Alobied, 1994). But, how can we measure the impact of this supposed "deterrent"?

Souryal, Potts, & Alobied (1994) argue in favor of PLA and provide sentiments glorifying and romanticizing sharia law and the concept of "Islamic justice." It's worth going over their claims. They argue that PLA: (1) deters and dissuades potential thieves; (2) keeps the bond among the community by preserving its collective integrity, since any threat to people's property is a threat to the community's wholeness; and (3) demonstrates how horrific the cost of betrayal of trust is in a Muslim community. They compare PLA to the court-ordered castration of compulsive rapists, the neutering of a pet, religious circumcision of male children, and cutting a tree. They further reason that the Hodud and qisās serve as a warning to others. The sharia apologists claim that the Hodud and qisās are there to benefit society at large (*maslaha*[12] or expediency), to which I would add the state, or what Foucault would call *raison d'état*. Therefore, they argue that the society (read the state) reserves the right to administer justice (read punish the criminals). They further add that corporal punishments, due to their cruel nature, deter the criminal from ever repeating their crime.

Rispler-Chaim (2007) indicates that current statistics from Saudi Arabia, and from Sudan and Pakistan in the 1980s, are often cited to prove that there is a clear link between the enforcement of physical punishments and the low crime rates in the given society (p. 77). Contrary to that, she claims, it is shown that advanced countries such as the United States and Britain, which hardly resort to physical punishment, suffer ever-increasing crime rates (Rispler-Chaim, 2007). Nevertheless, we should note that the crime rates could have been manipulated in Sudan and Pakistan to defend cruel punishments in order to justify the use of sharia as a penal code, although the code is 1400 years old. Thus, those statistics may not be as reliable as the PLA advocates claim.

Additionally, those in favor of the Islamic corporeal punishment focus extensively on how Westerners should or should not perceive the PLA that is performed in some Islamic countries. Their rationale is that since PLA is a punishment "indigenous" to some parts of the world, it should, therefore, be left alone. This reminds me of the old battle of "cultural relativism" that is still fought in the academy. There are still people who refuse to condemn female genital mutilation (FGM) as a sexist, misogynist, and disabling act, arguing that it is an "African" or "Christian" practice. But you never hear from the same people that the wage gap between men and women in the West is a "cultural" practice and should be left alone. Instead, they would argue that it is the most obvious form of gender discrimination (Kazemi, 2024b). Reducing historical social relations to cultural practices that happen in a sociopolitical vacuum is naive. Every disabling/wounding process, from FGM to PLA, should be examined in a historical and relational context, where unequal power relations can be exposed and not concealed under the cloak of "cultural difference."

The apologists rationalize PLA by claiming that Western societies are hypocrites for problematizing the implementation of sharia in some countries while they themselves engage in what Souryal, Potts, & Alobied (1994) call "social amputation" (p. 9) by imprisoning convicts' bodyminds, isolating them, and discriminating against them even after their release. With the same token, Miles (2002) accuses Westerners of being either ignorant or hypocritical when she compares the Islamic PLA and some contemporary Western legal and medical procedures, as she argues that the latter practices may also look ferocious in fifty years. She further argues that imprisonment or the idea of rehabilitating (read fixing, curing, normalizing) sinners/criminals has seldom made much headway in conditions of socioeconomic stringency, where lawbreaking among the masses threatens the privileges of a rule-making class. The critics also contend that the two disciplinary measures of capital punishment, which is still practiced in certain American states, and imprisonment, which is practiced in the entire Western Hemisphere, are also inhumane. It is interesting to note that the societies that practice PLA that defend their use of PLA in relation to the Western practice of imprisonment usually practice imprisonment and execution as well.

Souryal, Potts, & Alobied (1994)'s argument sounds rather "Orientalist" (Said, 1978) to me, rather than resisting "Orientalism," because it is obsessed with the ways in which "Westerners" understand PLA to be cruel. This, I believe, relocates us, the Middle Eastern people, at the periphery where we are always "seen" by the center/West as being either "barbaric" (which literally means foreigners) or not. The authors bring up Judeo-Christian traditions in an effort to demonstrate how "similar" they are to sharia. Again, I see this as an effort to put ourselves, "in relation" to the "better Other," to Westerners, and examine ourselves from their point of view.

Reading these critiques, one cannot help but assume that sharia law does not include imprisonment at all, though imprisonment is widely practiced in all countries where Islam is the religion of the state. The question is whether we can compare PLA to imprisonment. Can we imprison the bodymind for a lifetime but argue against cutting four fingers? One might prefer to have his four fingers cut off rather than be thrown in a small cell for forty years. This suggests that imprisonment is not humane, either. However, there is still a difference between the two regarding how they violate the bodymind. Imprisonment has its own critics, as evidenced by the prison abolition movement, which demands immediate abolition of incarceration, de-funding police, and divesting from prison corporations (Ben-Moshe, 2020). Therefore, when we are comparing different forms of disciplinary, punishment, and rehabilitative measures, we must be careful not to fall into "what-aboutism," or, in other words, an Olympics of sufferings. PLA is more contested than imprisonment, and that's why the latter is practiced in the world more than the former. However, this does not mean it is fine to keep humans inside cages. Many disagree with both and argue that systems of justice based on punishment should be eliminated altogether, replaced with a more restorative form of justice based on education, community-based healing, volunteer work, and the like (Ben-Moshe, 2020).

In an article, a Malaysian surgeon examines the ethics of the idea that doctors should, by law, participate in the punitive amputation of the limbs of persons convicted in a sharia court. The paper's main concern is how a modern medical practitioner should approach this ethical question (Das, 2020). The author proceeds from the viewpoint that Western assumptions that PLA is the "most barbaric punishment" are hypocritical at best, since there are U.S. states that still carry out execution by lethal injection, performed by a physician or supervised by one. After the eighteenth century and the arrival of modernity and the constitution of humans as subjects with rights (albeit only European humans and not African slaves or Native Americans, for instance), including the right to his/her body and dignity, even the punitive measure adapted themselves to this notion. In other words, in European societies, torture and limb amputation ceased to exist, at least officially, as a punitive measure. Bernstein reveals that although Westerners prohibited the use of torture at home, "it was increasingly used in imperial and colonial adventures" (Bernstein, 2015, p. 7).

For instance, at the time of European colonization of Africa (1884–1904), many slaves went through PLA and became disabled. In 1885, the Berlin Conference, which led to the "generous" division of the entire African continent among the European powers, donated the Congo Free State to King Leopold of Belgium as personal property. This notorious colonial ruler rushed to extract profits from his new colony by exploiting the abundant, inexpensive slave labor there. His agents treated the local population with great cruelty. In this twenty-year period, as European powers competed to exploit the wealth of Africa, between five and eight million Africans died from colonial violence, including systematic amputation and torture.

Additionally, most European schools of thought, as we know them today, agree that cruelty is the worst thing a person can commit against another and that unnecessary pain and suffering should be avoided or regarded as an ethical failure. Therefore, over the past 200 years, "overt state violence against citizens [read subjects of the state] was replaced by more insidious forms of penal violence, what Foucault denominates as *disciplinary regimes* [emphasis in the original]" (Bernstein, 2015, p. 8). For instance, torture was officially replaced with the right to due process and imprisonment and execution with life sentences (Bernstein, 2015). After WWII and the disaster of the Holocaust, the global community came up with a new notion, "crimes against humanity." This was a pivotal moment when humans developed a new concept to identify with and redefine at least part of their established criminology and legal apparatus around the social and collective notion of "humanity" rather than just the individuality implied by the terms humans or human. This is the point at which certain offenses became categorized as crimes committed against humanity as a whole, and not just the single person or group of people who were themselves directly physically harmed by a crime.

Political Economy of Punitive Amputation

From a political-economic standpoint, why do the sharia apologists not explain why Allah hasn't given humanity a plan to eradicate poverty, which necessitates robbery in the first place as a means of survival? Why hasn't "he" given us, or expected us to build (just like the prayer and fasting that we are supposed to do), an economic system that is based on equality and equity and not exploitation? The logic that robbery is a malicious act and should be punishable is usually held in societies ruled by either capitalism or, before that, feudalism, which are both based on class hierarchy and exploitation. In these economic systems, poverty is an inherent logic, as they are designed like a pyramid where working-class people's labor power is purchased for much less than its actual worth by the people at the top who do not need to work as much, since their money generates more money for them. In these systems, poverty of the working class is inevitable. Why does sharia not tell us how to eradicate poverty, as opposed to commanding us to amputate the limbs of poor people who have to steal to survive?

Rispler-Chaim (2007), who studies the use of PLA in the Islamic law, states, "The right hand is especially important, as it is used in eating, and it is also the hand used when taking an oath, which is also termed *yamin* in Arabic. The amputation of a hand is therefore primarily an attempt to degrade the owner of the hand, to bring upon the thief humiliation and shame ('ar, khizy)" (p. 79). It is interesting to note the normative assumptions in this speculation that the criminal must belong to the majority who are right-handed, and that disability is equal to "humiliation" and "shame." The rationale behind it is that "the organ [not the economic structure that causes poverty] that committed the crime has to be removed so that the rest of society may regain peacefulness and security in their daily life" (p. 79).

Bengtsson (2018), a theologian, who has examined Islamic texts to understand their treatment of disability and disablement, argues that first and foremost, Islamic history is intermingled with the history of spreading the message through wars. We now know that for every person killed in a war, as many as 100 more are left with disabilities (United Nations, 2007). These conflicts, since many nations resisted Islamic rule, turned into real battles, which increased the risk of permanent injury. These injuries, as Bengtsson (2018) argues, would locate the injured person as a community member in need of care and support. This was seen as a position of "dependence." Bengtsson states, "The Quran thereby illustrates how a *weak* [my emphasis] state paves the way for a system of religious- and individual-based charity" (p. 7). This meant that the Islamic system required community members to show support through "zakat," which is a charity model mediated by unequal relations of power that recenters/designates some as donors and others as recipients. The Islamic system outlined in the text (i.e., Quran, Hadith) suggests that the disabled person is seen as a member of the community of "believers." Therefore, this person "must submit to religious norms to obtain assistance" (Bengtsson, 2018, p. 7). It's imperative to understand that the Islamic system works based on "us versus them," or believers and non-believers. This is a value-based collective identity system embedded in both inclusion and exclusion. Also, it is important to note that "it [the Quran] contains no explicit decree regarding obligations of the state concerning, for instance, accessibility and rehabilitation" (Bengtsson, 2018, p. 7).

The Quran doesn't contain the world "disability." It instead orders the *ummah* to give *zakat* (obligatory tax) to the needy and "disadvantaged," which includes the disabled (Bazna & Hatab, 2005). It says not to kill your children—aimed at preventing people from killing their disabled children, as was prevalent in the ancient world. By establishing a broad category, such as "the needy," people with disabilities were foremost integrated into the heterogeneous group of the poor, which created a link between scarce economic resources and disability (Bengtsson, 2018). The maximum effort Quran has shown for the poor is thus *zakat* (Pervez, 1990, p. 3). The Quran stresses the principle that a community member has a responsibility to support and assist his or her own family members (Ghaly, 2010). "However, the Quran also demands that community members should devote themselves to regular charity that reaches beyond family members and occasional alms giving" (Bengtsson, 2018, p. 3). Bengtsson (2018) argues that "he [Allah] explicitly states that there should be a financial transfer system that moves resources from the rich to 'the needy.' 'Those who . . . practice regular charity,' the Quran reports, 'to them shall we soon give a great reward' (4: 162)" (p. 3). The overall goal for *zakat*, Bengtsson argues is for the *ummah* to establish a charity system and care for each other (2018). This brings me back to the initial point that charity is a system that exists precisely because there is inequality. Charity is required when there is structural inequality and injustice. If there is equality in a society, why would we need some people's "benevolence" toward others? Most religions naturalize the idea of charity as a "virtue" to be adopted, as opposed to aiming toward building a society that would not rely on charity.

Souryal, Potts, & Alobied (1994) claim that in the philosophy of Islamic justice blame is placed on the "sick" hand of the thief who has stolen, which makes it unsalvageable. Therefore, according to this rationale, the thief's hand is cut off as a way of "curing" the entire person and society. Note the similar language used to refer to criminals as a "problem" or "sickness" in society that needs to be "cured" by being cut off altogether. The ableist tradition embedded in the rationale of "natural" inequality is noteworthy here. Not only does sharia law not condemn economic inequality, it also sanctions "disabling" the poor for wanting to survive.

Embodiment, Wholeness, and Dignity

I have explored in this chapter how the theocratic state exercises its sovereignty, via the punitive/judiciary apparatus, on its subjects' bodily integrity. The penalty system as well as the use of a disability rhetoric, with its link to ignorance, are other examples of how the Quran has some contradictory traits regarding disability. The Quran does not present a clear reconciliation between disability and dignity (Bengtsson, 2018). On the one hand, it offers an inclusion-like discourse to count disabled people as community members (Bazna & Hatab, 2005; Bengtsson, 2018). But, on the other hand, it sanctions and deems necessary a punitive system (Quran, 5: 38) that includes disabling measures to actively render people disabled. Therefore, the covert logic here is that "the deviant body could also be used as a moral warning sign. Hence, how a certain disability came to be could affect the level of stigma attached to it" (Bengtsson, 2018, p. 5).

What is the relationship between embodied wholeness and dignity? Islamists claim that Allah has emphasized the importance of the wholeness of the body (Rispler-Chaim, 2007), and yet he orders limb amputation to punish criminals who steal and "disrupt the order" of society. Rispler-Chaim (2007) states, "It is astonishing, therefore, that in certain legal scenarios Islamic law prescribes, contrary to the above perception and to the general ethics of life, the deliberate violation of the wholeness and dignity of the human body as means of physical punishment. This implies that the law not only tolerates but indeed requires the creation of disabilities in certain people who were born with no disability, and thus punishes them for deeds which society abhors" (p. 75). The order here means a sense of security for *ummah*, a sense of wholeness and trust (Bengtsson, 2018; Souryal, Potts, & Alobied, 1994).

The first thing this logic recalls is the ideological and ahistorical view of *ummah* as some euphoric community that lives outside human society, which is not characterized by the same traits as other communities. The logic speaks of order as if the Muslim community is not embedded within the current global economy or culture. People steal when they cannot afford to buy. If there is no private property, and if things are shared by the community, then people cannot steal because they do not own anything privately. The order discussed does not aim at tackling the material conditions that force people to steal to survive. It treats stealing as a crime done out of malice and not out of need, since this order implies a euphoria where everyone has access to resources and does not need to steal. The logic fetishizes the wounded/amputated body and masks the violence that exists in a society that is run by exploitative economic systems.

Wholeness could mean dignity of the bodymind—the human bodymind deserving to remain whole, especially preserved from the violence of amputation, war, torture, and acid attacks. Nevertheless, I can foresee the critique that I have once again theorized disability as lacking, incomplete, broken, and fragmentary. In response, I argue that it is not disability that is inherently lacking, it is the theocratic state violence that produces disability as a "lack." In other words, I agree that "wholeness" per se can be interpreted as an ideology similar to "normalcy," but my intention here is to point out the violence that the state inflicts upon the bodymind of the poor while upholding the very same ideology of wholeness about the society that has presumably been violated by the "unruly" poor. In other words, it is the violence of PLA that produces disability as "lack" concealing the economic hierarchy that requires poverty to operate.

Bernstein (2015) states, "Torture and rape are paradigm cases of moral injury; interrogating them will lead to thesis that what is harmed in moral injuries is the dignity of the wholly embodied human subject" (p. 1). He further clarifies that to suffer devastation is to suffer loss of trust in the world. Trust, as a form of mutual recognition, is the invisible ethical substance of everyday living. To recognize another's standing as a person is to respect their dignity (p. 14). Dignity is a fragile social possession that is a product of everyday practices of trust that are now best protected by the rule of law. Bernstein (2015) indicates that dignity is a social possession protected by the rule of law (at least in the Western world since the Enlightenment era).

My question, in the context mentioned earlier, is what about the places in which universal human rights laws do not have jurisdiction, such as the IRI and Saudi Arabia? Dignity should not depend upon legal protection, or be contingent upon geographical location, although it is certainly important to uphold the law as a deterrence. We should note that the Universal Declaration of Human Rights is in conflict with national laws and constitutions in certain countries, such as Iran, or wherever Islam is the religion of the state. How can we protect human rights in the entire world when the international human rights law is an agreement between sovereign states, some of which actively violate the human rights of their citizens? The Transnational Disability Theory and Praxis, developed in Chapter 1, taught us to develop collective political consciousness going beyond international borders and to tackle injustices everywhere, not just in one's local context. Here is where transnational solidarity and global community-building, outside the official international relations between nation-states, come into play. One example is the transnational solidarity praxis (Kazemi & Karah, 2023) that overthrew the apartheid regime in South Africa, whereby the entire global community united and opposed the apartheid state by isolating and boycotting the South African government and imposing sanctions on it. A combination of internal and international resistance to apartheid helped dismantle a racial apartheid (i.e., the white supremacist regime). In fact, decades of domestic and transnational activism, as well as international economic sanctions, led to the end of the regime enforcing a strict racial segregation that allowed the country's white minority to colonize a country with Black majority and rule over them by holding them as inferior second-class citizens. The South African case is an apt example that shows the potential of transnational solidarity processes for social change in any context.

I have called my theorization of disability, the "transnational" disability theory, to emphasize the significance of organizing and building solidarity transnationally, beyond ties to the nation-states, international institutions, and the "rights-based" regimes. The fight for access and accommodation should complement the fight against cruel punishment and incarceration since they are deeply connected as disability issues. The current disconnection between these movements and revolutionary desires is detrimental to both, while building a potential alliance can bring them together and make them stronger. The fight for disability acceptance should not be carried out without declaring solidarity with those who continue to resist dehumanizing punishments like the PLA, flogging, stoning, and eye grouching, because they are analogous. This is exactly what a transnational disability praxis is all about: building alliances between seemingly different (disability) justice struggles all around the world and resisting reducing them to "cultural" differences. Disabling processes like FGM and PLA, aimed at violating the bodyminds, should be defetishized and treated as disability issues and not "cultural" practices. One way of seeing them defetishized is by foregrounding the actual practices of wounding, which is what I have been doing in this book: the historical materialist reading of these disabling practices.

PLA is a crime against humanity, as it destroys the wholeness of the body. One may argue, and rightly so, that other forms of punishment may also be crimes against humanity. However, the focus here is on the state act of "disabling a non-disabled body." As I argued in Chapter 3, the imprisonment and torture that lead more often than not to disability and trauma are also inhumane practices and should be abolished. PLA is against human dignity, which is why many countries have ceased to practice it.

What is it about dignity that we need to preserve, protect, and keep unharmed? When a person's dignity is damaged, the damage is not just inflicted on that person alone; rather, it is done to all humans, to humanity as a whole. The dignity of one person is humanity's dignity. This is what justice means. Justice prevails when every human's worth is equal to humanity's worth. When we say a crime is inhumane, we mean that it is a disgrace to all of us. At this point, one might ask: What about animals and the environment as a whole?[13] That is a valid question. However, it can be raised only if we consider ourselves separate from the cosmos. If we see ourselves as part of the entire universe, then not only must we not harm humans, but we also take it upon ourselves to respect the wholeness of other living beings.

Additionally, we do not need to generate justice; we just need to find the barriers that we have built against justice. Rumi, the thirteenth-century Persian poet, said, "Don't look for love, just remove the barriers within yourself that you've built against it." Dignity doesn't belong to one person. You cannot possess dignity. Dignity is a relation. Just like access, dignity exists between bodies not within them, according to what Tanya Titchkosky (2005)[14] has taught us. Disability justice is about dignity, about letting other bodies exist and breathe with dignity. When we do not provide access for different bodies, we are actively destroying dignity. Not just the dignity of the person denied access, but our own as well. The moral injury that Bernstein (2015) talks about is what disabled people deal with on a daily basis, because when your bodymind is not accommodated by the society within which you live, you become wounded/injured. This injury is a moral injury, because it harms your dignity. It may not be as apparent as the visible scars left by physical torture, but it cuts deep into your soul. The feeling that you're not welcomed in the world is devastating for disabled people. As such, justice is about dignity and vice versa.

There is much that can be learned from disabled people, as I have been emphasizing throughout this book. We, as a society, are not allowed to disable each other, because every human bodymind deserves to live as a whole and not be subject to corporal punishment. Limbs mark the boundaries of personhood. This is not to suggest that if you are missing a limb, you're not a person anymore. Rather, it's to say that we are not allowed to intentionally dislocate that boundary by amputating a person. People deserve to preserve the human cartography with which they were born. We can certainly add to them by giving everyone a chance to access prosthetics, but we cannot reduce it. We should not intrude upon each other's boundaries other than for a consensual, affectionate, and/or sexual interaction. We should form interdependent human cartographies and cherish access intimacies as opposed to wounding each other with exploitation and violence.

Public Spaces of Penal Spectacle

The last thing to discuss before concluding this chapter is the "public" performance aspect of PLA. Why is the punishment, as per the Islamic code of sharia, performed publicly? It is a religious requirement for the sinner, who has violated sharia, to be punished before other people. Saudi Arabia, for instance, as a Sunni-Islamic state, punishes sinners/criminals in public. Iran, as a Shia Islamic state, in most cases does the same. What happens when the sinner/criminal is amputated and disabled before others by a state that makes a claim to his/her body as property-subject or subject-property?

In his foundational text, *Discipline and Punish*, Michel Foucault (1975) illustrates the savagery of the French judicial system in punishing Robert-François, who was convicted of attempting a regicide against Louis XV. Foucault's depiction resembles a theatrical production, something ceremonial and spectacular. Mehdi Khorrami (2015) argues that Foucault's main purpose is not to tell a story of savage punishment of a citizen. Rather, his purpose is "to point out the relationship between theatrical and spectacular characteristics of these ceremonies and the sovereign power" (p. 24). Foucault gradually introduces us to a "reformist" transition "from sovereign power to new frameworks of power in modern societies" (p. 24). He brings us forward from a cruel punishment "ceremony" (e.g., quartering, limb amputation, and torture) to the modern-day forms of punishment that are less "spectacular" and "ceremonial" and more based on discipline and control (e.g., prison, school, psychiatric ward).

Khorrami informs the reader that in the case of IRI, punishment continues to be a "spectacle" and that it would be a mistake to examine the Islamic Republic's forms of public punishments using Foucault's theory alone. Darius Rejali (1993), the author of *Torture and Modernity: Self, Society, and State in Modern Iran*, demonstrates that the IRI contradicts Foucault's theory, because it is a modern state that "still" uses public forms of corporal punishment. Talan Asad critiques Rejali's argument saying that Iran is at best a modernizing society and not a modern society in the first place. Furthermore, Asad (2003) indicates that the modern states also use torture but not overtly and publicly. Khorrami (2015) argues that the IRI is a combination of medieval/premodern and modern qualities stating, "blatant torture and ritualized spectacles are part of the punitive-judiciary system [of the IRI]" (p. 24). PLA, public flogging, and hanging from huge cranes, Khorrami argues, "are not akin to surreptitious torture as an aspect of police work of modern control systems employed for the purpose of extracting information." These public forms of corporal punishment should be placed in precisely the same categories as the torture and execution of Damiens as Foucault describes, Khorrami argues. The penal exhibition under the IRI "aims to represent a sovereign power which, more than the many examples of absolute power which preceded it, defines its legitimacy and justification for such acts in terms of religion" (Khorrami, 2015, p. 25).

Since the rise of the state in its modern form, as Bargu (2016), following Foucault and Agamben, demonstrates in her book, *the Politics of Human Weapons*, the state treats the body as something-someone or object-subject that should be managed. There exist prisons, schools, hospitals, and psychiatric wards in the modern world; those institutions are the sites at which the state exercises its power over its subjects by disciplining them. The state performs what she calls "biosovereignty," which is the exertion of power over subjects' bodyminds and lives. Under a Shia theocratic state, the jurist is the representative of the divine, which renders him the true and only sovereign, with an authority that is therefore unimpeachable. Echoing Bargu (2016), I argue that biosovereignty is what the ideological-theocratic states exercise on the bodies and limbs of their subjects on behalf of Allah (i.e., who is believed to be the actual ruler and owner of the body). Power, whether exercised in the form of discipline or punishment, is always in a dialectical relationship with resistance, which is a response to power by the subject (Sakhi, 2014). By resisting sharia law, many people have been resisting the violence of PLA and the death penalty ordered by sharia. This resistance is a way of reclaiming our bodyminds.

Das writes that "the method of amputation was fairly standardized in medieval times. It was usually carried out in the central square of the town on Fridays after the noon prayer." (2020, p. 145). Let's return to the initial question posed earlier: What happens when the sinner/criminal bodymind is amputated and disabled before other people's eyes, by a state, which makes a claim to his/her body as property-subject or subject-property? Bernstein (2015) calls the places where the state carries out these acts "public spaces of penal spectacle." The Islamic state in modern times, given its archetype (i.e., the initial experience of the prophet forming a punitive-judiciary state and carrying out the PLAs himself), has always been devoted to exercising political power, which involves the power to discipline and punish the bodymind. Why the town square? Why the spectacle? Why does the state need to put on a show/ceremony—a show in which a human being's body is mutilated? Although a similar argument can be made about public executions, my interest here is not death, however tragic and deserving of attention, but disability. What is it about displaying an amputation that captivates the state? The first thing that comes to mind is the notion that it is meant to teach others a lesson, a rationale that authority figures typically use to justify their violence. What else could be there to discuss? Is the theocratic state disabling someone to deter other subjects from becoming thieves? Or is it disabling someone to demonstrate that sinners do not deserve to have a whole body by which they could work and earn a living?

The sharia apologists argue that the electrified cutting machine is not just supposed to amputate the "criminal" but to cut through the crime, because the logic behind it is that the crime and the criminal are the same (Souryal, Potts, & Alobied, 1994; Rispler-Chaim, 2007). This public ritual "desensitizes" people and makes cruel punishment, by Islamic state agents, "ceremonial." Punishing the criminal by making him an "invalid" before others is done as a way of "visual cleansing," getting rid of the impure by restoring the wholeness of the pure. This is where cleansing becomes visceral and a "lesson" for others to learn. The irony is that in the Islamic tradition, Quranic verses and the quotes from the Prophets/Imams claim that the wholeness of the body should be honored and always preserved (Rispler-Chaim, 2007), and yet, it sanctions limb amputation like a Yakuza Mafia godfather who acts in accordance with some underworld code. In fact, punitive amputation fetishizes the victims' disability by disintegrating the body of the individual under the guise of preserving the "whole" body of the collective. Fetishization of disability here aims at occluding the existing social order, as the root cause of poverty, under the guise of "fixing" the problem of "crime."

Theocratic punishments are about violating the body. Cleansing is supposed to be about pain and purification for the *ummah*; removal of "filth" is what is supposed to take place in the public ceremony of amputating a poor human being. Restoration of moral order in the body, minus the worldly crime, is the goal of this cruel ritual. One may claim here that once again I am perceiving disability as a "lack." This is not about disability. Disability is both the outcome in the process that humiliates and degrades a person in public, and the fetish that conceals the social inequality that have pushed the person to steal, and the violence of amputating them by placing the blame of poverty on them. This fetishization process transforms the poor into a disabled person whose bleeding wound is stigmatized, demonized, and fetishized all at once.

Mohsen Sabzichi, whose fingers were amputated for robbery, said that after the amputation procedure, he hid his hand from people. His shame was not from the disabled hand but from "how" it was acquired, which indicates the stigma of having a hand amputated by the state as a punishment for theft. Disability is a social relation, a contract, whereas PLA has additional layers of meaning associated with it. It is attaching a stigma to an already-disenfranchised body, adding to the stigma experienced. Sabzichi said, "I am ashamed of my fingers, so I hide them in my pockets."

By performing the PLA in a class society, the Islamic state actively punishes the poor by disabling a non-disabled or further disabling a disabled. PLA results in a disability caused by ideology enacted by humans, because ideology plays a significant role in this procedure as it provides the necessary justification to convince people to wound their fellow humans and yet masks that justification. This is the same as the fetishization process that I talked about in every chapter. Ideology fetishizes the existing inequalities in a society by creating more inequality (disability). PLA is a form of public torture that destroys human dignity by enabling the state to disable the bodymind of the poor, which is in contrast with what Islam claims to uphold: the "wholeness" of the body. Inequality cannot be cured by creating more inequality, and to end all forms of violence against the bodymind we should care about each other's struggles and build transnational solidarity as disability praxis.

Ableism should be resisted along with incarceration, FGM, PLA, eye grouching, etc., not separately but along with them. All the same, we should be able to critique any ideology, whether Islam or any other religion or code, without the fear of being accused of Muslim-phobia. Islam is not a race or ethnicity but a set of ideas that can and should be critiqued. The prison abolition movement can and should take a stand against sharia law and its dehumanizing practices because they (opponents of sharia or proponents of secularism as well as prison abolitionists and social justice activists such as feminists) are fighting the same fight for human dignity. If any critique of sharia is silenced under the banner of Muslim-phobia, we can never end disabling practices like the PLA. We should also remember that the disability caused by PLA is not "just" a disability but a disability fetish that does the free labor of concealing state violence and other violent relations including inequality and poverty.

5

Burning Wounds

Acid Attack, Disabling Gender-Based Violence

> My face suddenly felt tight, and it was burning all over. The smoke emanating from my face was suffocating me. Fearing that the acid would eat up my face, I ran home. My mother opened the door and went into shock to see her daughter's face being swallowed up by acid fumes. I received third degree burns on my face, right hand and chest. My features were completely distorted, and it was difficult for my own friends to recognize me. Since my eyelids had shrunk, I couldn't close my eyes, and this made it very difficult for me to sleep. Every night, I'd sit on my bed waiting for dawn.
>
> —Shirin Fuwaley, attacked with acid by her husband

> A woman burned by acid is like a living corpse. Those who commit such vengeful acts seek to sentence their victims to a plight worse than death.
>
> —Uzma Saeed, a lawyer working with a women's nongovernment organization in Lahore, Pakistan

We know that gender-based violence (GBV) is a worldwide issue that disproportionately affects women and girls. Throwing acid on others (most victims of which are women and girls) falls under the category of GBV, "because gendered roles and hierarchies within families and society not only motivate perpetrators to commit the crime, but also provide them with a sense of impunity" (Siddika & Baruah, 2018, p. 153). However, throwing acid on others rarely falls under the category of "disabling" violence, despite the fact most survivors, two of whom quoted at the beginning of this chapter, describe the harm that they endure as an attack that distorted their body, or a death sentence. In this chapter, I discuss why and how patriarchy, ableism, misogyny, and theocratic state violence under the Islamic Republic of Iran (IRI) disfigure and disable women victims. I foreground the materiality of ableism and its intersection with religiously-sanctioned toxic masculinity to theorize the "logic" behind acid attack as a form of social control. Furthermore, I discuss the centrality of the theocratic state as a vehicle through which the violence against women gets sanctioned, mobilized, required, and even performed, while enabling the perpetrators to walk with impunity, receive a minimum sentence, or even remain anonymous. Theoretical contributions of this chapter include how an acid attacker attempts to control the body and sexuality of woman forever, which I call "futurity in ableism"; disfiguring woman's body as a form of masculine "conquering" of a land by making it undesirable for other men; and interpreting insensitive social attitudes targeting acid survivors, as a form of what I call "ableist anti-catharsis."

Throughout this book, I have been talking about becoming and remaining disabled/wounded as a result of exploitative power relations (e.g., patriarchy, torture, imprisonment, theocracy, capitalism, imperialism, nationalism). In this chapter, in order to identify and theorize the transnational disability praxis in the form of solidarity movement(s) that have been initiated to resist GBV and disabling violence and to support the survivors' livelihoods, I discuss the role that the transnational disability and feminist activists in the diaspora play to raise awareness and financial support for acid survivors in Iran constituting the infrastructures of care for them where the state fails to intervene. Before ending the chapter, I discuss how the Islamic Republic mobilized state thugs to attack "bad-veiled" women with acid like "vitriol morality police." Although I have interviewed a dozen survivors for this research, due to spatial constraints, I include here a detailed narrative of a woman survivor from Iran who has lost both her eyes and has become disfigured as a result of an acid attack by her ex-father-in-law. After telling the survivor's story, I discuss the physical, medical, and special barriers she faced as not only a blind and disfigured woman but as a stigmatized victim of acid.

Aesthetics of Surviving an Acid Attack

The acid attack survivor, Masoumeh Ataei, one of the founders of the *EHGHA*, which in Persian/Farsi stands for "Association for the Support of Acid Victims," was invited by social media (Instagram) to take part in this research study via telephone. I selected the participant on Instagram after seeing her public posts about her struggle with an acid attack injury that took away one of her eyes completely and the other partially. Masoumeh Ataei is a well-known and outspoken survivor who introduced me to other survivors. While narrating her life story and the events that led to the attack, I present a feminist reading of Masoumeh's life trajectory, which reveals that she has had to deal with different forms of family as well as state-patriarchal violence both before and after the attack. I discuss Masoumeh's living conditions after the attack as a blind and disfigured woman and a mother who has had to navigate the inaccessible, non-accommodating, ableist, religious, and patriarchal Iranian society for more than a decade now. I demonstrate how perpetrators who throw acid on others count on society's already-existing sexism and ableism to isolate and discriminate against their victims even before purchasing acid. Additionally, I discuss the chain of acid attacks in the city of Esfahan, which is believed to have been "organized and staged by religious fundamentalists in position[s] of power along with members of the Parliament to create a state of fear and insecurity and target women's bodies and psyche" (Amani, 2014, np).

My intention here is to go beyond the "already-available narratives" (Hesford, 2004) utilized to account for acid attacks, such as "backward rural patriarchy" and "aberrant third world," or even "complex, layered structural conditions of vulnerability" (Chowdhury, 2015, p. 9). Given that "gender violence is inextricably linked to structural violence" (ibid.), I use a Disability Studies (DS) lens to theorize the disability relations that render the victims disabled and fetishize their wound by active and continuous state violence that is both ableist and misogynist.

Vitriol Attack and Toxic Masculinity

An acid attack, acid throwing, vitriol attack, or *vitriolage*, is a form of violent assault involving the act of throwing acid or a corrosive substance onto the body of another with the intention to punish, disfigure, maim, torture, or kill (Chowdhury, 2005, 2015; Mannan et al., 2004; Welsh, 2009). Perpetrators attack their victims by throwing corrosive liquids at them, usually at their faces, burning them and damaging skin tissue, often exposing and sometimes dissolving the bones. Chemical burns incurred through such an assault often result in facial disfigurement. Facial disfigurement is stigmatized in the normative culture and has been described as "the last bastion of discrimination" (McGrouther, 1997, p. 2). Blindness, eye burns, and severe physical and psychological scarring (read stigmatizing) of the face and body are among possible long-term consequences of acid attacks (Bandyopadhyay & Rahman Khan, 2003; Mannan et al., 2004; Swanson, 2002; Yousaf & Purkayastha, 2015).

Acid violence was prevalent in the United States and England from the eighteenth century to the mid-twentieth century due to easy access to sulfuric acid, which was manufactured on an industrial scale in these countries. Stricter regulations limiting easy access to corrosive chemicals, a tougher justice system, and the rise of feminist consciousness and movements precipitated a decline in the number of such cases (Chowdhury, 2005; Yousaf & Purkayastha, 2015). Although these cruel assaults are more often linked to patriarchal societies in contemporary times, statistics from the Health and Social Care Information Centre from the U.K. show that in 2019, 62 percent of victims treated in England following acid attacks were male. However, globally, it is estimated that 80 percent of victims are female (ASTI, 2024; Evans, 2013). Although acid attacks occur all over the world, this type of violence is most common in the global south, especially in South Asia. According to Acid Survivors Trust International (ASTI, 2024), however, the U.K. has one of the highest rates of acid attacks per capita in the world "with a 69% rise in the number of attacks in 2022. Acid attacks peaked in 2017, with 941 recorded cases. The figures then steadily dropped to reach 421 in 2021."

Men are the primary victims of acid attacks in the U.K., with most of them usually victimized in gang-related violence. Gang culture recognizes masculine ideologies of "toughness" as strength and protection. It sees acid attacks as "shameful" and "degrading" for the victim, signaling the latter's "failure" to protect himself (Evans, 2013). Ironically, sulfuric acid, used as a weapon, is on the rise in its birthplace, Britain, where it was first manufactured (Jack, 2017). Jermaine Joseph Lawlor, a former gang member who now works for a charity that provides help for survivors, said (quoted in Evans 2013, n.p.):

> If someone sees a knife wound or a scar on your face there's a chance a stereotype is going to be created that [you] don't mess with me, I'm negative, I'm a bad boy—but with an acid attack it's so degrading. It's not a knife attack, it's not a gun attack, it's an acid attack—we don't want to kill you, but we want to humiliate you.

Research shows that there is a significant difference between the intention of throwing acid on women versus men. It's believed that acid attacks on women are intended to disfigure them, isolate them, and make them "undesirable" to other men (Chowdhury, 2015; Cambodian Acid Survivors Charity, 2010; Mannan et al., 2004; Welsh, 2009; Swanson, 2002), whereas acid attacks on men are intended to humiliate them (Evans, 2013). This is to say that, according to the norms and discourses of the patriarchal and misogynist culture, if men are attacked by acid, they were weak and unable to protect themselves. However, if women are attacked, it means they will be "lonely" (read without a male lover according to the cisheteropatriarchal logic) for the rest of their lives. These are profoundly different discourses and public beliefs, and their very contradictory nature signals the need to explore further the reason behind scarring the other in the context of patriarchal society.

Masculinity is socially constructed as "the ability of men to protect, defend, and sustain their property, including their homes and families" (Anwary, 2003). As such, masculinity is an embodied behavior to perform, a role to play, to assure others that the perpetrator is "actively in possession" of masculinity. This is why Kalish and Kimmel (2010) argue that in the context of male violence "extreme alignments to and hyper-performances toward embodying hegemonic masculinity influenced the actions of the perpetrators." Connell (2005) defines masculinity as a scaffold that is varied across cultures and contexts and undergirded on the normative gendered-performances complacent with hegemonic masculinities. Perpetrators of acid violence are mostly men, and "toxic masculinity—the desire to permanently victimize someone while demonstrating his own power and brutality—is almost always the underlying cause regardless of whether the victim is a woman, man or transgendered person" (Baruah & Siddika, 2017). Hegemonic masculinity is a gendered ideology with one person "living up" to it and its sympathizers expecting him to do so. A case study, titled "Conflict Dynamics of Acid Violence," found that "the root cause of acid violence [is] in patriarchy and hegemonic masculinity" (cited in Chowdhury, 2015, p. 4).

Although acid attackers rarely die by suicide, the case of acid attacks has subtle similarities with the case of school shootings in the United States, which sometime end with the perpetrator ending his own life after killing plenty of people. We know now that the perpetrators do not make a decision to murder several people overnight. They are often humiliated by the people around them for not "living up" to the masculine expectations of the normative culture that expects "toughness," strength, and heterosexuality, among others (Oliffe et al., 2015). To this list of expectations, I add able-bodiedness and able-mindedness.[1] The perpetrators have often been insulted at times, called names, and told that they were homosexual. In order to prove otherwise, they demonstrate their "toughness and strength" in a militarized fashion by shooting at defenseless others and, finally, by showing the "courage" to end their own lives (Kalish & Kimmel, 2010). This shows that the normative culture of our society is also guilty of pushing perpetrators (even with its implicit biases and expectations) to the point where they feel helpless and, therefore, forced to comply with the normative culture's expectations. The same happens in the case of acid attacks. Society expects and allows an aggrieved male to "man up," pushing the perpetrator to meet toxic masculinity's expectations of owning and controlling women and their bodies and sexualities, as opposed to respecting and loving them.

Acid survivors invariably face societal isolation, ostracism, social anxiety, avoidance, negative self-perception, and decreased self-esteem, with little or no chance of ever finding employment. Added to the stigma of visible disfigurement, the acid survivor is most likely to experience both physical and psychological trauma (Mannan et al., 2004; Lansdown, 1997). The psychological morbidity of burn survivors has been extensively described (Meyer et al., 2004), although consistent throughout the disfigurement literature, there appears to be no direct relationship between the severity of a disfigurement and psychological distress (Robinson, 1997). Furthermore, Mannan et al. (2004) reported, "It was shown that a higher proportion of females had psychological morbidity when compared to males, while location of assault and relationship to the assailant was positively correlated with an increased likelihood of distress in females" (p. 236). Despite the growing interest in facial disfigurement and deformity, studies have been almost exclusively focused on Western populations. This lack of research diversity is important since "visible disfigurement might be expected to predominate in communities where there is less access to health care" (Mannan et al., 2004, p. 236). Therefore, potentially interesting groups are those (mainly) women assaulted with acid in Iran, who have resultant severe facial burns and blindness. Women in Iran have increasingly suffered these horrific attacks in recent years (Amani, 2014; Esfandiari, 2014; Dehghanpisheh, 2014; Middle East Eye and Agencies, 2015).

Disabling Patriarchy and Theocracy

> Men stand superior to women in that God hath preferred some of them over others, and in that they expend of their wealth; and the virtuous women, devoted, careful (in their husbands') absence, as God has cared for them. But those whose perverseness ye fear, admonish them and remove them into bedchambers and beat them; but if they submit to you, then do not seek a way against them; verily, God is high and great. (Quran 4.34)

It is not easy to determine factors that precisely constitute the religion in a religious society. Is it just faith, a set of norms, one's cultural heritage, one's community, one's beliefs, a text like the Bible or Quran, or one's moral compass? To prove or deny that something has been clearly said by their God or is required of the followers of a certain faith, some refer to the religious texts/scripture or its various interpretations. Some believe that religion is more than just an ahistorical text but a long set of customs, values, and norms enmeshed with the history and culture of a certain community. In the current chapter, just like the previous one, I discuss the role of Islamic jurisprudence or sharia, taken up by the IRI, governing the lives of Iranians in facilitating a disabling process, acid attack in this case. When I critique Islamic law and how it is enforced, I can foresee critics saying "don't blame Islam; it's not Islam; it's just a patriarchal interpretation of Islam." Let me be clear that the point here is neither prosecuting Islam nor exonerating it. A religion taken up, enacted, sanctified, and institutionalized by a state, is no longer just a religion that may or may not be intrinsically good or bad; rather, it is a state apparatus with enormous power and the country's resources at its disposal. Also, a religion turned into a religious state is no longer a benign text on one's bookshelf but a class system that has possession of a country's myriad institutions, armies, weapons, criminal justice system, police force, and wealth. Therefore, when I critique Islam, the Islamic state, or Islamic law, I am not just critiquing an ideology but an ideology that has the power to change the material reality of people whose lives it indiscriminately rules while denying them the choice to believe or reject that ideology.

Furthermore, acid attacks do happen in many different countries like India, Cambodia, Pakistan, and Iran, and are not peculiar to any one religious or cultural context. I also know that countries with the same religion, like Pakistan and Bangladesh, or Pakistan and Iran, are not homogeneous contexts mirroring the same social fabric or gender politics. Therefore, when I say we need to question and critique religious or any ideological factor contributing to acid attacks, I am reserving the right to be critical of any religion and ideology that has the power to enable these attacks, justify them, or let the perpetrators walk with impunity.

Foregrounding her analysis of acid attacks in Bangladesh, Chowdhury (2015, p. 172) states that "processes of globalization have frequently made women's positions less secure and weakened the so-called 'patriarchal contract,' or men's obligation toward women and their families." She further adds that "In sum, the changing gendered social order, continuing devaluation of women as women, globalization, and structural adjustment policies of the government have contributed to the precipitation of gender violence in the national context of Bangladesh" (p. 168). What is missing from this argument, though, is the role that religious society and religious cultural practices and assumptions play in oppressing women and protecting men's superiority.

On the other hand, Anwary (2003), who conducted comprehensive research in Bangladesh on women survivors of acid attacks, demonstrated that the main goal behind committing this heinous crime, which was committed mostly against women in Bangladesh, was ending the victim's career and social life. This is consistent with the findings of my research on Iranian women who fell prey to this type of attack. Anwary, however, exonerates Islam from having anything to do with creating or fostering a patriarchal culture in Bangladesh, declaring that "recent Bangladeshi national complexity, not the Islamic culture of Bangladesh, is liable for acid attacks" (p. 3). Yousef and Purkayastha (2015) and Chowdhury (2005) have also made similar claims. Chowdhury (2005) states: "It is a misconception that acid attacks against women are peculiar to Bangladesh and that attackers are Islamic fundamentalists who punish women for 'immodest' behavior" (p. 165) Neither Anwary nor Chowdhury mention that although not in Bangladesh, there have been cases of religious-fundamentalist groups or governments like the Pakistani Taliban or the Taliban in Afghanistan that threatened acid attacks against girls who wanted to go to school, never mind other forms of their repugnant violence against women under a gender-apartheid system working through legal mandates that relegate women to a lower status compared to men (Khan, 2012).

As is clear from the example I provide here, neither under Taliban nor under the Islamic Republic has punishing women for "immodest" behavior been a myth. Unlike Anwary and Chowdhury, I argue that religious ideology, in this case sharia law, is one profound reason for the culture of impunity for male attackers in Iran. In most acid cases, the gendered nature of this abhorrent violence is either overlooked, ignored, or not taken seriously by the judicial system, and if it was taken seriously, the law protected the male assailants anyway.

Chowdhury (2005) and Anwary's (2003) hasty retreat to hold only globalization and a host of other gender-related problems (such as hegemonic masculinity) accountable demonstrates that they are reluctant to even slightly criticize Islamic ideology and governance for "allowing" men to harm women and walk with impunity. Throughout this chapter, I engage with the intricacies and nuances of living under sharia law and being victimized by an acid attack in order to unravel the ways in which sharia facilitates men's escape from accountability for their acts of GBV.

Inconveniencing Patriarchy and Arousing Its Ire

Masoumeh Ataei's father was the patriarch of the household, expecting all his daughters to follow the path he chose for them. Masoumeh loved art and was interested in pursuing a career in graphic design, which she had briefly studied in high school. Even choosing graphic design as a major at high school caused a serious fight with her father and made it difficult to obtain his approval. She became an outstanding student at the school of art, mastering skills in visual arts, graphic design, and professional drawing. Her hard work and passion garnered several awards and prizes for best photography and poster designing, among others. However, not even those awards were sufficient to convince her father to grant his "approval" for Masoumeh's participation in the University Entrance Exam. According to Masoumeh, his main problem was his disapproval of the universities and colleges where men and women are "mixed" (not segregated based on gender)—attending the same classes and sitting next to each other.[2] He perhaps preferred even higher education institutions to be segregated, just like the rest of the educational settings in elementary and high schools in Iran.

So far, we can draw from Masoumeh's words that, on the one hand, her father was a fanatic who believed that women should be controlled and "managed" as second-class citizens who belong to their fathers, and later to their husbands, who then should decide for their bodies, sexuality, future, and career goals (if they are to have any at all). Further, the gender-apartheid system under the theocratic regime of the IRI (Mojab, 2001; Kazemi, 2024b) facilitated these patriarchal desires by segregating the schools, buses, mosques, etc., and granting men the control of women's lives.

Masoumeh, just like many women who live within religious, patriarchal, and fanatic families, thought that after getting married, she might be able to do many things she had always wanted to but was never allowed to pursue. This was based on a hopeful imaginative investment in the next man who would possess the power to "allow" her to do the things she liked. This was hoping for an emancipation through the next man in her life, or rather, stealthily gaining freedom from her father's household while transitioning to another. Unfortunately, the husband turned out to be worse than the father. As Masoumeh put it, the experience of marrying him after leaving her father's home was like "climbing up a puddle and falling into a well." The husband disciplined her, just the way the father used to. According to Masoumeh, he was the only biological child of his family, and everything had revolved around him his whole life. His parents just said "yes" to whatever he wanted or did. Even when he made mistakes, they approved of him and his actions.

Masoumeh's husband had started violently beating her right after they got married. After a month, Masoumeh sought divorce at family court with her body filled with bruises and the scars left from being beaten by a leather belt. Her father was not supportive of Masoumeh, leaving her to weigh the options of leaving her husband and going back to live under her father's rule or bearing with her husband's abuses. She faced the decision of choosing between two violent men. She opted for the husband's house over her father's, because at least in her husband's house she had a certain level of independence, which she lacked in the latter. That limited independence was important to her, since beyond her husband's abusive behavior, she had a space for herself to live, even in loneliness. Nevertheless, she applied for divorce multiple times—knowing that she did not really want to go back to her father's house, but she could not put up with her husband either.[3] Every time, he would promise he would not hit her ever again, and yet he would continually break that promise—it was the typical cycle of abuse.

A year after their wedding, Masoumeh found out she was pregnant. Six years of marriage was like a "battlefield," in Masoumeh's words. Her husband did not have a job; instead, he was an epicurean and a "fun"-loving person with a wealthy father who supported him financially. Sometimes he would not come home for three days, and if Masoumeh demanded an explanation, he would beat her. All he wanted was for her to remain silent and accept everything he did without objection. During their constant fights, her husband would beat her until she begged him to stop, and he enjoyed that so much. In contrast with what he demanded of Masoumeh when it came to his behavior, he was extremely jealous and insecure about her social interactions with other men, even if the man was a cab driver. Masoumeh argued against this, asking why it was fine for him to do whatever he wanted but not for her. This is a fundamental question that women in Iran, India, Pakistan, Saudi Arabia, and many other countries ask themselves. The answer is a short one: "discrimination justified by sharia law."[4]

You might ask yourself, why did she not leave him? I learned that one barrier to Masoumeh's path to emancipation was financial dependence from the men in her life. If she had gone to college, she might have garnered a career for herself. This makes me think about the roots of this barrier. Her father did not allow her to pursue higher education. Was the father afraid of Masoumeh's independence as a "free" woman to do whatever she wanted with her life, body, and sexuality? Was he really afraid of the "mixed" (not segregated based on gender) nature of university environment? Or was he afraid of what a college education could have given Masoumeh, such as a job, independence, and financial security? Was he afraid of the colliding and collapsing boundaries between who held power and who did not? If education would have garnered Masoumeh power, can we say that the father was actually afraid of losing his patriarchal power over Masoumeh's life, body, and sexuality as a result?

After their baby was born, her husband became jealous of the baby and the love Masoumeh was giving him. Things got worse. One day, to hurt Masoumeh, he placed the baby in the car, locked the doors, and left. Masoumeh was watching from the window of her apartment and screaming for help, the baby was crying in the car, and her husband simply enjoyed the scenery. Masoumeh called the police. They came, opened the car doors, and took the baby out.

It was at this point that she decided she could take no more. It became unbearable to live in the same place as her husband. Her son was still an infant, and Masoumeh did not want him to become like his father when he grew up. The baby had already started to throw things just like his father did when they would fight. When their son was one-and-a-half-years-old, Masoumeh suggested to her husband, again, that they should divorce, but he did not accept that. Therefore, one day when he was not home, she packed everything, including her dowry, and left forever. Since her parents' house was small and had no room for her furniture, she dropped it off in her uncle's backyard and went to her parents' house with her baby. Her father, expectedly, was not supportive of her decision to seek a divorce, so he did not receive Masoumeh with much hospitality. She then went to her uncle's house, held a garage sale, and sold her dowry. With that money, she rented a flat and moved there with her son. Although, she did not have any income, her mother secretly brought her money sometimes. Masoumeh demanded divorce, but the husband continued to resist.

Masoumeh retreated to the *Mehriyeh*[5] (or *Mahr*) option by demanding it. Masoumeh's mehriyeh was 150 gold coins, and she demanded to have them. He did not pay the mehriyeh and Masoumeh filed a lawsuit against him. The court issued an arrest warrant for Masoumeh's husband and he was arrested and taken to prison. Her father-in-law agreed to pay the mahr in installments and brought a gold coin every month for two to three months but stopped after that and instead went to talk with Masoumeh. She clarified that all she wanted was divorce. Her father-in-law went to the prison and talked to his son. He agreed to sign the divorce in return for being relieved of paying the mehriyeh.[6] He demanded custody of his son, which the law gave him easily. Since the child was almost two years old, he had to stay with his mother until he was seven, after which the custody automatically would have gone to the father. He had visitation rights every two weeks. However, after a while, Masoumeh discovered that he had developed a drug addiction and used needles in front of the child. She returned to the court to demand the visitations stop. The court demanded that the father could only see the child in a public space, such as a park. Instead, the boy's father stopped visiting him altogether, but the father-in-law asked to replace him and visit the grandson every two weeks in a public place with his mother present at all times. He would pick up the mother and the child, take them to a park or restaurant, and bring them back after a few hours. Sometimes, he would talk to Masoumeh about getting back with her husband, while making promises to financially support them.

Within a year, Masoumeh had taken a hair stylist course, secured employment as a stylist, and opened a small hair salon of her own. She also found a job as a drawing instructor in an art institution. The two jobs brought her the financial stability she was looking for. The father-in-law was surprised to see the business sign for the hair salon and became enraged about Masoumeh's ability to pull herself up by her own bootstraps. He couldn't take Masoumeh's success. His son, Masoumeh's ex-husband, on the other hand, had become homeless, a heroin addict who was going down quickly while Masoumeh was going forward in her life and becoming more independent. Masoumeh's ex-husband sometimes reached out to her and threatened her by saying that he would "run her over with a car" or "destroy her life." He saw her as responsible for his own misery. Simultaneously, he thought that his father had deceived him by convincing him to divorce Masoumeh.

Masoumeh had empowered herself with the small business, new apartment, income, and a career. When her father or brother wanted to comment on her clothing or makeup, she would immediately shut them down by saying they could only comment on the ways she lived her life, if they were supporting her financially. Now that she was completely independent, they had no right to interfere in her life.

Gradually, Masoumeh started noticing certain signs in her ex-father-in-law's behavior that frightened her to some degree. He started to exert a sort of an "ownership" over her, her body, and her sexuality. This might have stemmed from what they call "honor." "Honor" means extending and sustaining men's ownership of/over women's bodymind, sex(uality), and genitals. "Honor" is the foundation of patriarchy in general, and theocracy in particular. "Honor" is violence per se, both as a socially constructed concept and the material reality of actively possessing a woman's body and sexuality and threatening her for attempting to reclaim her body/sexuality, and eventually killing or disabling her by acid attack, mutilation, beating, beheading, genital burning, and murder.

The former father-in-law tried to establish his "masculine" presence as a guardian over Masoumeh's life, who didn't want to be possessed by anyone. Masoumeh's attempt at reclaiming her life could have been the actual trigger for the perpetrator to plan his vicious attack against her. He was probably afraid of her determination to control her life, instead of leaving it up to her ex-husband, his son. While they were in public places, such as a park or restaurant, if any man paid any attention to Masoumeh, he would pick a fight with the man. Simultaneously, he peeked on Masoumeh's cellphone the entire period they sat together during the visits. Sometimes, he would even go to the extent of asking about the identity of those who had called or texted Masoumeh.

On one occasion, when Masoumeh, her son, and the ex-father-in-law were eating outside, he got visibly agitated when he noticed that a young man at a nearby table seemed attracted to Masoumeh. On another occasion, after the ex-father-in-law noticed the business sign outside Masoumeh's apartment, he said, "You put a sign, didn't you?" Masoumeh replied, "Yeah, so I don't starve." The response was an allusion to her mother-in-law's words, when she once said to Masoumeh, "You will starve, if you get a divorce and live on your own." The incident with the young men paying attention to Masoumeh and the incident where her father-in-law's anxiety over her emancipation through financial independence was aroused by him noticing the sign for the hair salon are both significant in constituting a way for us to imagine what might have gone through the perpetrator's mind before committing the heinous acid attack. This is consistent with Chowdhury's findings that one motivation for men throwing acid against women is an attempt to end their public lives and their economic and social mobility (2005).

At some point in our conversation, I revealed to Masoumeh my suspicion about the father-in-law's possible feelings or sexual desire for Masoumeh beyond the conventional level of "caring about the mother of his grandson." Unfortunately, she confirmed my suspicion by saying that she had noticed it too, shortly before the attack. Masoumeh even told her lawyer about this, but he discouraged her from publicizing that information, saying that the father-in-law could file a lawsuit against her if she failed to "prove" her point, given the misogynistic context surrounding her both legally and culturally. Therefore, Masoumeh remained silent about the father-in-law's malicious intentions. He had asked Masoumeh to "be with him" and had been rejected by her, which could be the main trigger for his eventual rage and attack. Usually, the logic behind these patriarchal claims is "if you're not mine, then you shouldn't be anyone else's either," which re-establishes what we have been discussing here and calling "ownership" over a woman's body and sexuality.

On one occasion, he had claimed that twelve years after separating beds with his wife, Masoumeh had "awoken" a strange feeling (read sexual attraction) in him once again. Then he went further and said that he would do anything for her, anything that the young men attracted to her would not even have the resources to do, only if she accepted him. This dialogue took place the last time they met before the attack, where Masoumeh got angry and asked him to stop coming to see the grandson. Otherwise, she threatened that she would revoke the visitation rights by filing a harassment charge against him. He responded very calmly that he would stop coming and that he would not bother her anymore.

He called after two days and asked to visit his grandson for the last time to give him a gift. Masoumeh didn't even think for a second that the "gift" would be acid—thrown at her.

Masoumeh's ex-father-in-law took his grandson to a park near a lake located in a small suburb, called Baharestan, near Esfahan. Masoumeh also had an errand to run in Baharestan, so her ex-father-in-law offered her his car. She got the car keys, but before taking off, the old man (the ex-father-in-law) said, "I have bought you something, but to prevent you from falling prey to your curiosity, I will hide it properly in the trunk." It didn't occur to Masoumeh that the gift in the trunk was a container full of acid. She took the car, ran some errands, and returned to the park. That night, Masoumeh wanted to go to her parents' house, which was located in Shahreza, a small town near Esfahan, and an hour's drive away from Baharestan where they were. He asked her to drive, which wasn't unusual for him to ask, since he claimed his eyes could not see well at night.

Masoumeh had a good excuse for wanting to go home quickly; her parents were accustomed to sleeping early, so she needed to get there before they went to bed. Masoumeh's son had fallen asleep in the back seat, so once they arrived at her parents' house, she needed to carry him inside. The old man opened the trunk, and inside was the "gift"—wrapped in a nice paper, just like a real present. He said, "I got a present for him [the grandson]." Masoumeh's hands were full carrying her son, so she offered to take the child inside and come back for the gift. He accepted the idea. He started unwrapping the "gift" while saying, "I want to surprise you, let me unwrap it." He asked Masoumeh to close her eyes to take away her body's natural reaction to something being thrown at her. Naturally, humans would turn their head away, if they see something coming at them, so he took away her possible opportunity to turn her head.

Masoumeh closed her eyes, and then all she could feel was burning, the feeling of extreme heat inside her entire existence. She didn't even know what acid was or what it could do to the human flesh until that moment. All she thought about now was that she was burning with the boiling water that he emptied on her. She didn't think for a second that this was a corrosive substance. The liquid, as she remembers it now, was a dark sticky substance like a condensed syrup or sap. She smelled something rancid, which puzzled her even more about what was happening to her, and why. She noticed that her *montow* (Islamic covering that women are forced to wear under the IR regime) was fragmentizing and crumbling off. Her shawl (hijab, the headscarf women are forced to wear at all times in public) started shrinking quickly like a burning scrunching piece of plastic. The old man throwing the acid targeted Masoumeh's face, but since she was standing inside the door, some of the acid splashed on the door. Thus, the acid had even penetrated the door and the asphalt. Even the tiles on the front pavement had holes in them. Still standing in the semi-open door, Masoumeh tried to open her eyes after she felt the liquid. The sticky liquid was still pouring down her face. The acid was penetrating her skin slowly and yet quickly. Masoumeh started screaming, "I'm burnt!"

Her parents, half asleep, came downstairs wondering where the fire was, since all they knew was someone screaming, "I'm burnt." Masoumeh could not open her eyelids as they were stuck together. She was madly looking for the water hose to cool off, although she couldn't find it. Instead, she was desperately wandering around while bumping into the walls and other things in the yard. She heard the car starting, so it was clear the old man was fleeing the scene. Her mother got to her and removed her shawl and montow, trying to prevent the dark penetrating liquid from eating up more of her daughter. She also turned on the tap and poured it on Masoumeh's entire body. It was too late though; Masoumeh had already lost almost both her eyes to the sticky black liquid. The eyelids stuck together and wouldn't open, no matter how hard the mother tried to separate them.

Impunity for Femicide, Wounding Women, and Acid Attacks

The old man was arrested and convicted of the acid attack and sentenced to only five years in prison; after eighteen months, he was granted advanced parole due to old age. The most unbelievable part of the story is how some perpetrators convicted for an acid attack are allowed to go home for the weekend every week for the duration of their sentence. This shows that the Islamic Criminal Code doesn't perceive men who throw acid on women a real danger to society. People who blind women, take their appearance away, and change their lives forever are not seen as a danger to society. The new law, however, which has been passed in Iran but is not yet enforced states that no parole or furlough can be granted to perpetrators.

This acid attack happened in 2009. The punishment for an acid attack in the Islamic Retribution Law hadn't changed from 1958, until in May 2019, Masoumeh and a few other survivors organized and lobbied the Islamic parliament to change the punishment from fifteen years' imprisonment[7] to a maximum twenty-five years in prison without a possibility for parole. The change was not retroactive, meaning it only covered future cases and not previous ones like Masoumeh's. The resistance she and the other survivors faced from many in the parliament was preposterous for Masoumeh. According to her, the initial proposal suggested a life sentence (which is the case in Bangladesh) for acid attacks, but the parliament rejected the bill and ratified only a maximum of twenty-five years in prison.

The prevalence of acid attacks in a country under theocratic rule has something to do with the overall view of women in sharia law as second-class citizens and the main source of temptation and "sin" for men. We know that the basis of a theocratic state is the Quranic verses, the Prophet's tradition (Sunnah), and hadith. Mohammadbagher Majlesi, a renowned Shia jurist, quotes Prophet Mohammad about the people he observed in hell on his famous ascent to Heaven in the *Miraj* night. Literally every single person the Prophet visited in hell was a woman. Mohammed said, "I was shown the Hellfire and that the majority of its dwellers are women."[8] Furthermore, the Islamic Criminal Code in Iran is not kind to women at all. For instance, a man can have four wives (al-Bukhārī, 2019). Or if a father murders his own daughter for any reason such as "honor," he doesn't get *qisās* (retribution, which is execution for murder, literally meaning "eye for an eye"). Instead, he just needs to pay the daughter's blood money (*diya* or the financial compensation paid to the victim or heirs of a victim in the cases of murder, bodily harm, or property damage). It is an alternative punishment to qisās, which for women is half that of men. The 2013 penal code that replaced an older version makes diya for men and women equal in cases of homicide. However, according to Tavana, a civil society organization, it is unclear if the diya between men and women is equal in cases of bodily harm such as acid attacks. It appears the final judgment has been left to the Iranian courts to decide (Tavana, 2014).

Under Iranian law, acid attack as a crime has two aspects. One is the public aspect, which is the way it hinders the maintenance of the social order by creating panic and fear among people. The private aspect concerns qisās, which is a common way of seeking justice under the Islamic Criminal Code. Qisās, or the proportionate punishment for the type and extent of the crime that has been committed, is determined and enforced separately. Rispler-Chaim (2007) states:

> An intended injury that does not end in killing or loss of life (*al-qisās fima dun al nafs*—retaliations for less than the life) means that the intended injury has destroyed an organ or several organs, but no death ensued. For this Qur'an 2, 194 reads: "And one who attacked you, attack him in like manner as he attacked you. Observe your duty to Allah and know that Allah is with those who ward off (evil)." The rule is that for each organ that was intentionally injured, the same organ in the criminal must be injured or amputated, if this "equality" can be followed. This is an implementation of the biblical law of "an eye for an eye and a tooth for a tooth." For a victim's eye that was put out, for example, it is suggested that wet cotton be placed on the equivalent eye of the criminal, and a hot mirror be pressed against it until the eye loses its sight. (p. 84)

For example, if an attacker blinds someone by acid or any other means, the victim can ask for qisās. The IRI is afraid of the publicization of the horrific logic of "eye for an eye," which is the basis for the inhuman law of qisās in sharia law, which seeks justice in doing the same to someone who has committed a crime. The idea is that there could be a global backlash that would find the qisās law extremely inhuman and savage, given the anti-torture law that most countries in the world abide by. The IR state tortures its prisoners, as I explained in Chapter 3, and amputates crooks for stealing, which I discussed in the previous chapter. Therefore, torture is at the heart of the state's treatment of its citizens, and the sharia law facilitates it.

Furthermore, the victim could ask for a perpetrator's eye to be blinded just as theirs was blinded. However, a licensed medical examiner must determine whether a victim has lost their vision completely before they can ask for qisās. This was the case for Masoumeh. However, qisās for men is twice as that for women, thanks to the unequal nature of the sharia law. In 2019, it was announced that the 2013 penal code that made the diya equal for men and women will be implemented in the case of bodily harm as well as homicide. As such, men's and women's diya has been equal since, although it is not retroactive. Therefore, in Masoumeh's case, which happened in 2009, the women's diya was half of men's, which meant that for both of Masoumeh's eyes, the old man would have had to give up one eye.

Additionally, Masoumeh emphasized that the diya law at the time, or even now, does not consider that the young woman who has been attacked was only twenty-six years old, while the perpetrator was seventy years old. All the courts said was that since Masoumeh was a woman, her two eyes were equal to one eye of the old man. Since Masoumeh lost both eyes, she was required to pay half of the blood money for the old man's eye, to have him blinded in one eye. Masoumeh was furious, expressing her disbelief at how unfair and discriminatory the Islamic Criminal Code is that a female victim should have to pay money to the culprit to get qisās while she has lost both her eyes. For the skin burns she experienced, no qisās could have been requested, since that only exists for limbs, which can be counted. For skin, only diyeh is determined as needing to be paid to the victim.[9]

Overall, after final calculations, Masoumeh was told that if she insisted on qisās, she'd need to pay (45 million Toman or $4500 USD in 2009), which is considered a lot of money for a working-class woman divorcée who was almost blind by then. The logic is that men are breadwinners, so their lives are worth more. Masoumeh said laughingly, "I too was a breadwinner; I had just started to make money and raise my family."

Masoumeh could not wrap her head around the old man's motivation to do such a thing to her. Their relationship appeared "normal" before the incident. Masoumeh was nice and respectful to the entire family. For instance, she even celebrated her ex-father-in-law's birthday for him, which made him cry saying that no one had ever done anything like that for him. Surprisingly, he even brought the birthday gifts to the court, which surprised the judge and made him question the old man's intention for bringing the gifts to the court showing how nice his daughter-in-law has been to him. He said, "Yes, she was so good, but she didn't remain my daughter-in-law [read in my possession]."

On the one hand, in her mind, the old man wanted to take revenge. He threw acid onto Masoumeh to make her "undesirable" for other men. Additionally, the old man claimed to have "healed" his son's old wounds of contempt for Masoumeh over her courage to have left an abusive relationship. On the other hand, as soon as the old man told his son what he had done to Masoumeh, the ex-husband became very excited. He felt rejuvenated, went sober, and stopped taking drugs. He even re-married and started a new family. Chowdhury (2015) states, "The choice of acid as weapon is symbolic at multiple levels. It disfigures (so [the victim] will no longer be desirable to anyone else), permanently marks (leaves an imprint on her body of the violence that is intended to shame her for defying his authority), and potentially impairs vision and hearing (she is no longer readily employable and thus inhibiting her economic mobility as well as social mobility)" (p. 8).

The next abusive roadblock against Masoumeh, set up by the old man and his son, and facilitated by the sharia law observed by the IRI, was discrimination against her. When Masoumeh's son turned eight years old, the law stated that custody of him automatically goes to his father. The family wanted Masoumeh to let go of qisās in return for custody of her son. The father, who was previously completely absent from the child's life, suddenly showed up as a caring father and filed a custody request. The patriarchal anti-women family courts under the IRI immediately displayed their ableist attitude by declaring Masoumeh "unfit" for parenting due to her newly acquired disability. Masoumeh objected to the court's decision and argued that she was not blind when she got divorced and took sole custody of her son, and that it was this man's father who had brutally attacked her and blinded her. The judge, of course, stated that these were two "irrelevant" matters that should not be brought up in the context of the custody decision. Masoumeh resisted the judge's comments by saying that no one should expect her to give custody of her son to a family that attacked her with acid. The ex-husband argued against Masoumeh's claim and stated that whatever his father had done had nothing to do with him and that he was responsible for his own actions.

The judge told Masoumeh that she had forty-eight hours to turn the child over to his father. Masoumeh refused and said that she would never do such a thing. Subsequently, she moved to Tehran and ignored the court order, no matter how many times she was served with court letters. Her father, who still lived in Shahreza, phoned her one day and told her that her photo appeared in a daily newspaper as someone who had "kidnapped" a child, for which she could have gone to prison for fifteen years. At this point in our conversation, Masoumeh laughed bitterly, saying, "Five years for throwing acid, fifteen years for not wanting to give your child to criminals."

Masoumeh's lawyer advised against holding on to the child and argued that it was better for Masoumeh to take the child to his father and avoid persecution. At this point, the ex-husband's family contacted Masoumeh with an indecent proposal, saying, "If you don't want anything bad to happen to your son, let go of the qisās, and in return, receive the custody of your son." The lawyers, this time, advised Masoumeh against accepting the proposal, arguing that the ex-husband wouldn't be able to raise a child and that he was just using the custody order as a way to render her powerless so she would stop requesting qisās. Their suggestion was for Masoumeh to go ahead with qisās and wait for the ex-husband to return the child to her. Masoumeh told them that they did not know that family, and that she would never leave her child with them, since they would get back at her by tormenting the innocent child. Masoumeh's fear was not irrational after all, since the ex-husband told her that "whatever" happened to her would also happen to her son (read being subject to acid attack).

Masoumeh's son was only three years old when he woke up to his mother's screams for help as she was burning with acid. Besides the night of the incident, the next day, he had witnessed his mother's arrival from the hospital, where they had bandaged her entire head and face like a mummy. Deleuze & Guattari (1987) write "[the face] is a whole body unto itself: it is like the body of the center of significance to which all of the deterritorialized signs affix themselves, and it marks the limit of their deterritorialization" (p. 587). Since Masoumeh had a beauty salon, and he was used to often seeing her with a beauty mask on, he thought that the bandage for the burns was the same as a beauty mask. He kept asking, "Why doesn't my momma remove her mask?" Those experiences, coupled with the father's threats that he would burn his child with acid just like the old man had done to Masoumeh if she didn't take back her qisās request, made the child extremely anxious and stressed about his safety. He at times told his mother that the father's family wanted to drown him in a bathtub filled with acid. As such, Masoumeh chose her son's safety, mental health, and well-being over her right to qisās, because she wanted to live without the anxiety of losing him to another acid attack or some other harmful action of his father's family. Masoumeh went to a notary public and requested a notarized recognizance from the family that under no circumstances should they try to go near her son, in return for the unconditional and permanent custody of the child and the permanent surrender of qisās.

Controlling the Body and Sexuality Forever: Futurity in Ableism

According to Baruah and Siddika (2017) "acid attacks are often specifically used to ruin a woman's future romantic prospects, her career, financial security and social status." Chowdhury (2015) also argues that "systems [of patriarchy and misogyny] when threatened, lead to expressions of hegemonic masculinities manifested through domination and control" (p. 4). In Masoumeh's case, the father-in-law became most upset when he saw the sign for Masoumeh's newly established hairstyling business, which would have rendered her completely independent. Masoumeh's father-in-law decided (in his mind) to take away her ability to live alone, her job, her financial independence, her ability to be an independent mother, her future, her sexual interactions with romantic partners, her sight, her career, her beauty, her mental health, and more. Women's independence, ownership and control over her body, affection, and sexuality, as well as her financial independence, threaten patriarchal structures that sustain men's dominance in society—just like Masoumeh Ataei's financial independence and sexual autonomy threatened the ex-father-in-law's "masculinity," or control over her.

Without unpacking ableism as it interacts with other forms of societal oppression such as patriarchy and sexism, it would be impossible to find out the reason behind committing this horrific GBV, namely the acid attack. The first question that comes to mind is why someone would do such a thing to another person. The ex-father-in-law attacked Masoumeh while counting on society's already-existing pitfalls and barriers for disabled women. He deliberately counted on those barriers to carry out their share of the job to oppress her further. He already knew how difficult it was for a disabled person, never mind a disabled woman, to live in an inaccessible, ableist, sexist, judgmental, and patriarchal society like Iran. He already counted on those systems of oppression and people's negative attitudes toward disability to turn the wheels and do their job to make her life unbearable. Therefore, he was not the only culprit in the picture. We, as a society, were and are all in this with him; we are his accomplices. We, as a society, perform the aforementioned social relations and disabling processes in extended modes of consciousness from the past. As such, the culprit counted on the surrounding society (i.e., historically and socially constructed assumptions and norms about the desirable body and the beauty standards for women) in which Masoumeh must operate to finish the job for him. The post-attack world was one he knew and assumed would make Masoumeh's life miserable. This was all meticulously planned far before the actual attack took place. Please note that I perceive the acid attack not just as a GBV but also a "disabling" and wounding process/act mediated by gender and class relations.

Some of the male attackers, who have been interviewed, have confessed that what they wanted was to do something to the victim so nobody would look at her (Baruah & Siddika, 2017). What they mean is a multilayered social matrix. First, they want to control the victim's social life, which includes attractiveness, dating, sexual interaction, aesthetics of the body, and marriage. Second, they want to exert a "durable control" over the body of their target. In other words, by burning the body, they want to ascertain that no other person would be interested in that body. This is exerting your control over the body forever, because the scars, possible blindness, and disfigurements caused by acid are almost irreversible. Most important for my argument here, these accurate, yet inhuman, calculations happen against the backdrop of an ableist, sexist, and misogynist society in which women are supposed to be non-disabled, desirable for men, attractive from a heterosexual standpoint, "pretty" (according to the popular culture's standard), and "normative." Without a society possessing these features, the perpetrator might never commit the crime of throwing acid.

To theorize and critique "cure" as an ideology that feeds ableism both as culture and temporality, Alison Kafer (2013) shows through what she calls the "imagined future body" (p. 57) that ableism functions through negating the materiality of an existing disabled body in the here and now to imagine a future for that body without a disability. To reshape Masoumeh's present, violently, the perpetrator relies on the ableist future that would inevitably harm her imagined disabled body. The acid attack was intended to suspend Masoumeh's body in the here and now and imagine a future where a disfigured, blind, and, hence, "undesirable" Masoumeh would be replacing her.

Kafer suggests that seeing disability as self-evidently negative is a political decision based on ableist thinking that wrongly assumes and constructs the inherent superiority of able-bodiedness and able-mindedness over disabled bodies and minds. I am not suggesting that the unannounced desire, "presumed consensus," Antonio Gramsci's (1971) "common sense," or the cultural agreement that a disabled person will inevitably become undesirable after acquiring a disability is the only reason behind throwing acid. What is clear, however, is that the ableist assumption that a future with a disability is an undesired future is certainly an assumption on the mind of the perpetrator. Perpetrators decide to commit the crime of acid throwing based on their assumptions of "predictable behaviors" from the surrounding society. In other words, perpetrators count on society's deep-seated ableist attitudes toward disabled people, especially disabled women, and count on the society's historical discrimination against them.

The perpetrator wants to own the target's body forever, even symbolically, by making the body "undesirable" for other men. He knows that a burned face/body will be undesirable for most men in a sexist and ableist society. He knows it because everyone knows it, because it's common knowledge, because the normative culture is violent against disabled women. The perpetrator counts on all these factors before committing his crime. Therefore, the society is also guilty of being ableist and sexist in the first place. The perpetrators are products of the society in which they live. By arguing this, I mean to hold us, all of us—the culture, the social structures—responsible for constantly reproducing an ableist and sexist society as a suitable context for acid attacks to occur.

Conquering the Body

Colonial and imperialist conquests are obsessed with depicting their success as sexually piercing the land (McClintock, 1995). McClintock begins the first chapter of her book, *Imperial Leather,* with Adreinne Rich's words: "I am not the wheatfield. Nor the virgin land" (p. 20). From the outset, she shows us the interwoven structure and co-functionality of gender and colonialism. Rich is speaking to the dual image of her gendered body as the land and the fruit to be harvested/conquered, and the colonial land as inherently virgin (read feminine). McClintock illuminates for us the "long tradition of male travel as an erotics of ravishment" (p. 22). She demonstrates in her book that the colonizers of the New World, from Columbus to Coleman's Mustard

Company, have imagined the Indigenous land as a woman's body to be conquered, impregnated. This gendered viewpoint, McClintock argues through a psychoanalytic tack, helps us uncover the contradictory duality of the male consciousness upon entering this feminized "terra incognita." She describes the male conqueror as "suspended between an imperial megalomania . . . and a contradictory fear of engulfment" (p. 26). She painstakingly demonstrates that the driving forces of imperialism, nation-building, and expansion are male fear and male lust. This is why Indigenous land is often referred to as a "virgin" if it hasn't been "penetrated" by other colonizers. The look at the history of art shows us that women's bodies and sexuality are perceived as "nature" itself—fertility, nation, futurity—which need to be "penetrated" and "impregnated" by (male) builders who plant the seeds. Even in militarist language mobilized during military invasions, sexual language and a gendered framework are utilized to describe invading "other" lands as if sexually piercing a woman's body.

Furthermore, historically, woman's virginity has been instrumentalized as a means to control and discipline woman's sexuality, pleasure, reproduction, and socialization (e.g., marriage). There are still parts of the world where virginity is highly monitored, and its violation before marriage could mean no marriage proposals for the woman who has lost it. Deflowering women has been perceived as owning the woman and her vagina at the same time. However, feminist movements have become a tool by which women reclaim their bodies and exert control over their own sexuality and reproductive rights, although as a continuous and constant struggle. Now, despite the changes that the feminist movements have brought about, women still deal with all sorts of violence. However, the social atmosphere is different, since there are some legal consequences for domestic violence, sexual assault, and other forms of corporal violence. Given today's patriarchal, sexist, and "normative" culture, having sex means enjoying, interacting with, and exerting control over the woman's body just once, and not always. This means that interacting with a body for a few minutes or more does not mean owning that body forever, as would have been the case decades ago.

Therefore, for a sexist man who wants to own the body of his target "forever," things have dramatically changed. One way in which men can exert their control over the bodies of their target, especially if they have been rejected and deemed undesirable by their target, is to make sure no one else can perceive the target's body as desirable. This exertion of control, which could take the form of an acid attack, they think, can act like a remote control on the target's body. They think, "If I can't have her, then no one should have her." This stems from a patriarchal and misogynist notion that is still obsessed with "owning" a body as if it is an object, without considering what the person, who lives in that body, desires. This dehumanization of the target and objectification of her body occurs long before the acid is even purchased. The woman, who rejects the perpetrator, is, in his view, a piece of property that he has been denied the chance to own. The target is already an object in his eyes, before the actual acid is purchased.

"Conquering" the body in the perpetrator's view is like sabotaging a piece of property so it cannot be used by anyone else, particularly by other men (Ridley, 1986). This is what I mean by conquering the body. Chowdhury (2005) states, "Women [attacked by acid], symbolically the honor and possession of the patriarchal family and community, are hence marked as 'spoiled goods'" (p. 164). It is the process by which the dehumanization of a person completes its course. In an interview, a perpetrator stated, "I was so sad, I sat inside a cab and smoked. The cab driver said, 'Go do something to her,' and I did." I call this phenomenon a patriarchal form of biosovereignty, in line with Banu Bargu's (2016) definition of the term, which explains the sovereign's power's metamorphosis from exercising it on life to "over" life. By throwing acid on the woman's face, the perpetrator aims at exerting ownership over the body like a ruler exerting sovereignty over his subject's life. Bargu's biosovereignty is relevant here as it can explain not only the perpetrator's desire to exercise ownership over her target's life but also his aim at disciplining the body that has rejected him in the first place.

Barriers: Inadequate Medical Care

I asked Masoumeh about her experiences with the sudden loss of sight at the age of twenty-six with a burned face and a three-year-old child to raise in an inaccessible and misogynist society like Iran's. First, she informed me that she had partial sight for up to a month after the attack. For instance, if a person was four to six inches away from her, she could see them. The problem is that doctors do not know much about eye injuries caused by chemical burns, as they are not as prevalent. First, she was treated by an ophthalmologist in a hospital in Esfahan, who was a well-known specialist in the city. At the beginning, Masoumeh's brother asked the doctor what the best course of action was at that time, such as traveling to a more medically advanced country where they may have been able to treat her eyes. He responded by saying, "Even if you take her to the other side of the world, the right medication in the next few months is this brand of eye drops that I have prescribed for her." Masoumeh used those drops, but she gradually lost her sight completely in both eyes. After a month, she couldn't see anything at all.

After her case got some publicity, a journalist advised Masoumeh's brother to bring her to Tehran where better medical facilities and hospitals existed. Masoumeh went there and visited an ophthalmologist experienced in working on Iran-Iraq War veterans, who had sustained chemical injuries.[10]

During the first visit, he tossed out the eye drops the other doctor had prescribed for Masoumeh. "What stupid doctor believes that a burnt eye can absorb drops? You should have undergone a surgery, whereby your eyelids would have been unhinged," the doctor shouted. Masoumeh told him that she did not have any idea about what needed to be done at the moment. The doctor said that it was too late for anything to be done at that point.

Masoumeh believes that all the doctor in Esfahan needed to admit[11] was that he did not know how to deal with a chemical burn. In addition, Masoumeh thought that the first hospital in Shahreza that she was taken to after the attack lacked the particular equipment that is used to open burn-stuck eyelids so that the inside of the eyes can be rinsed with water. This is done because usually a corrosive substance precipitates the eyelids to stick together. Interestingly, Masoumeh's cousin, who happened to be working in the hospital in Shahreza, told Masoumeh that she and her colleagues had asked hospital management on multiple occasions to purchase that equipment for the hospital as it was necessary and not expensive at all, but the administration simply ignored their request. When Masoumeh was taken to that hospital right after the attack, she was told that in order to access advanced equipment, she had to go to Esfahan, which was an hour's drive from Shahreza.

Notable here are the multiple layers of the medical-industrial complex in Iran, governed by austerity and the global neoliberal model. The system is inaccessible, violent, doctor-centered, and lacks necessary equipment, as opposed to being universal, patient-centered, and equipped with proper medical devices. Iran is a rich country, however, given its abundant resources, oil supplies, and small size, compared to its neighbors. Therefore, it should be expected that the hospitals would be stocked appropriately to treat their patients. However, the reality is that the country is run under kleptocracy,[12] and its corrupt leaders use political power to appropriate the wealth of their nation by embezzling or misappropriating government funds at the expense of the wider population.[13] Had the doctor admitted from the beginning that he did not know how to deal with a corrosive chemical, Masoumeh could have been treated by a doctor who had more experience dealing with eye burns. The same can be said about the hospital that lacked the right equipment, even with its staff reminding the management about the necessity and inexpensive price of it. What is clear is that the perpetrator is not the only person responsible for Masoumeh's loss of sight. The inadequate care she received in multiple hospitals since the attack also contributed to her loss.

According to many acid attack survivors whom I have interviewed, as soon as they are released from the initial hospitalization following the attack, their medical insurance stops covering attack-related medical expenses. In other words, the medical insurance only covers the initial intervention immediately after the attack, which involves rinsing the victim's face and body, along with the initial hospitalization for severe burns. This is an important point because acid attack survivors have to undergo many surgeries after the attack, sometimes up to seventy, in order to have an "acceptable-looking" face (this is the phrase survivors used). The pressure is especially greater on women because of the "compulsory aesthetics of femininity" and the pressure on women to "look good." Therefore, stopping insurance coverage after the initial intervention is unfair, inhumane, sexist, and ableist and represents the collateral damage of a patriarchal society. Additionally, the surgeries are not always aesthetic interventions but rather necessary operations to improve the quality of life for the patient, such as helping an organ to work properly.

At this point, the question arises as to who should pay for these numerous surgeries, given the lack of insurance coverage as well as the lack of social and legal measures to demand perpetrators pay for the typically expensive aesthetic surgeries. Masoumeh said laughingly, "You should get lucky to have a rich perpetrator who would pay for your surgeries. But if he wanted to give you money, he wouldn't have attacked you in the first place." Basically, there is no resource for survivors to take advantage of except relying on philanthropists or fundraisers inside and outside the country and within the Iranian diaspora.

According to Masoumeh and other acid survivors, there are no subsidized special services available for them, such as free psychotherapy or medical treatment. With no social safety net in place, the attack is just the first hole in the dam, the beginning of a flood of problems ranging from physical health issues to mental health concerns, along with poverty, "undesirability," and lack of access and accommodation for the blind. I asked if Masoumeh had signed up with the national organization for the vulnerable populations in Iran, which is called *Behzisti* (i.e., state welfare organization). This overwhelmed and underfunded organization, with its underpaid staff of mostly poor women, is responsible for looking after many disenfranchised populations, such as orphan children, disabled civilians, homeless and battered women and children, and so on. As a blind person wanting to sign up with Behzisti, she said, "You have to go through myriad of exams and jump through multiple burning hoops, [then] you may qualify to be covered by Behzisti." It takes a year or two to qualify and for the agency to determine the severity of your disability, which they classify under one of three degrees: weak, mild, or severe. After two years, you enter a new phase, where an overall assessment takes place that lasts another two years. Finally, if you successfully pass all these steps, you can get 53,000 Toman ($3 USD) a month, which is enough to buy a few apples in Iran. Since Masoumeh has a son, they gave her 70,000 Toman ($4 USD) extra, enough to buy a little more than a loaf of bread. After they found out Masoumeh had a small income from teaching pottery, they stopped the paltry payments. In 2020, the authorities decided to increase the financial support by 100,000 Toman ($5 USD)[14] per person, which is still a very small amount, given the cost of living. Besides, the Human Rights Watch (2017) reported that Behzisti's staff treat their disabled clients with extreme disrespect, and there is no accountable system in place for the latter to complain about or appeal the decisions made by Behzisti.

People with mobility issues go through a different route to obtain assistance, filled with its own difficulties. Before the COVID-19 pandemic swept through the world, Masoumeh made a living by teaching blind people how to work with accessibility features like voice-over on their phones, teaching pottery, and selling her pottery products. Simultaneously, she worked at the "White Cane Center," a non-profit organization sustained by public donations. There, she learned elementary pottery before moving on to a private education center that was more advanced. Eventually, she went back to the White Cane Center and became a pottery instructor. She also made major progress in learning how to work with an accessible phone and started teaching others. The center hired her as a paid instructor one day a week. Overall, however, especially after the pandemic, she generally relies on philanthropists who support her with living expenses.

In 2012, a philanthropist and feminist, Y. N., brought Masoumeh to Maryland in the United States and facilitated her visit to the ophthalmology section of the Johns Hopkins Hospital, where Masoumeh underwent three operations free of charge. Masoumeh was surprised that the hospital did not charge her at all for the operations, while in Tehran, *Labbafi-Nejad Hospital* requested one million Toman or $1000 USD (in 2009) before even admitting her. Masoumeh's brother stated that at the time, the family was not able to carry that much cash with them in the midst of the emergency, and so the hospital refused to admit her. The brother went to fetch the cash. Therefore, Masoumeh had to stand in the hospital's parking lot for seven hours, with the direct sunlight beating down on her newly burned skin, hand wounds becoming infected by the minute, and an unimaginably depressed and traumatized mind. During the attack, some amount of acid dripped on her hands and damaged the nerves. As such, she couldn't move her finger for a while. Even though hospital staff could see that a woman was burned with a corrosive chemical, they refused to let her in until she paid the requested amount. The journalists who had come to see what was happening to Masoumeh felt bad for her and attempted to raise the funds needed for her admission right there in the parking lot.

By the time her brother brought the money, hospital staff declared that it was now too late for admission, and that they would need to come back the next day. Masoumeh compared her experience in the Labbafi-Nejad Hospital in Tehran to her experience at the Johns Hopkins Hospital in Maryland, where she did not have to spend a penny for her treatment. It is interesting that in a country with no universal healthcare system, an Iranian visitor, seen as a "non-resident alien" by U.S. immigration authorities, was treated for free. Apparently, according to the hospital staff, the facility was able to provide complimentary treatment to one patient a year for a tax break.

Masoumeh's hostess was Y.N., who had reached out to Masoumeh through an online campaign on Facebook that a group of feminist activists had launched to fundraise and gather support for Masoumeh. She hosted Masoumeh for a year in Maryland while providing continuous support. When the final surgery was completed on Masoumeh's eyes, which involved stem cells, she was told that she needed to come back in eighteen months for a follow-up. Not only did they provide complimentary medical treatment, but they also provided her with enough medications for the entire eighteen months that she needed to wait for the stem cells to work. Unfortunately, though, circumstances did not allow Masoumeh to go back to Johns Hopkins for a follow-up visit. Her hostess moved to a different country, so Masoumeh had no one else in the United States to sponsor her stay. In 2019, I would have hosted Masoumeh, but President Donald Trump's travel ban on Iranians would have prevented her from entering the country anyway. It is an interesting example of how global politics impact people at the micro level, such as a blind Iranian woman's access to medical care in the United States.

Access and Accommodation

> I am not a regular blind person; I am a blind person with special circumstances
>
> —MASOUMEH

The first barrier Masoumeh encountered after the attack that left her blind and disfigured was having to personally go to the police station to press charges against the old man. They didn't accommodate her condition, being a burn victim, who had to remain in the hospital for a while. They required her physical presence in the station and didn't accommodate her. The trial lasted six years, and eventually Masoumeh had to give up on the eye qisās to secure custody of her son. It's interesting that during the custody battle, Masoumeh's numerous medical reports indicating her physical abuse at the hands of her ex-husband were by no means enough to convince the judge that he, as a father, wasn't fit to look after a minor. He reasoned that being a bad husband didn't mean he would also be a bad father. The judge, however, was convinced that as a burned/disfigured and blind woman, Masoumeh wasn't "fit" to look after her son. For this reason, and to show the judge that disabled people can and already do have a life, Masoumeh hired a blind lawyer to represent her in court. Mr. K., the new lawyer, told Masoumeh that the judge had no right to declare her "unfit" to receive custody of her son. He also appeared in court and said to the judge, "Just like I, as a blind man, can earn a living and provide for my family, so can Masoumeh." However, thanks to the male-dominated legal system under the IRI, nothing convinced the judge, and eventually, Masoumeh was only able to keep her son because of her ex-husband's decision to trade custody for his father's eyes (to not become blind according to the qisās).[15] Nevertheless, the ex-husband's family kept harassing Masoumeh via phone and continued to threaten her and refused to pay diya for her injuries.

Furthermore, I wondered what barriers Masoumeh had to face as a newly blinded and disfigured woman in a world that was not only ableist and sexist but also expected her as a woman to meet certain "beauty standards." She said that, at first, she was reluctant to leave the house unless going to medical facilities for her surgeries and appointments. Even on some of those rare occasions, she would cover up her face, which is not a conventional thing to do for women in Iran, unlike some other places where the use of burqa is common. Therefore, she was already purposefully stepping outside the "norm" to prevent people from seeing, or reacting to, her "nonnormative" face, because in the ableist culture, a covered face is perceived as less "disruptive" versus a disfigured face. It is interesting to note how we contract, perform, and measure "normalcy" (Davis, 1995), and what McRuer (2010) calls, "compulsory able-bodiedness" by self-policing. The latter behavior, Foucault (1975) thought, was something we inevitably develop by living in modern societies, where every move taken by us is under surveillance.

Using a ridesharing application (called Snapp in Iran) is easy for Masoumeh, as she uses the accessibility feature (voice over) on her phone to call for a ride. Since she cannot see the plate number of the car, sometimes her mother or her son walk outside with her to make sure that she gets in the right car. Once inside, drivers often ask her companions where Masoumeh wants to go, as if Masoumeh is not there, assuming that she doesn't know where she's going because she has no sight. Masoumeh usually responds before her companions can do so, letting the driver know that she herself can communicate effectively. Sometimes Masoumeh requests accommodation by asking the driver to get out of the car and assist her once he arrives at her door. Usually, the cab drivers who are summoned by phone or smartphone applications stop the car somewhere near the address they are supposed to go and wait for the passenger to find them using the make, model, and color of their car, which is shown on the application. This is of course a normative assumption, presuming that the passenger is sighted.

Public transportation systems have their own issues. In Tehran, the subway's automated stop announcements sometimes do not match the name of the stations at which the train is actually arriving. Masoumeh has at times followed the instruction from the announcement and has gotten off at a certain station only to find out that it was not the destination announced. Also, the subway stations per se are not accessible for blind people, since the tactile lines on the floor that are supposed to be trackable by blind people's white canes sometimes end abruptly in the middle of the station without any further guidance. Authorities often claim they have made certain places accessible, but in reality, they are not accessible to blind people at all. This is like the "imaginary access" that Tanya Titchkosky (2008) has discussed in her article, "to pee or not to pee" that a building can show off an accessibility sign but lack actual accessibility.

People whom Masoumeh encountered, whether on the street or in medical clinics, were often curious about what had happened to her. Masoumeh described it as follows: "You're already devastated and under enormous pressure, and people keep asking questions. What's happened to you? 'What a pity'? 'Why'? You respond to one of them, and walk three feet away, when the next person asks the same question." Masoumeh also talked about people's never-ending stares, whispers, attitudes, and hurting assumptions, such as believing that you "must have done something wrong to deserve this," which is similar to the "rape culture" assuming that what the victim has done or worn must have caused the rape and not the rapist. Unfortunately, many disabled people around the world experience what we call the religious/moral model of disability, whereby one's disability is believed to be a punishment (i.e., karma) or a test from God. The attitude stems from the ableist belief that God imposes disability on people as a divine punishment for having committed a sin in the past or for not believing in him.

Ableist Anti-Catharsis

Another vicious and pestilential encounter was when people would see Masoumeh and become ecstatic and "grateful" for not being (like) her. They would even whisper quietly "*Khoda-ro-shokr*" or "*alhamd-o-lellah*," meaning "Praise to God," or "Thank God," which is said by Persian-speaking people when they are grateful for something. This attitude/reaction serves almost as an "anti-catharsis" moment when the encountering of something "tragic" is received with a euphoric feeling of relief, because one realizes they are just a witness, not a protagonist. I call this "anti-catharsis," because catharsis is about purification as a result of witnessing something tragic, not to celebrate it as a moment of dissociation. Many disabled people are forced to experience this bitter encounter. Other survivors I've interviewed have shared similar stories about times they heard similar phrases.

In these encounters, which I call "ableist anti-catharsis," the non-disabled person uses the disabled person's disability to feel good about their own lack of disability. This phenomenon is like "inspiration porn,"[16] but in this case, the non-disabled also uses that as a moment of prayer/conversation/gratitude with the higher power or deity who is supposedly responsible for this outcome. This encounter is violent, because it reduces the disabled person to something to avoid, something adverse, and it also attempts to objectify the disabled person, reducing them to a sort of "rosary" to use in prayer. In this phenomenon, the expression of "gratitude" to God, or the saying of a prayer, is done audibly and publicly, so as to assure that the disabled person witnesses it. As such, this is not a spiritual moment but a social encounter, a violent one, where one's mere existence is objectified.

In another "ableist anti-catharsis" encounter, Masoumeh was standing inside a subway train holding the bars. Two women standing behind her started talking about the burn scars on her hands, having guessed that it must have been an acid burn. Since it usually happens in the form of a violent attack (on women by men), compared to other types of burns, an acid burn has a different social reception, a stigma attached to it. The social context behind a burn scar caused by acid allows people to judge the incident and the victim by making assumptions about what "she must have done" to "provoke the attack." According to Masoumeh, one of the women whispered multiple times, "Praise to God." The second woman reported to her friend the brilliant discovery that the scar on Masoumeh's hand must have been an acid burn scar and continued by saying, "these girls go get boyfriends, and then the boyfriends throw acid at them." Masoumeh, at this point, turned around and said that although she could not see, she could still hear.

This violent encounter yet again demonstrates the lack of feminist consciousness in those women who assumed that what happened to Masoumeh was an expected thing that happens to woman who get boyfriends, as an unavoidable bitter reality. This implies the incident could have been avoided, had Masoumeh controlled her body and sexuality. Sexist beliefs like this are the foundation upon which patriarchal society reproduces itself—by our actions, thoughts, and attitudes toward ourselves and other women. It is the belief in controlling women's sexuality that causes or facilitates acid attacks in the first place. That is why it's ironic that those women's assumed narratives were yet again about controlling women's sexuality, as opposed to questioning the patriarchal society that "allows" a man to commit such horrific violence against a woman.

Raising Disability Consciousness

I spoke with Masoumeh about how the religious patriarchal culture "allows" men to attempt to "possess woman as their property," and she agreed. At this point, I felt like there was a pedagogical relationship between us, as well as a survivor–activist and witness–researcher connection. This shows that her activism and my activism intersected at a critical juncture I call "feminist solidarity." Without having the terminology for it, Masoumeh was building a community of survivors with whom she politically organized, suggested modification to the existing legislation, started a professional association, fundraised, and so on. I, on the other hand, organized with survivors of violence in order to be/come a witness of, with, and for their struggle against barriers that continue to wound them.

I asked Masoumeh if she was concerned about blind people's rights before the attack. She said, "No, not at all." Masoumeh added, "I did not know we had so many blind people around us." Masoumeh wasn't a disability-rights activist, but she had "become" one after "becoming" blind. These two becomings didn't transpire at the same time. It took Masoumeh years to accept her bodymind the way it is, even more to realize that the barriers she faced as a disabled person are socially imposed and politically justified. It is this moment when one becomes aware that the barriers that they are forced to overcome are not imposed on them by their disability but by the structural inequalities that have not been designed to accommodate disabled people. This moment comes when political consciousness in a social and political subject emerges. Using Marx's consciousness theory, by political consciousness I mean gaining critical awareness that your oppression is a direct result of unequal power relations between you and your oppressors. Our consciousness should result in concrete sensuous activity; otherwise, we will not have understood Marx properly. He emphasized the unity of thought and action as a way forward to ending ideological abstraction. Our political consciousness, having arisen from knowing those experiences, should result in political action. Otherwise, we will produce a new ideological layer to be added on top of the abstraction that is already wrapped around people's experience of disablement (especially in the global south).

Disabling State

Throughout this book, I emphasized the importance of paying attention to the ways in which the state (in this case, the IRI) facilitates not only becoming disabled but also remaining disabled through its authoritarian rule, ableist ideological bureaucracy, mandated discrimination against women, and animosity toward freedom of expression, freedom of the press, and feminism. Not only does the state fail to help the victim, it also hinders the disabled person's access to funding if they publicize their ordeal, by blocking their bank accounts, like it did with Masoumeh after she shared her story with an exiled dissident overseas. After the attack, Masoumeh was banned from speaking to activists and talking about acid attacks. Additionally,

EHGHA, which Masoumeh and other survivors founded, wanted to create a video about the necessary first aid steps to take after an acid attack (e.g., rinsing the affected area with plenty of water, avoiding applying anything other than water to the affected areas, etc.). However, the state refused to issue a "certificate of approval"[17] for it. In Iran, under the Islamic regime, nothing can be released to the public without permission from the state, as there is heavy censorship implemented on everything shown on the media—even in private social media accounts, never mind more public platforms.

The state strives to display an "acceptable" image of itself for the world to see that is not based on the truth of what goes on in the country. Resistance to the video provides confirmation that there are likely many acid attacks in the country, the publicizing of which would further damage the Islamic state's image in the world. Acid attacks, therefore, are much more common than the regime wants to acknowledge. A doctor, whose identity I cannot expose for security reasons, was able to obtain a rough estimate of the number of hospital-visits for acid burns in 2018. According to him, there had been more than 180 cases of acid burns in Iran in that one year alone.[18] One anonymous acid survivor I interviewed believed that the Islamic Republic's attempt at hiding reality and delivering a false image about itself is a historical process and not an isolated incident. She said what Holocaust-denying President Ahmadi Nejad said while visiting Colombia University was part of the same policy of lying to the entire world: "We [in Iran] don't have homosexuals like in your country [the U.S.]" (Wright & Branigin, 2007). Denying the Holocaust, as well as the existence of LGBTTQI persons, are all part of the propaganda that the IR regime (re)produces through cultural production, such as its operation of seventy television channels outside the country alone (Ghasseminejad & Nader, 2020)—never mind the ideological educational system and state-sponsored national media it maintains for domestic consumption.

Acid as Morality Police

"If you don't observe your hijab, then you will be sprayed with acid." This was an anonymous text message received by a woman in Iran whom the Iranian Students' News Agency identified as *Haniya* (Dehghanpisheh, 2014). On the other hand, as of October 2014, at least eight (some believe that the number was thirteen) acid attacks occurred in Esfahan, Iran, leaving one woman dead and many more with severe burns to their faces and hands and blinded in one or both eyes (BBC Persian, 2014). These women were all driving when they were attacked. An Iranian journalist, Elahe Amani (2014, n.p.) wrote, "They were accused of being 'bad hijab' ['bad veilers' or those with 'improper veiling,'] claiming they were 'sullying' their family 'honor' by committing 'indecent behavior.'" The families of the women do not come forward, though, afraid of the possible consequences of accusing the Islamic state of anything. The chain attacks raised fears and prompted rumors that the victims were targeted for not being properly veiled, one of the many reasons that the morality police arrests and punishes women in Iran. These women are still traumatized seven years later, and no one has ever been arrested regarding these attacks (IFP News Agency, 2018).

Interestingly but not surprisingly, the cases were closed immediately and the journalists who were investigating the cases were arrested instead (Ioannou, 2014). Since every city's Friday Imam is appointed by the supreme leader himself (Azadi, 2020, p. 2), many believed that the Esfahan's Friday Imam's sermons enticing violence against "bad veilers" had given the green light to the regime's followers or *basij* (paramilitary) militia to go forward with the attack (Dehghanpisheh, 2014). Amani (2014) wrote that the chain attacks in Esfahan appeared to be "organized and staged by religious fundamentalists in position of power along with members of the Parliament to create a state of fear and insecurity and target women's bodies and psyche" (n.p.). The evidence includes the fact that all the women attacked were behind the wheel, and all the attacks took place between 7:00 and 7:30 P.M.

The Friday Imam's circle, seen responsible for the attacks, are infamous members of the "unofficial" National Suppressive Forces Network serving the supreme leader directly as a shadow force to the country's official police and anti-riot forces (Veisi, 2020). It is believed the Friday Imam had given the regime's supporters, those who are close to the power core in the system, the go-ahead to scare women who are not "properly veiled" by throwing acid at them in the streets. Middle East Eye (2015) wrote, "the violence led to chatter on social networks that there had been up to 13 such attacks on women for being 'badly veiled' while driving their cars." The brutal attacks raised fears among all women. Some reported having water thrown at them in an attempt to terrorize them, as they automatically assumed it was acid instead. This became a means of intimidating all women who stepped outside their homes.

Additionally, *Shargh*, a major newspaper in Iran, printed that further examination showed the same chemical was used on all the victims (Amani, 2014). Elaheh Amani (2014) wrote,

> [Incidents in other places are] isolated cases caused by jealousy and anger. However, for a whole host of reasons, the spate of acid attacks in Esfahan is an organized, serial, and premeditated crime by nonstate actors protected by the Islamists in positions of power in Iran. The offenders in Iran will never express that they are 'sorry' for the harm they caused to their victims.

Instead of bringing those responsible to justice and holding them accountable, Islamic Republic's then prosecutor-general, Ebrahim Raissi (accused of participating in the 1988 massacre of political prisoners) said on October 27, 2014, "We cannot close our eyes to the media crime of disturbing public opinion." Ali Younessi, a notorious former Minister of Intelligence and adviser to the former President Hassan Rouhani, said, "An Iranian cannot have committed such a violent act," but "if the person responsible turns out to be Iranian, he must be under the influence of counter-revolutionary groups based abroad" (Amani, 2014).

Despite all the repressive measures that the IRI took, many poured into the streets and protested the attacks. Brave Iranian men and women demonstrators gathered outside the courts in Esfahan and the parliament building in Tehran on October 22 and demanded an "end to violence against women" (Esfandiari, 2014). Interestingly, Masoumeh was also among them, and she can be seen in photos of demonstrators. The slogans chanted in the protests in Esfahan and Tehran included: "Where is my face," "A secure street is my right," "Death to the *Daesh* [ISIS] School of Thought," "The silence of authorities, is support of Daesh," "You cannot force compulsory hijab," "Esfahan is our city and security is our right," "Security and freedom is our right," and "Acid attack is a crime, and the judicial system is supporting it" (Esfandiari, 2014).

Since the 1979 revolution, the gender reengineering policies of the IRI, which have resulted in a gender-apartheid system, have been reflected in numerous suppressive measures on women's full participation in society. Although hijab appears as just a gendered dress code, in reality it is a means to an end, an insurance policy for enforcing second-class citizenship and facilitating sexual segregation and discrimination against women. Note that schools, mosques, and public transit buses are sexually segregated in Iran. Women are banned from engaging in certain activities in public, including singing, dancing, going to sport stadium and from certain professions, such as those of real estate agents, judges, and even more recently, working in coffee shops. They are also prohibited from riding a bicycle. Mandatory hijab in Iran is not just a piece of fabric but the tool of gender segregation and indication of an essentialist gender ideology, and a gendered social marker that subjugates women to less-than-human status who do not have the same rights as men.

In 1979, Ruhollah Khomeini declared the hijab like a *fatwa* without any referendum or input from women. Women immediately resisted the oppressive order but were brutally suppressed by the regime supporters and Islamists and abandoned by the progressive leftists and secular who thought this was not a "priority" for the revolution. Therefore, the clerics won and took women back in history and took their many rights that they had won suffering and fighting for decades. Immediately after taking power, Khomeini changed the national civic law to the sharia law. In 1963 when the Shah started his so-called white revolution and gave women the right to vote and a host of other civic liberties, the only person who went on the offensive was Khomeini. He did not care about the constitution or any rights that people had gained fighting. All he wanted was for the sharia law to prevail, and he managed to carry out his mission.

Even to this day, many Westerners treat hijab as something legally required, as if it is a democratically ratified law. Western women politicians, such as France's Ségolène Royal, Belgium's Christine Defraigne, Italy's Federica Mogherini, or Britain's Catherine Ashton, who visited Iran, on official trips, wore hijab, and when called out by the Iranian feminists for being hypocrites, they repeated the same argument that the Islamists do, that they are just respecting the "law" and "culture."[19] It seems unlikely that they do not realize that in Iran and the Taliban's Afghanistan, hijab is a sexist dress code enforced by men on women, many of whom are coerced to do so against their will. Women receive prison sentences for refusing hijab, Western politicians cannot claim that hijab is a cultural "thing"[20] that should be "respected."

Khomeini's mandatory hijab "law" resulted in Iranian women's widespread protest on the streets on March 8, 1979, commemorated as International Working Women's Day. Women poured into the streets, whether with a hijab or without, marched side-by-side, and demanded freedom of choice on the issue of wearing the hijab. Under this law, women must wear loose clothing, known as hijab, that covers the head and neck, as well as a *montow*. Women who do not comply are arrested by the Morality Police Force (i.e., "Guidance" Patrols, supported by *Basij*), who consist of thousands of undercover agents to enforce Iran's Islamic code of conduct in public. Until the 2022 protests, Iranian women passively resisted this oppressive hijab law by wearing a "thin" or "short" veil that hardly covers the hair as well as "tight" clothing/montow, or coats reaching mid-thigh—an ensemble often denounced by conservatives as "bad hijab"—instead of a traditional *chador* that covers the whole body. This so-called bad veiling has been a way for women to resist the oppressive order of mandatory hijab. Iranian journalist Amani (2014) wrote:

> In recent years, other than the recent cases of hijab-related incidents [acid attacks by regime thugs] in Esfahan, Iran, there have been hijab-instigated cases of acid attacks reported in Afghanistan to prevent girls from attending schools in 2008 and also one case of acid attack in Gaza that a group called "Justice Sword of Islam" took responsibility for. However, the incidents of acid attacks in Esfahan, is

[are] the most organized, serial, and ideological case[s] conducted by religious extremists, Islamist plainclothes non-state actors with the intention of creating an environment of fear and intimidation for women who are not observing the "True" Islamic Hijab.

Women under sharia law, such as those in Gaza, have also been threatened and victimized with acid for "bad veiling" (Abu Toameh, 2006, 2007; Milton-Edwards & Farrell, 2013; B'Tselem Report, 1994; Hammami, 1990). "Bad veiling" could mean different things in different Islamic societies depending on which traditional clothing for women is considered "Islamic enough" in that society.

Most recently after the "Woman, Life, Freedom" protests in 2022 in Iran, which resulted in women's nonviolent, but active, resistance against mandatory hijab, the regime has taken new restrictive and discriminatory measures to target women and girls. The IRI has confronted women who resist the mandatory Islamic dress code by preventing them from entering public spaces, commercial buildings, taxis, restaurants, and banks, as well as fining them, imprisoning them, harassing them and their families, and stopping them from receiving their university degrees. Punishments also include placing women under surveillance for six months, imposing restrictions on foreign travel for up to a year, and excluding them from government or public positions.

Also, between November 2022 and April 2023, several girls' schools were attacked by a mysterious chemical substance (Iran Wire, 2023), which has led to health complications and even death in schoolgirls attending those schools. It has affected 13000 students. While the state has not taken a full responsibility for the attacks, it is certain that just like the Esfahan's chain acid attacks, there have been ideological and material incentives to entice this type of violence, not to mention the impunity in place for the offenders.[21] Besides, the regime has targeted young school-going girls by surveilling the school cameras to identify the protesting students, arresting them, threatening them, raping them in detention, forcing them to attend "psychological training" (CNN, 2022) to unlearn "antisocial" behavior (e.g., attending antistate protests), or forcing them to watch pornography to threaten and warn them against "women's emancipation" and its supposedly "immoral" implications for the society (Ghadarkhan, 2023).

Care Activism

What can be done about these heinous attacks and the survivors' living conditions? As feminists and disability-rights activists, what can we do to prevent these misogynist attacks and also support the survivors? In this regard, there is much to learn from women in South Asia. Anwary (2003, p. 309), who studies the work of nongovernmental organizations (NGOs) and women's organizations that provide services for acid attack survivors in Bangladesh, writes: "Programs and activities of one particular organization by the name of *Naripokkho* includes research, campaigns, protest work, discussions, advocacy, cultural events, alliance with other human rights organizations, and monitoring of state interventions to combat violence against women. The group organizes workshops for survivors and their families, helping to rebuild their confidence, returning them to an active life within their communities, and allowing victims to come together and realize that they are not alone (Asian Women's Resource Exchange 2002)."

It is important to note that each country's exposure to the transnational presence of NGOs and other members of civil society determines the amount of support that social movements in that country receives. For instance, Iran's Islamic state has isolated the country internationally for over four decades by sustaining an antagonistic relationship with the West. The Iranian state's anti-Western attitude[22] has increasingly isolated the country day by day to the point that many transnational companies and NGOs have no presence in the country even though they operate in most other countries in the world (DW, 2015).

However, with so much effort and sacrifice, small initiatives have been relatively successful. One initiative included a few survivors, such as Masoumeh, founding *EHGHA*, which provides limited financial, emotional, legal, and medical support for survivors. Additionally, Masoumeh started her own, more visible activism by using her cellphone to videotape her visits with survivor friends and allies who had also been attacked by acid. Masoumeh asked many survivors to join her in the videos she was making about her life and other people like her. Some did, while others declined to do so simply out of fear, since the IR state discouraged them from publicizing their cases. In one instance, a survivor told Masoumeh that her lawyer advised against talking to the press, reasoning that doing so would complicate her court case and put her at a legal disadvantage. A women's rights and anti-mandatory-hijab activist, Masih Alinejad, helped her edit the videos and put them together and create documentary-like footage that was shown on a Persian-language news channel, *Manoto*, which broadcasts from the U.K. The documentary went viral and attracted many people's attention to the acid attack problem and the inaccessible environment for blind people in Iran. The positive achievement was that many people who watched the video deposited money into the account numbers that Masoumeh shared on her social media accounts, in order to raise funds for her survivor friends who had received little to no support from the state and needed financial support.

Unfortunately, and predictably, the ramifications were devastating for Masoumeh in Iran, as the regime forbids Iranians from doing interviews with the Persian-language media outlets based outside Iran. The regime perceives them to be "anti-revolutionary" and "antagonistic" toward the IR. Masoumeh did participate in an interview with the same channel that had broadcast her documentary and that put her in trouble. She was summoned to a revolutionary court and threatened with a block on her bank accounts by the Ministry of Intelligence if she continued to interview with those channels. She was provided a few pages to explain why she had talked to the U.K.-based media outlet. She defended herself by stating she had no ill intention and that she simply spoke about her private life and the problems she faced as an acid victim. She told the court that she underwent thirty-seven surgeries (four to five million Toman or $200 USD[23] each) over the nine years since the horrific incident and that she did not have the money to pay for any of them. It was other people's financial support that allowed her to have the operations. She tried to make the court realize that, without receiving any help from the "sacred state," as its leaders call it (Kalantari, 2016), the only resource available to survivors is publicity and philanthropy. The state had only paid three million Toman ($3000 USD), nine years earlier in 2009.

The interrogator/prosecutor simply took a quick look at those pages, barely reading a couple of sentences, and wrote on them, "There's no way that the accounts could be unblocked." Masoumeh became infuriated and sarcastically said, "That's fine with me. I will go and live in a tent as a homeless person now that I have no access to my accounts." They said that if she wanted to have access to her bank accounts, she needed to do something for them, such as asking the U.K. television channel to remove everything they had broadcast or published about her life. "How can I deny myself and my life?" she asked the court. She tried to reason with them and explain that after the videos were posted online, there's nothing she can do to change that. The court was unconvinced, so Masoumeh had to stop interviewing with foreign television channels in order to access her accounts again. Nevertheless, the documentary was extremely useful in raising funds for her survivor friends who do not receive any support from the state. The Islamic Republic does not even support its war veterans,[24] never mind its female, civilian survivors of abuse. The state also ordered Masoumeh to stop posting about acid attacks on her personal social media accounts. Masoumeh asked feminist activist Masih Alinejad to help publicize her case while not mentioning her name, as her own accounts had been blocked by the state.

Masoumeh believes the state fears people like her who encourage other survivors to speak up, tell their stories, and ask for other women's solidarity. That is what she did in the documentary. She allowed other survivors to tell the world about the barriers they faced in financing their reconstructive surgeries and the economic insecurity they face simply trying to survive with a disfigured body, and often blind eyes, in an ableist society. As such, the state was infuriated because it just wanted to oppress them and suppress their voices, but Masoumeh was not silent. Instead, she was overcoming those barriers and seeking solidarity for the systemic problems she and her friends faced.

Because the account number that Masoumeh originally posted had been publicized by Masih Alinejad on Instagram, the court decreed, "The account will never be unblocked." So, when Masoumeh's funds were finally to be released, she was ordered to open a new account to receive the deposit. From that point onward, the state was determined to block the stories of Masoumeh and other survivors from being publicized. Even when a domestic television channel went to Masoumeh's house and recorded her life, the government would not allow it to broadcast the documentary. Masoumeh reached out to the network and asked why they did not show the footage; they said the state had forbidden them from showing it.

Transnational Disability Praxis

My goal throughout this book has been to highlight the experience of disabled people in the global south and to find ways in which solidarity and disability consciousness can be built and fostered among us. Transnational Disability Praxis helps us to re-theorize disability relations from the standpoint of marginalized disabled people in the global south. I have attended to this praxis or ethical commitment by consciously using "reflexive/relational" thinking and acting as my ethical commitment to conduct emancipatory (not just participatory) research, which leads to political praxis. Research becomes emancipatory when you try to make a difference in the lives of people you study, organize with, and struggle along (Barnes, 2003). Bannerji (1995) and Gorman (2005, 2016) define the "reflexive/relational" method of "going beyond the immediate experience and trying to understand how that experience has been organized through social relations and forms of consciousness extended from the past." I have done so in this chapter by witnessing the oppression that the disabled survivors have endured, being present to report this violence, and finally understanding the unequal power relations that affect their lives. This political/ethical commitment to conduct emancipatory research through reflexive/relational thinking and acting, as a general orientation and way of proceeding, has framed this research-activism journey throughout. One way in which this transnational disability praxis is performed is by building solidarity transnationally and transcontinentally with acid attack survivors in Iran.

There are transnational community organizations, non-profit groups, and even businesses that have shown solidarity with Iranian acid survivors and their cause of stopping acid attacks and supporting survivors. The short-term goals, such as access to medical care and aesthetic surgeries, are the ones that some philanthropists, activist groups, or local businesses, like *Negin Patisserie*, actively try to fulfill for survivors. Negin Patisserie is a bakery located in Toronto, Canada, and is run by an immigrant woman from Iran (who happens to be my mother) who usually employs disabled immigrant and refugee women with mental health concerns as well as former political prisoners. To facilitate emotional and financial support, Negin, the owner and head chef at Negin Patisserie, personally reaches out to the women survivors and their families on social media. She also fundraises for the survivors while spending time educating her costumers at the bakery about acid violence and creating a culture of acceptance and care. Other philanthropists, such as Y.N., personally procured Masoumeh's medical care abroad and took her to the United States—she did the same for another survivor.

Furthermore, community members inside Iran and transnational donors outside Iran facilitated Masoumeh's access to much of the care she has needed since the attack. However, the next impossible step was raising £80,000 for an upcoming surgery. Masoumeh has a chance to regain her sight, but only in one eye. What needs to be done for Masoumeh's eye at this point is a complex process called *keratoprostheses* that can only be performed by a handful of doctors in the entire world. As such, she is apprehensive about lying on the operating table before knowing the surgery will succeed. Masoumeh has identified a doctor in the U.K., who has always conducted this surgery successfully, so she has decided to go to the U.K. and ask the British surgeon to operate on her eye himself. However, the British National Health System does not cover visitors' expenses. I have been in contact with multiple grassroots organizations and charities seeking their support and to request that they lobby the government to not charge Masoumeh, as her attack was the result of GBV. We have made some progress so far. In collaboration with Negin Patisserie, I have also been fundraising for Masoumeh's possible surgery in the U.K. in order to find accommodation and temporary residence for Masoumeh and her son in the country. I reached out to the disability community on social media and asked for help in locating an individual or an organization in Brighton willing to provide complimentary accommodation for Masoumeh for the duration of her treatment. Luckily, someone from Brighton contacted me and expressed interest in hosting Masoumeh when she visits the U.K. for her surgery. She introduced herself as a nurse who works at the same hospital as the surgeon Masoumeh has picked to perform her surgery. As soon as some of the funding was secured through donations, Masoumeh applied for a U.K. visa, but her application was denied as she had not been able to convince the officer that she had enough funding and that she was going to return to Iran after the surgery. To prove that she was going to return to Iran after the surgery, she even decided to leave behind her son, who is her assistant and visual aid at this point, and travel alone with no knowledge of English to a foreign country. However, not even that convinced the authorities the second time when she reapplied. Fortunately, the surgeon has agreed to travel to a third location to operate on Masoumeh but given the magnitude of the logistics involved in a medical travel process like this, Masoumeh is once again in the waiting game, hoping to hear back from a multitude of sources about whether things are going to work out in her favor.

Curative Culture

As we discussed extensively in Chapter 2, the Iranian society both within and outside its geographical borders very much holds ableist attitudes toward disability and it perceives disability as a "lack." Since working with the Iranian subjects of violence, I have stretched myself between their needs and my discipline's politics (i.e., DS' uneasy relationship with cure). This has not been an easy task. I have often asked myself whether I can avoid apologizing for "cure seeking" even while narrating its violent excesses. In her work, *Curative Violence*, Eunjung Kim (2017) maintains these tensions throughout her analyses, by enabling us to imagine possibilities for disabled lives that are free from violence when care is seen "as a negotiation rather than a necessity." I lived most of my adult life in Canada, where universal healthcare, although of low quality according to "first world" standards, is available. My research, however, is situated in Iran where healthcare is expensive and access to it is not available to all while the ableist and "curative culture" prevails inside the nation and in the diaspora.

Eunjung Kim (2017) argues for ways to rethink "cure" as "a set of political, moral, economic, emotional, and ambivalent transactions that occur in social relations" (p. 41). This observation is accurate in many contexts including Iran's. Not all disfigured/disabled Iranian acid survivors, for instance, have access to reconstructive surgeries, while they desperately need them to look "acceptable" (this is the word one of them used to describe her face after multiple surgeries). Whether or not this "acceptable" face can once again fully participate in a patriarchal and ableist society, the "curative" culture in/of Iran, tries to do what Kim (p. 3) describes as that "properly govern[ing] the body and its social relations." The attack was also done to do exactly this. As such, the violence of acid and cure have a symbiotic relationship. In other words, if the survivors lived in a society that didn't demand what McRuer (2010) call "compulsory able-bodiedness," they would not suffer as much as they do, encountering the ableist violence that doesn't "approve" of their blindness or disfigurement. And it is exactly the knowledge of this system of oppression that enables the perpetrator to throw acid on the victims to "punish" them and "control" them while relying on the ableist violence to do its job.

It is important to ask the next question: whether the public's participation in Masoumeh's fundraising campaign for an advanced eye surgery is to support a disabled woman survivor of GBV or is just an attempt to help build a future "without a disability"? Is the public interested in "letting" Masoumeh access social inclusion by helping her achieve a "normative future"? This is similar to the concept of "time machine" that Kim (2017) suggests, by which the disabled subject citizen is required to disappear from here and now, only to occupy a temporal space in an unknown future, except that it's known for its "lack of disability." In any case, a better future is considered a future without disability, even though we may not know about anything else that this unknown future entails. Kim would ask whether Masoumeh's present life and existence are considered a "lost time" by this curative and ableist logic, because she is blind here and now. So, when people donate to Masoumeh's campaign, are they caring for a disabled person, or mobilizing her on the path to cure? Is this care or violence? Is this "curative violence" as Kim has taught us, or is this a layer of infrastructures of care for the disabled? How easy is it to dissect the two? As Kim (2017) has shown us, "a pre-disabled past or a healed future-to come" (p. 227) is usually what is preferred.

Furthermore, Alison Kafer (2013) shows in her book, *Feminist, Queer, Crip* that the persistence and prevalence of narratives that promote that to have a disability is to have no future, that to be disabled is a future that no one wants, and that a better future for humankind is one with no disability and no disabled people in it. For most of us—including many disabled people—this drive for a future without disability is simply common sense. Kafer (2013) does not simply argue against the unyielding drive toward eliminating disability that many DS scholars have shown that happens through medicalization of the bodymind, preventing disability through prenatal testing, preventing the admission of disabled immigrants (one way of enacting able-nationalism or building an able-bodied nation [Mitchell & Snyder, 2015]), and overcoming it through disability disavowal. Instead, Kafer (2013) explains that the "presumption of agreement" about the benefit of creating a future without disability is itself a brigadier barrier in achieving social justice and full inclusion for people with disabilities. Going back to Masoumeh's eye surgery campaign, can we conclude that Masoumeh's wish to regain her sight is a wish for a future without disability and a non-disabled self? And if so, what about the community she has developed through the fundraising campaign? What about the collective who have gathered to support Masoumeh's journey to a very complex surgery in the U.K.? Building a community, this collective sensibility offers redemptive possibility while resisting the liberal modern notion of the triumphant individualism favored by the most. How can we resist what Kafer (2013) describes as a desire for a future empty of disability while showing solidarity with a woman survivor of GBV?

Nevertheless, we need to be careful not to equate Masoumeh's desire for cure with "false consciousness." I am reminded of Liz Crow's words, where she states (1996; emphasis in original):

> Impairment is problematic for people who experience pain, illness, shortened lifespan or other factors. As a result, they may seek treatment to minimize these consequences and, in extreme circumstances, may no longer wish to live. It is vital not to assume that they are experiencing a kind of *"false consciousness"*—that if all the external disabling barriers were removed they would no longer feel like this. We need to ensure the availability of all the support and resources that an individual might need, whilst acknowledging that impairment can still be intolerable. (p. 217)

Crow (1996) cautions us that dismissing someone's impairment and the pain and suffering caused by it is denying aspects of that person's existence. Margaret Price has also reminded us we need to acknowledge one's truth, whether or not we ideologically agree with it, and understand that it is not just structures of power that govern our lives, but the livability of our lives in our bodyminds. Therefore, pain as a valid sensation and embodied experience, Price (2015) argues, should be acknowledged as a core component to our collective ethics of care.

Conclusion

In this section, I painfully unearthed how the violence of theocracy and theocratic state apparatus is instrumental not only in the creation of disability in women but also in rendering invisible the social and economic impact of ableist and sexist violence in their lives. I started from the story of one woman, discussing her struggle with not only the ableist society but also the theocratic state's facilitation of her wounding by justifying the violence based on sexist ideologies, providing impunity for the perpetrators, if not actively throwing acid on women victims, and refusing to care for the victims. Furthermore, the man who throws acid on an ex-wife or ex-girlfriend to make her "undesirable" for the next man has probably the same logic as the man who throws acid on women who, according to the Islamic state's standards, look "bad-veiled," as they both want to control women's bodyminds and sexuality inside and outside the domestic sphere, and by relying on the ableist and sexist world conceal their violence. Again, like we discussed in the previous chapter, disability is not just the outcome of this process but also the fetish that conceals the existing inequalities in the society.

It is impossible to get close to acid without risking a horrific burn. However, it is not that difficult to get close to people who have had a compulsory encounter with it. Unlike acid's cruel nature and permeating spirit, its women survivors are gentle, kind, brave, strong, and indomitable. One of them, Masoumeh Ataei, said to me, "My isolation is what the acid thrower wanted. I won't let him have it." In my first encounter with the survivors, they got a chance to share their story as it permeated their skin, eyes, flesh, beliefs, and lives in general, just like the acid did. The trauma of being burned with a corrosive chemical is multilayered and complex due to its violent nature being embedded in ableism, sexism, and misogyny.

Acid dissolves the skin and eats it up, cell after cell, until it reaches the flesh and even the bone. Acid attack is a form of torture that almost never ends, as it is aimed at controlling the victim forever. Complete recovery from an acid burn is almost impossible, since it requires numerous reconstructive surgeries, depending on the resources available to and accessible by the victim. It is also a traumatic experience of torture, in which the victim's trust in the world is shattered. Bernstein (2015) informed us why torture is an unsettling experience: we operate in the world with a relative trust, without an assumption the people we encounter intend us harm. When we leave the house, we do not expect to come back blind and burned. Acid attacks shatter that trust, because their first element is surprise. Acid is thrown at the victim by another person. It is a weapon by which the perpetrator attacks you, without giving you a chance to fight back. Acid burns you, meaning from the moment it touches your skin, with the face the typical target in most cases (eyes, nose, ears, lips, cheeks), it burns like hell. It feels extremely hot on your skin. As you burn, you are often stumbling on things around you, closing your eyes seeking to avoid the intense pain. You may never be able to open them again after that moment, however, as the acid glues your eyelids. Often, people around you do not know what to do. It takes a while for them to call an ambulance. By the time you get to the hospital, the shock has eaten up your soul, while the acid has eaten up your flesh. It is extremely painful, just like other burn incidents, but unlike many of those, this one is not an accident caused by negligence or pure coincidence. Rather, it is an attack by another human. Therefore, you often remain in absolute fear as the perpetrator might come back and burn you again. Additionally, the second layer of trauma kicks off when you look into the mirror—assuming you can still see yourself. You often look like a different person, someone you do not know, a person with a new face.

The new face is a surprise to your loved ones as well, because they are not used to it. The agony is inexplicable. The world as you knew it before the attack ceases to exist. A new scary, thorny, murky road is born out of that. It is a strange place called "the world that I live in now." This world requires adaptation, which is the first step of dealing with the trauma of distrust. Living in a world that leaves you burned, scarred for life, often blind, and disfigured, is not easy. Then there are society's ableist attitudes about feminine aesthetics, with people asking questions like, "Who will marry you after this?" The queries are like the sprinkling of salt on your open wound. You ask yourself whether your entire existence should be reduced to a man's impression of your face. People stare. People judge. People ask, "What happened to your face? Why did this happen to you? What did you do to provoke him?"

In the end, the words of Rev. Martin Luther King Jr. seem relevant: "In the end, we will remember not the words of our enemies, but the silence of our friends." Let's never stay silent in the face of this abhorrent violence.

CONCLUSION

Healing Wounds

Transnational Disability Praxis and Active Witnessing

Gorman (2005) defines witnessing as an act that "involves politically conscious human beings who can analyze their own roles in the story, and also provide the critical context for understanding the power relations *in order to change them*" [emphasis in the original] (p. 8). She asserts that in the process of witnessing, what the researcher experiences (i.e., receives and interprets by her/his senses) should be combined with her "understanding" of those unequal power relations. Only then can the unity of experience and analysis occur as I, the researcher, (re)present/report/narrate the disabled survivors' experiences. The point of witnessing, as Gorman (2005) suggests, is "be[ing] present in the experience/analysis" (p. 9). Inspired by her work, I explored the possibility of bearing witness to oppression as a research avenue. Throughout this book I documented the firsthand experiences of disabled survivors of violence, which I argued can become a point of departure that provides a powerful locus for expanding the notion of "experience" within Disability Studies (DS). I have chosen to engage in witnessing, because it provides a context and corroboration for the stories of institutional and violent situational survivors who have told their stories.

When the roof of sorrow caves in I roll into myself like a snail except not tender nor sweet, and wonder why. This was my feeling most of the time as I was interviewing and organizing with my participants, the living witnesses of massive atrocities such as the 1988 massacre of political prisoners, many of whom had already served their sentences in Iran, and catastrophes, such as acid attacks. As an activist, I generally try to change the future and present, but this time I was so angry and sad that I couldn't change the past. What can we do with something that has already happened in the most devastating form? Activists work hard to create change by resisting the dominant discourses and structures of power. But can one change what has already taken place? At this juncture, what is the job of a witness? What is witnessing? Is witnessing a call for action and a form of care—an element constituting the infrastructures of collective care?

Sharon Oster (2014) writes that "bearing witness is no silent, passive act; it demands an ongoing dialogue and our active interpretation of survivor accounts" (p. 307). On the other hand, Ann Kaplan (2005) defines "witnessing" as "prompting an ethical response that will perhaps transform the way someone views the world or thinks about justice" (p. 123). The conventional deal is that the witness (testifier) is an active interpreter of what has transpired, a "remnant," something or someone who can convey a truth that has happened to him/her and others who might not be there to testify for themselves. Witnessing and "proxy witnessing" are important ways in which to mobilize the knowledge that we are granted by the testimonies we get access to, as a witness or proxy witness. Primo Levi (1989), a Holocaust survivor, defined the term as a way of accessing someone's testimony who has ceased to speak, through other people who continue to speak "for"[1] that person. This knowledge is not just there in the words in the testimonies and the meanings behind them. It is rather the possibility of social change and political consciousness that we now have to mobilize as witnesses. By possibilities, I mean the new teachings and modes of consciousness that the testimonies encapsulate.

The prison survivors, for instance, whose stories I told in Chapter 3, arose from the prison with new forms of consciousness that constitutes a social and political foundation for the next generations, including mine, to analyze their own role in history. My generation was born in the 1980s when the generation before me were either perishing in the battlefield with Iraq or getting tortured and executed in political prisons in Iran. When I mention these two groups in the same sentence, I do not mean to equate them as they were fundamentally different in a sense that one group opposed the regime and the other went to war for the regime. As such, their politics and ideological alignments were significantly different. I am mentioning the two together because those contradictions are precisely what my generation have inherited and had to work through to define and find its own place in Iran's history of social and political struggle. Therefore, the knowledge that has arrived in my hands has been gained, constructed, lived, and passed on, with unimaginable effort, pain, agony, struggle, resistance, suffering, and trembling, which renders it a treasure for not only for the Iranian people but for humanity in general.

Mojab and Taber (2015) argue that the knowledge arising from surviving and resisting state violence should be mobilized, transmitted, and taught to others. Whether it is a testimony or autobiography, it stems from a place of memory, and therefore, they call it "memory pedagogy." Teaching memoirs, they argue, carry transformative possibilities, such as remembering together as a form of collective praxis, and building transnational solidarity with marginalized communities whose stories we hear. Mojab and Taber (2015) write:

> Feminist studies of violence suggest that remembering experiences of violence is essential to resistance, recovery, and the process of rebuilding community (Osborne, 2014; Smith & Watson, 1998). Community begins to be reestablished when people are able to remember together, giving testimony to their experiences and having others bear witness to their experiences. Individuals and communities can form a sense of purpose by transforming the act of remembering and witnessing to a living document for social action. (p. 2)

Feminist and Disability Consciousness

In the Introduction, I pointed out that one of the purposes of this project is to bear witness to disabled survivors of state violence, namely, war, incarceration, torture, Punitive Limb Amputation (PLA), and acid attacks, by actively defetishizing their disability. By defetishizing, I meant carrying out a thorough analysis of these categories, in order to unveil the social relations behind their creation and to name the processes that render people disabled. This unveiling process is equivalent to a defetishizing process, which I argue has a revolutionary capacity to produce nonideological knowledge and praxis. Over the course of developing the Transnational Disability Model (TDM), I strived to understand how all of this shapes the articulation of TDM praxis and consciousness in the broader disabled people's liberation struggle against disability, race, class, gender oppression, and state violence. Besides being rooted in the material world, this transnational model means: (a) we can imagine a world with no borders and avoid trying to impose a universal disability identity upon all disabled people while perceiving ourselves as one oppressed group; (b) we can resist the "whiteness" and the Western-centeredness of the field and build transnational solidarity using multilingual approaches to disability expression and knowledge production (Kazemi & Karah, 2021c); and (c) we can start imagining an organized and diverse group of people with collective disability consciousness with no universal disability identity and no necessary ties to nation-states (i.e., circumventing the international borders and nation-states, as local and global blocks of power or empires); (d) we can foreground the dialectic of disability care as well as building the "transnational infrastructures of care" including solidarity and active witnessing (Kazemi & Karah, 2023); and (e) we can reimagine disability justice as a global project and hold ourselves accountable vis-à-vis transnational contexts.

In Chapter 2, I told the story of wounds created by war: the story of disabled war veterans and civilians of the Iran-Iraq War, in the middle of which I was born. I also discussed how the ideological category of "living martyr," manufactured by the state, has hindered the way for disabled veterans to seek and get support (e.g., cure, medical intervention, accommodation, housing) and has fetishized their disability by concealing the structural violence they face as neglected citizens. The social and structural pressure to take on and perform the manufactured identity of a "living martyr" has only contributed to their further disablement, mental health crises, suicide attempts, and even death. I also discussed the dysfunctional bureaucratic system of disability measurement, based on the medical model that the state uses to determine the extent of the benefits veterans receive and called it, "soma-technologies of disability measurement," which hinders veterans access to rehabilitation by demanding them to "get worse" to receive a higher disability percentage. This system prevents veterans from developing collective political consciousness, considering themselves as being in the same boat by forcing them to compete with another for a higher percentage as opposed to caring for one another and feeling united.

In Chapter 3, I told the story of wounds created by torture: the story of those who participated in the 1979 revolution in Iran and became disabled/mad under unimaginable torture in the dungeons of the new Islamic state. Using more than thirty interviews and a twelve-year long ethnographic work, I theorized the enigmas and aporias of madness in prison, foregrounding the material reality that the Iranian political prisoners in the 1980s went through, the ways in which their bodymind acquired disabilities/wounds throughout this process, and how their bodyminds responded to this violence. I also explained the disability-care dialectic in and among political prisoners so as to understand what constituted the infrastructures of collective care and interdependence between them in response to the imposed disablement and madness.

In Chapter 4, I told the story of wounds created by state punishment: the story of those whose fingers or limbs were amputated by the judiciary system in Iran in compliance with the Islamic Criminal Code for petty theft while the high-ranking state official embezzled millions with impunity. I also discussed the exercise of biosovereignty (Bargu, 2016) by the state as torture and disablement via judicially-ordered amputations according to sharia law in Iran, the public spectacle it produces, and the process by which it attempts to "cure" crime by "producing" disability and restore the "wholeness" of the Islamic society by dismembering the poor's body.

In Chapter 5, I told the story of wounds created by gender violence: the story of women who became blind and disfigured as a result of acid attacks. I foregrounded the dilemma of simultaneously thinking about cure and disability consciousness by seeking transnational care, solidarity, and support as the foundations of disability praxis while working toward the elimination of ableism.

In all these stories, there is a common thread; the survivors of violence became and remained disabled. My active witnessing what Schaffer & Smith (2004) define as "recogniz[ing] the humanity of the teller and the justice of the claim; to take responsibility for that recognition; and to find means of redress" (p. 3), or my attempt at healing these wounds, is what mediates the diffusion of the story from its origins to the reader's consciousness. My feminist and disability consciousness (this can also be a site where a class consciousness of disability might be formulated) was galvanized as part of my affective and vulnerable witnessing in relation to the populations, communities, and individuals with whom I organize, suffer, sympathize, and demand justice. Sakhi (2017) reminds us that social justice and the justness of social relations/interaction/contracts have to be foregrounded based on ethics and ethical subjectivity and "response-ability" in relation to others. Questioning the ethics of social relations, or human-to-human relations, is absolutely necessary if we want to have an alternative arrangement that is ethical.

According to Sakhi (2017),

> Far from given, humanity is always actively created within our mutual subjective–objective life experience by our nonindifferent (in)action as both singularity and sociality. Therefore, if inspired by [Hannah] Arendt, we see humanity as "the paradoxical plurality of unique beings" (1958: 176) achieved through "constant establishment of new relationships within a web of relations" (1958: 240), then our struggle for social justice is also always-already an ethical project. (p. 161)

What is relevant then to my project here is attending to these two aspects simultaneously, which requires our "creation and constant recreation of an active human subject who relates to itself through its response to the others, conscious and responsible for its response-ability" (Sakhi, 2017, p. 161). If I want to be response-able toward my participants and the research projects

I have described in this book, then my engagement with data sources should be ethical—as we learn from Sakhi and Arendt. I call this conscious, ethical, and response-able engagement "active witnessing"—a method of transnational disability praxis.

This active witnessing, thus, means not only being politically conscious of what kinds of wounds these peoples have sustained, but also "doing" something about it. Marx believed that knowledge is not separate/separable from the physical body, and therefore not separate/separable from the material world. Marx (1845/1976), according to his own words, was out to change the world, not just interpret it. My rationale in performing an embodied active witnessing is based on the dialectical and historical materialism thinking that the material world cannot be dissected from our consciousness; therefore, we live what we know, and we do what we know. This is how research can become emancipatory and not just participatory, when you try to make a difference in the lives of people you study, organize with, and struggle along (Barnes, 2003). The key point in possessing knowledge is what we do with that knowledge, the actions that stem from that knowing. Witnessing implies the mobilization of a particular knowledge that needs to be passed on and communicated with others. It is this mobilization that helps larger communities build their political consciousness and "act" according to the new knowledge that they have gained. Remembering, commemorating, honoring, and showing solidarity, for instance, are among the actions that show if a certain event has been recognized by the public or not.

This thinking and acting as part of active caring and witnessing is played out differently for/with each group of disabled survivors. As it pertains to the prison survivors, for years, I made myself available as a counselor for the survivors who often dealt with post-traumatic stress, anxiety, and/or depression. The sessions provided me with invaluable knowledge about their experiences and struggle in and after prison, especially since many of them live in exile in Europe and North America. This means that on top of being a survivor, they have had to leave the country often "illegally" and seek asylum somewhere else, not to mention the world's unwelcoming attitude in regard to asylum seekers. As demonstrated in Chapter 3, many of the survivors have acquired physical and psychological wounds due to physical, sexual, and psychological abuse that they have had to endure during their time in the Islamic Republic of Iran's prisons. Besides providing therapy sessions for them, in which I learned a lot about how real fights for social justice are fought, I learned how they navigate the "justice-seeking movement." Therefore, the fight is not over for them. It is not like serving your prison sentence and now getting over it and living your life. It is rather like living a lifetime of struggle and actively fighting the state even from exile.

Here I do not mean to paint a picture of their lives that is filled with gloom and doom. On the contrary, I have been fascinated with how resilient these people are, how they have managed to change the world around them by taking brave steps for social justice and social change. Even though they are mostly forced to deal with trauma, dispossession, and displacement, they passionately care about the world and strive to make a difference in any way they can. Furthermore, they care about Iran and whatever that goes on there in terms of social, economic, and political issues, such as women's oppression, poverty, etc. In my work with them, I have been captivated by how they manage to bring the qualities and skills that they have developed in prison to their daily life. Post-traumatic stress is understood as a "disorder" by the "psy" apparatus and its professionals, however, scholars like Burstow (2015) have shown us how at times of trauma people are capable of developing excellent survival skills to protect themselves during and in the aftermath of the trauma. These survival strategies may seem "nonnormative" from the point of view of the public, but for them, it is an excellent "response" their bodymind has developed to the "nonnormative" circumstances.

In reciting the testimonies of the survivors whom I interviewed, I seek to demonstrate the process of construction of difference through the atrocious crimes of a fundamentalist state. At this impossible disjuncture, I stand with an impossible task on my hands: witnessing the witnesses and testifying their testimonies through ethical practice; (re)telling their stories of degradation of life, health, sanity, and bodymind, while resisting the ableist normative culture, history, and society with unresolved tension. However, I also need to resist euphemism, the urge to glorify violence, because that is part of the crime and its fetishization.

In relation to acid attack survivors, my short-term goals, as a feminist and disability activist and active witness, have been to start a network, document cases of acid violence, connect to survivors via social media, record their stories, empathize with them through phone calls, show feminist and disability solidarity, and engage in care activism with them via social media to raise awareness around the barriers they face in society on a daily basis (Kazemi & Karah, 2023)[2]. While we, as a network, have gained more visibility, which has been one of our goals from the beginning, other burn victims, even survivors who acquired their disability in an accident (not in a deliberate attack) have joined us and declared their support and solidarity. This seemed like the first time that acid survivors and burn survivors started communicating together realizing that the differences aside, they were fighting a similar battle. What materialized here before us as these seemingly different groups came closer to one another was building bridges, instead of more barriers, or turning mirrors into windows, which is the essence of solidarity.

Karah and I have called this phenomenon, "crip solidarity" (2023, p. 311). Additionally, I have connected many women survivors to doctors and dentists whom I know in Iran. I call these informal channels, "care infrastructures," or "informal disability justice pedagogy" (Kazemi & Karah, 2023), which emerge where the state fails to provide formal care. In this case, these informal channels are cultivated transnationally, which are part of transnational disability praxis. This type of praxis can be detected in the activism we carry out to overcome multiple social, institutional, and economic barriers to facilitate survivors' access to care. I think as part of our feminist solidarity we have been there for them as allies and sisters who care about them and understand the necessity of the battle they are fighting. This type of solidarity is either missing from intersectional transnational struggles for freedom or shown selectively in certain contexts and not others (Kazemi & Karah, 2023).

Transnational Care Infrastructures

Going beyond the postcolonial obsession with how we are viewed by the Westerners, my project here is to evoke solidarity and compassion to end violence. This is not to say that the people whose stories you heard in this book are helpless victims who may or may not be "exotic" and "vulnerable" enough to evoke empathy or sympathy. Rather, I foreground their agency and consciousness in this book, while demanding your solidarity and not pity. Remember the racial apartheid in South Africa and the world's collective will and determination to put an end to that system. Why not show solidarity with each other and those who are struggling against unlivable conditions? Why not show solidarity with Iranian women who have been living under a gender-apartheid system for the past four decades?

Fully aware of this book's absence of narrative conventions, I demand your care, affective response, and solidarity. Solidarity is not charity. Nor is it something to give. Rather, it is something to "show," a resistance to the divisive and fragmenting lies of structural power embedded in binary thinking. Going beyond national, racial, and ethnic binaries, it is a call for standing together beyond subjectivities fractured by identity and geopolitics. It is like waving at the other person to assure them that you are there, and then joining them and politically mobilizing with them. Therefore, I have not told the stories of violence and resilience in this book to evoke the Western or at least English-speaking readers' pity fulfilling the already-existing tropes of the vulnerable war casualty, acid victim, torture victim, etc. I want my readers to feel moved enough to show solidarity, to go beyond the politics of "representation" and conventional narrativizing tropes, to get in touch with their humanity. Solidarity is essential for marginalized communities' mental health and sense of well-being.

Dawn Shickluna (2020) proposes the possibility of engaging with life narratives of trauma and testimonies to challenge the dominant discourses that separate private memory from public and historical memory, and instead emphasize the connection between personal and political, paving the way for a transformative solidarity building through what she calls "radical survival narrative pedagogy." This radical survival is a kind of transnational praxis that encompasses collectivity and solidarity through, for example, "narrative pedagogy," a cross-reading of women survivors' autobiographical narratives, documenting their experiences of structural violence and connecting their experience and the knowledge arising from that experience. These threads, Shickluna (2020) argues, "call us to consider how we may renegotiate and reconstruct dominant ideologies, post-trauma/survival subjectivities, and experiences of state-violence" (p. 28).

Similarly, Doris Rajan, in the case of building solidarity among marginalized women, namely, refugee, Indigenous, and disabled women, calls it "critical-feminist pedagogy of solidarity" that through community development strategies would unite these groups of women and enable them to challenge structural violence that they have had to experience (Rajan, 2019). Rajan contends that to address the structural violence in our lives, the process of solidarity building should aim at transforming the way we (marginalized groups, such as disabled survivors of violence) think about violence in our lives, and address its root causes not just manifestations. In other words, Rajan (2019, p. 82), following Marx, suggests that to change the social relations that rule over our lives, first we need to understand those relations by coming together with those who we have key commonalities with that may not be apparent at first sight. Further, this process of solidarity pedagogy, Rajan suggests, can be galvanized by thinking collectively through effective dialogue, developing shared language, strategies, and actions, and questioning our own participation in reproducing those relations. While I concur with Rajan in calling for the necessity of grassroots solidarity building among marginalized people themselves, I also deem necessary an engagement between those who are in pain and those who are not, the superior and the inferior, those who are privileged and those who are marginalized. I argue that a true transformation cannot take place, at least not in today's globalized world, unless those who are not in pain show solidarity with those who are. It is at this critical moment that hope can appear on the horizon.

Furthermore, the right-leaning discourses have unfortunately long hijacked our agency as women from the global south to have a say in anything by considering us as inherently backward, uncivilized, submissive, even hijab-loving, cultural selves. The left, on the other hand, has mostly (if not only) critiqued the Western humanitarian discourses and Western Orientalism and Western representation of Middle Eastern women without touching religious fundamentalism, Islamism, clerical fascism, and dehumanizing practices such as the sharia law, out of the fear of reproducing Orientalist discourses (Said, 1978). When can we finally have permission to critique Islamic law while asking our fellow humans for solidarity without apologizing for Islamism and its inherent patriarchy, ableism, and violence? When is our turn to ask for solidarity just like our brothers and sisters do across the Western world in the Black Lives Matter and LGBTTQI+ movements?

One way in which we can bring disability praxis and transnational solidarity together is by generating transnational platforms that are multilingual in nature, since proficiency in "official" languages such as English is a massive barrier for many to access other people's thoughts or to share theirs (Kazemi & Karah, 2021c). This can be done by adding a "global" section to the existing academic journals, periodicals, and conference proceedings that promote engaging with data sources from the global south centering "structural violence and the forms of resistance to it," as Hemachandran Karah and I have by launching the "Disability and Multilingualism: A Global Perspective" section with the *Review of Disability Studies: An International Journal*[3] (Kazemi & Karah 2021c). "Creating a space for transnational solidarity praxis as a framework, political endeavor, accessibility commitment, and a cultural setting is where languages and disability expressions appear more than an identity marker or private possession of a community" (Kazemi & Karah, 2021a, 2023). Creating sections like that can complicate what disability is as a wound, and what it means to become and remain wounded/disabled under exploitative social relations and oppressive historical continuities and discontinuities. Initiatives like that can challenge what "we think as 'normative' disability consciousness, 'normative' disabling conditions, and 'normative' disability expression mobilized by patriarchal, colonial, fascist, theocratic, and imperialistic legacies" (Kazemi & Karah, 2021b, n.p.). Materializing transnational solidarity in the form of solid actions like the one described here can defetishize disablement by unmasking the naturalization of structural violence (Kazemi & Karah, 2021c). A transformative approach to transnational disability studies should be emancipatory in a sense that it not only does explain the social relations and processes involved in wounding bodyminds but also possesses a revolutionary potential for ending those relations and stopping violence.

Another way is generating archives documenting how disabled/mad people survive as they develop informal channels of care and mutual support to sustain themselves with resilience. Disabled people around the world have long found ways to survive despite living under ongoing systemic neglect. Their survival happens largely through innovative informal strategies in favor of resilience and resistance. Although such informal infrastructures of care are present everywhere alongside institutional arrangements, they have not received much scholarly attention and are not yet fully understood and documented. It is absolutely necessary to build digitally accessible "crip oral history archives" (Kazemi, Gold, Karah & Hande, 2025) concerning such informal care infrastructures from around the world and take a step toward building transnational disability solidarity as praxis (Kazemi & Karah, 2021c, 2023).

The Vulnerable Witness

The term "vicarious trauma" is a term that describes the phenomenon generally associated with the development of trauma in helping professionals, who are exposed to the trauma of their clients (Pearlman & Saakvitne, 1995). Vicarious trauma transpires when one individual helps a trauma survivor (Kaplan, 2005). Although witnessing might partially include vicarious traumatization as a desire to help the other who is in pain, witnessing in a larger sense has the capacity to mobilize public recognition of what has happened to the survivors, why, and what to do next to prevent further harm in the future (Kaplan, 2005).

After working with acid attack survivors both as a researcher, co-activist, and ally, my relationship with my face (as the first organ that is fully exposed to the outside world) has transformed, just like it did with my body and the notions of pain, exposure, and vulnerability after working with torture survivors. The acid attack usually targets your face whereas incarceration and torture demand and capture your entire body. Talking to burn survivors has changed my ideas about beauty, attractiveness, femininity, aesthetics, masculinity, and my own face/body. It is difficult to fully distinguish trauma from vicarious trauma. Developing "vicarious trauma" sounds too liberal for someone who has written this book, if you know what I mean. Throughout this project, I have been talking about internalizing resistance, inheriting pain and political consciousness embedded in the historical struggle for justice, and cultivating other people's pain inside ourselves to learn to empathize. As such, it may seem "too liberal" to talk about vicarious trauma that I, as a frontline activist-witness, experience. Since I embarked on the journey of interviewing acid attack survivors, burn survivors, disabled people, former political prisoners, and trauma survivors, I have developed a new relationship with myself and my surroundings.

As a DS scholar, I resist using psychiatric language, such as psychological "disorders." Instead, I consider my new ways of relating to the world, a response to what I have witnessed about my research participants–allies. This new response comprises a distrust in the world, which Jean Améry and, inspired by him, Bernstein (2015), told us about. The distrust in the world is a response to trauma that the survivor experiences after the trauma-inducing incident is over. The world changes in the victim's eyes, from a relatively benign world to an extremely dangerous one, in which incidents like rape and torture transpire. In my case, ever since I have started conducting interviews and immersing myself in their stories, I apprehend sudden explosions to take place in my face. I expect my oven to explode for no apparent reason. I expect my car to explode. I constantly await a blow of air and fire to burst.

But why an explosion? Why not acid throwing? Why not imprisonment? An explosion is a sudden end to the world, destruction of everything you know and have, a sudden blow to reality as it is experienced "normally." Everything that survives the explosion can never be restored to its former status. It changes forever. Perhaps my mind has perceived my work with my research participants as an explosion in my consciousness, a sudden blast, and something that changes you forever. The stories they have confided in me, the looks we have exchanged with some of them, the tears we have shed over Skype, and the laughter and friendship that I will forever cherish are those sudden explosions. Now, with this book as living proof that those acts of organizing politically, community-building, witnessing processes, and confiding in each other, I can claim that my understanding of disability/madness/wound has evolved in diverse ways. Today, I theorize disability not just from my point of view, me as a person or a Middle Eastern feminist woman who has survived a war. Rather, I theorize this from a collective point of view of many different disabled people and their allies, from war veterans to burn survivors. Each and every one of them has taught me a new way of understanding disability from "limitation" to radical possibility to uniqueness, to a sign from God to illness. I resisted some. I welcomed most. However, the explosion has done its job. I no longer am the person who started writing this book. I hope it changes you the way it changed me.

Let me end this book by a poem from Sa'adi:

Human beings are members of a whole	بنی آدم اعضای یکدیگرند
In creation of one essence and soul	که در آفرینش ز یک گوهرند
If one member is afflicted with pain	چو عضوی به درد آورد روزگار
Other members uneasy will remain	دگر عضوها را نماند قرار
If you have no sympathy for human pain	تو کز محنت دیگران بی غمی
The name of human you cannot retain.	نشاید که نامت نهند آدمی

Notes

PREFACE

1. This movement was first initiated by families of the executed or forcibly disappeared prisoners in the 1980s and kept growing as the regime executed and disappeared more Iranians. Today, the movement comprises many families including those whose loved ones were shot during the street protests in 2019, the families of the passengers of the PS752 Ukrainian flight shot down by the IRGC's missiles, and the "Woman, Life, Freedom" movement's martyrs and disabled/wounded.

2. See Mesdaghi (2012); Sakhi (2017).

3. See Shelly Chan (2018) and Aihwa Ong (2011) for discussions on overseas Chinese investment and Chinese neoliberalism; Shelly Chan, *Diaspora's Homeland: Modern China in the Age of Global Migration* (Durham, NC: Duke University Press, 2018); and Aihwa Ong and Li Zhang, "Introduction," *Privatizing China: Socialism from Afar*, ed. Aihwa Ong and Zhang Li (Ithaca, NY: Cornell University Press, 2011).

4. See UNHCR (2023).

5. This discussion has first appeared elsewhere. See Kazemi (2024b). Used with permission of The Ohio State University.

INTRODUCTION

1. See for example Meekosha (2011); Barker and Murray (2013); Ghai (2012).

2. To address other forms of exerting power over the developing nation by developed nations, few scholars have talked about imperialism as a disabling force. Priestly (2001), Gorman (2016), Puar (2017), Meekosha (2011), and Erevelles (2011), among others, have talked about imperialism as a form of indirect occupation and exploitation. These scholars theorize disability by taking into account the economic and political relations/condi-

tions that have historically produced "disability" by violence. In this book, I am building on their works.

3. It is important to acknowledge several other political economists such as Prabhat Patnaik, Silvia Federici, and Glen Coulthard who have theorized imperialism and its delivered violence in different ways, such as accumulation through financialization, accumulation through encroachment, accumulation by primitive accumulation through exploiting women's labor, and primitive accumulation through colonizing Indigenous land, and so on.

4. I provide two examples in the final section of this chapter.

5. If you're born with a certain disability or acquire a disability in an accident, I do not consider that a wound. However, there are congenital disabilities created as a result of violence, such as poverty or chemical and nuclear weapons. In Japan, for example, after more than seventy years, there are still children born with disabilities as a result of the effects of the U.S. atomic bombs in Nagasaki and Hiroshima (Oftedal, 1984). The other possibility is malnourishment of pregnant mothers that could lead to disabilities in the child. Therefore, even disabilities that one is born with could have been caused by violence. In this project, I discuss "wound" as a disability caused and/or sustained by state violence or other violent relations.

6. Care does not always carry a positive connotation for disabled people. Care can also harm people. Many antipsychiatry theorists, for instance, have talked about the harmful effects of electroconvulsive therapy on mad or mentally disabled people. See Burstow (2015).

7. See Barnes (2003); Shakespeare (2006); Oliver (1983).

8. See the works of Mia Mingus (2010), Leah Lakshmi Piepzna-Samarasinha (2018), Patricia Berne (2018), Leroy Moore (2017), Eli Clare (2017), and Aurora Levins Morales (2018), among others.

9. There are scholars (such as Nancy Krieger and Camille Nelson) from fields like law, epidemiology, medical anthropology, and global health who may not identify as disability studies experts but have extensively produced materials that inform DS in one way or another. João Biehl, for instance, through vivid cases and bold conceptual work, has done excellent work on global health and access-to-care activism exploring grassroots mobilizations for the right-to-health and for state accountability in Brazil.

10. Sami Schalk and Jina B. Kim (2020), for instance, offer a feminist of color approach to disability studies that centers Black, Indigenous, and feminist of color experience at the heart of any conceptualization of disability relations and politics.

11. See the works of Nirmala Erevelles (2011), Rachel Gorman (2016), Sami Schalk (2018), Jina B. Kim (2017), Julie Avril Minich (2014), Lezlie Frye (2023), Mel Chen (2012), Liat Ben-Moshe (2020), Cynthia Wu (2018), Jasbir K. Puar (2017), Eunjung Kim (2017), Robert McRuer (2006, 2010, 2018), Leah Lakshmi Piepzna-Samarasinha (2018), and Therí Pickens (2019).

12. See the works of Tsitsi Chataika (2012), Anita Ghai (2012), Clare Barker and Richard Murray (2013), Helen Meekosha (2011), Shaun Grech (2009, 2012), and Karen Soldatic (2014), among others.

13. See for example Lopez & Murray (1996); Burke, Degeneffe, & Olney (2009); Barker & Murray (2013); Ghai (2012); Tsitsi Chataika (2012); Carrigan (2012).

14. Turkey was never colonized (although Russia, Britain, France, Italy, and Greece did try in World War I). However, Britain and France took over some parts of the Ottoman Empire.

15. The discussion about the inadequacy of postcolonial critique in disability studies to tackle the new forms of regional imperialism in the Middle East and beyond, for the

first time, appeared in the *Journal of Disability and the Global South*. See Kazemi, Gold and Karah (2024). Materials used with permission from Disability and the Global South, https://dgsjournal.org/wp-content/uploads/2024/10/dgs_11_01_02.pdf.

16. See for example Grech and Soldatic (2016); Kim (2011, 2017); Puar (2017); Erevelles (2011); Priestly (2001).

17. This revolution was the first major democratic revolution in Asia, Africa, and Latin America. See Mojab (2015).

18. Saba Kord Afshari and Yasaman Aryani, both in their twenties, are among the women who unveiled publicly and received sentences of more than ten years.

19. I use, reluctantly, the terms "Muslim majority," "Islamic society," "Islamic country," or "Muslim woman." It would be inappropriate to characterize individuals, societies, cultures, or countries by their religion or, rather, the dominant religion practiced. For a similar objection to the term "Muslim society," see Zubaida (1995) and Mojab (2001).

CHAPTER 1

1. My discussion of the TDM, for the first time, appeared in the journal of *Critical Disability Discourses*. See Kazemi (2017). Used with permission from Critical Disability Discourses, https://cdd.journals.yorku.ca/index.php/cdd/article/view/39729/35971.

2. See Fritsch (2010), O'Brien (2005), Shildrick (2009).

3. Realpolitik means pragmatism in politics and international relations, prioritizing reality over ethical, moral, or ideological considerations.

4. Such as white, European, English-speaking, bourgeois, heterosexual, and non-disabled.

5. My discussion of building the TDM based on the case study of the Iran–Iraq War was initially discussed in the journal of *Disability Studies Quarterly*; see Kazemi (2019b). Used with permission from Disability Studies Quarterly, https://dsq-sds.org/index.php/dsq/article/view/6496/5412.

6. In Chapter 5, I discuss examples of this mobilization such as the digital multilingual oral history archive.

CHAPTER 2

1. "Ahmad Shamlou (1925–2000) is an Iranian poet and journalist. Nominated for the Nobel Prize in 1984, Shamlou is one of Iran's most revered modern poets and one of the prominent leaders of Iran's modern literature literary movement. He is the author of over 17 volumes of poetry (over 800 pages). Shamlou lived in exile in the United States and England for three years, but returned to Iran shortly before the 1979 revolution. Between 1979 and his death, he remained in Iran and continued to write poetry and criticism despite the unabashed hostility toward his writings from the Islamic Republic. The clerics viewed Shamlou as an anti-Islamist nationalist, a traitor and a Westernized writer. However, because of his popularity, the new regime did not dare to arrest him. They did, however, ban the publication of his poems and writings for many years. He died on July 24, 2000, at age 74" (Wolpé, 2018). Material used with permission from the Bamdad Foundation and Sholeh Wolpé.

2. Sholeh Wolpé is an Iranian-American poet, playwright, and librettist. Her most recent work include *Abacus of Loss: A Memoir in Verse* (University of Arkansas Press) and *Attar: The Invisible Sun* (Harper Collins 2025). Wolpé's translations of the twelfth-century Sufi mystic poet, Attar, *The Conference of the Birds* (W.W. Norton), and of the twentieth-

century Iranian rebel poet Forugh Farrokhzad, *Sin: Selected Poems of Forugh Farrokhzad* (University of Arkansas Press), have garnered awards and established Wolpé as a celebrated re-creator of Persian poetry in English. She is the Writer-In-Residence at the University of California, Irvine. She divides her time between Los Angeles and Barcelona.

3. The result of this study was first published in the *Canadian Journal of Disability Studies*; see Kazemi (2019a). Used with permission from Canadian Journal of Disability Studies, https://cjds.uwaterloo.ca/index.php/cjds/article/view/530.

4. The observations that I made reading the survivors' stories, memoirs, testimonies, eyewitness accounts, and online posts/comments are extensive in number and internal richness. I am aware that every story of disablement is important and deserves attention. However, for the purpose of this case study, I had to select a handful of them to (re)tell. Out of 500 narratives/comments that I read for this study, I sampled and translated 78 of them based on maximizing variance in order to cover/represent most forms of oppression that the disabled veterans endure (see Kazemi, 2018). Maximizing variance is a purposeful sampling strategy that aims to sample for heterogeneity and maximum diversity. I put only a few of them in this chapter that pertain to the analytical themes rooted in the discussion of "fetishization of disability by the state." I remain in debt to every other disabled veteran or civilian whose story I have not had the chance to narrate. The few stories/comments that I have chosen for this chapter are key in understanding both processes of producing and perpetuating disability in the survivors.

5. Inspired by Erick Fabris, I use this term to demonstrate the horrible effects of psychiatric medications that are used to silence disabled individuals as opposed to caring for them in humane ways (Fabris, 2011).

6. For proper pronunciations, see the "ijmes" transliteration system for Arabic, Persian, and Turkish at the Review of Middle Eastern Studies Journal.

7. The veterans' access to medications is hindered for a variety of reasons. Although the Islamic Republic of Iran's propaganda demonizes the Western world especially the US for "imposing" the economic sanctions against the country to dissuade them from pursuing a nuclear bomb, the sanctions have never involved medication, food, and humanitarian aid. The real reasons behind the lack of access to medication is the ever-increasing inflation, poverty, structural corruption, and the state's destabilizing behavior in the region. This behavior, which involves sponsoring terrorism, using Afghan refugees as militias, recruiting child soldiers, and supplying Shia militia with weapons to undermine the security of multiple countries such as Iraq, Syria, Lebanon, and Yemen, has provoked the economic sanctions against the Iranian banks and deterred the global financial institutions and pharmaceutical companies of doing any transaction with the Iranian banks. Transparency International's Corruption Perceptions Index ranks Iran one hundred and fifty-one out of 180 countries (Corruption Perceptions Index, 2024). Moreover, to hide its sponsorship of terrorism which is done through a host of illegal activities such as smuggling illicit drugs and human trafficking, the state fails to ratify and accept the Financial Action Task Force (FATF), the inter-governmental body against money-laundering, which is a global requirement for transparent trade and money transfer. Currently, Iran is on FATF's blacklist and is considered to be a "high-risk jurisdiction" for corruption, money laundering, and the financing of terrorism (FATF, 2020), because it fails to ratify the Palermo and Terrorist Financing Conventions, in line with the FATF standards. This prevents Iran from accessing the world's banking system and being able to pay for the medicine and supplies that it needs to purchase from the world market. FATF Annual Report states (2020), "Until Iran implements the measures required to address the deficiencies identified concerning to countering terrorism-financing in the Action Plan, the FATF will remain

concerned with the terrorist financing risk emanating from Iran and the threat this poses to the international financial system."

8. For a discussion of the gendered nature of care see the works of Evelyn Nakano Glenn (2012) and Nirmala Erevelles (2011).

9. Negin Goodrich (2013) reveals that in Iran, there is legislation in place to protect the rights of people with disability, such as *The Comprehensive Law to Protect Disability Right*, which was ratified by the Iranian parliament in 2004. Such legislation is supposed to benefit both the population with disabilities in general, and disabled war veterans, in particular. However, these regulations are often not enforceable because there is no proper system in place for their execution as planned on paper (Goodrich, 2013). There is a gap between legislation and the everyday experiences of disabled people. The veterans' requests are legitimate and have been predicted in the law, but most of those laws are never enforced. And no person or organ is ever punished for violating them.

10. See, for instance, Fashnew (2016); Namehnews.ir (2013); Nasr (2014); Soleiman Nia (2012).

11. See veterans' comments in Entekhab.ir (2016); Fashnews (2016).

12. See the Human Rights Watch's report (2016) on the state's crackdown on media freedom in Iran.

13. See for instance Ahmadi (2022) and Hamshahri Online (2022).

14. It is worth mentioning that it is not easy to find credible academic sources concerning the Iranian state's corruption due to the extreme censorship of the media in Iran. Clearly, no scholar is allowed to investigate state corruption or publish any critique of the "sacred" state.

15. See veterans' comments in Fashnews (2016); Irna (2014); Javanonline (2014).

16. See, for instance, Fashnews (2016); Javanonline (2014); MehrNews (2012).

17. See Alef.ir (2010); Javanonline (2014); shohadayeiran.ir (2016).

18. See for instance Afkarnews (2013); Alef.ir (2010); Javanonline (2014); shohadayeiran.ir (2016).

19. See Alef.ir (2010).

20. See Alef.ir (2010).

21. See for instance Kaleme.com (2016); Mehrnews (2012).

22. The discussion on the "living martyr" first appeared in the special issue of *Review of Disability Studies: An International Journal* in 2024; see Kazemi (2024a). Used with permission from Review of Disability Studies: An International Journal, https://rdsjournal.org/index.php/journal/article/view/1127.

23. The day that the battle of Karbala happened, and Imam Hussein was killed.

24. See Bastani (2019).

25. See myriad movies in this genre that the state calls the "sacred defense": *The Scent of Joseph's Shirt* by Ebrahim Hatamikia (1995); *From Karkheh to Rhein* by Ebrahim Hatamikia (1993); *In the Name of the Father* by Ebrahim Hatamikia (2006); *The Glass Agency* by Ebrahim Hatamikia (1998); *The Marriage of the Blessed* by Mohsen Makhmalbaf (1989); *The Third Day* by Mohammad Hossein Latifi (2007); *M for Mother* by Rasoul Mollagholipour (2006); *The Red Ribbon* by Ebrahim Hatamikia (1999); and *Chronicles of Victory* series (aired on national television) by Morteza Avini.

CHAPTER 3

1. The word "broken" has dual use in the prison literature. One refers to breaking inside, submitting, and "converting" to what the totalizing system wants from you, Islam in this

case. Another refers to psychological breakdown, or a psychotic break. In *Ghosts of Revolution*, Talebi (2011) means the first interpretation. Therefore, "unbroken" here means someone who still believes in the legitimacy of his/her cause.

2. See Akhavan (2017); Sakhi (2017).

3. Even in 2021–2022, an unprecedented trial took place in Stockholm, Sweden, which under the authority of Universal Jurisdiction prosecuted and found guilty an IRI state official, Hamid Nouri, who had been involved in the 1988 Prisoners' Massacre in Iran. In 2024, Nouri, unfortunately, was returned to Iran as part of a shameful prisoners' swap deal between Sweden and Iran, which felt like a slap in the face of family members whose loved ones were hanged and dumped in unmarked graves during the 1988 massacre.

4. Normalcy is not a "natural" state but an ideology (Davis, 1995), a socially constructed phenomenon that masks material reality. If normalcy is defined in terms of a point of reference for assessing whether behavior is abnormal or non-normative, we need to first assess the pre-existing conditions in which the behavior has occurred. Therefore, I assess the prisoners' behavior not against a fixed medicalized normative notion of human conduct; rather I contextualize it in relation and response to the ruling relations, controlling the ideological prisons at the time.

5. One form of torture that produced many mad people was the so-called "Resurrection"/"boxes"/"graves"/"machines"/"the human-making factory" or (*kārkhāneh-ye-ādam sāzi*), "the human-making machine" or (*dastgah-e-ādam sāzi*), that was tested in Ghezelhessar prison from the fall of 1983 to the summer of 1984. "Prisoners were forced to squat for hours in boxes in the form of coffins ('the Grave,' also known as 'Resurrection'), with Quranic incantations sometimes blared loudly at them, during which time they were intermittently beaten and whipped on their heads and faces" (Iranian People's Tribunal, 2012, p. 34).

6. The notion of madness as "response-ability" of political dissidents has first appeared in *Handbook of Disability* edited by Marcia H. Rioux, Alexist Buettgen, Ezra Zubrow, and Jose Viera (Springer, 2022). See Sona Kazemi and Hemachandran Karah, "Madness as Response-ability against State Terror: A Case Study from Iranian Revolution," in *Handbook of Disability*, edited by Marcia H. Rioux, Alexist Buettgen, Ezra Zubrow, and Jose Viera (2022), 1–19. Used with permission from SNCSC. https://link.springer.com/rwe/10.1007/978-981-16-1278-7_40-1.

7. There are no exact figures of the number of victims due to the suppressive political climate and severe censorship in Iran. Nevertheless, to this day, there are around 5,000 known names of victims that have been documented by the families, political parties, and human rights organizations (Iranian People's Tribunal, 2012, p. 5).

8. See Agah, Mehr, and Parsi (2007); Talebi (2011); Mesdaghi (2006); Parvaz (2002); Parsipour (1995); Baradaran (1995).

9. "Sleep deprivation was employed when prisoners were taken to trials or interrogations in the dead of the night" (Iranian People's Tribunal, 2012, p. 34).

10. "Prisoners were sometimes forced to stand still for long periods of time: reportedly anywhere up to 72 hours. Variations included standing on one leg or standing barefoot on ice. This was at times combined with psychological torture: on one reported occasion, prisoners were left standing blindfolded in front of a wall and every once in a while, one was taken away, with no further news about him" (Iranian People's Tribunal, 2012, p. 33).

11. "*Bastinado* is an excruciatingly painful form of torture in which the soles of a victim's feet are whipped; the victim is first tied to a bed, either on his back or front, with a blanket thrown over his head or a dirty sock or rag stuffed in his mouth. This was the most common form of torture used in interrogation and was inflicted on virtually every-

body. Survivors said without exception that bastinado was performed with whips made of electric cables, up to half an inch thick" (Iranian People's Tribunal, 2012, p. 31).

12. "Many witnesses underwent or witnessed *ghapani* during their interrogation. *Ghapani* involves the suspension of a victim in the air by his arms, one of which is twisted behind his shoulder and the other wrenched behind his back; the victim's hands are bound together with sharp handcuffs and tied to a chain or rope from the ceiling. The handcuffs were tightened with every move the prisoner made, thus increasing the pain. The torture on occasion began with making the victim lie down on the floor on his chest, before yanking the chain so that he was raised from behind; victims were left in this position for hours" (Iranian People's Tribunal, 2012, p. 33). One of my participants, Siavash said, "Ghapani after 14 hours renders you disabled. But if they hang you from the ceiling with ghapani you become disabled in one hour."

13. Ayatollah Montazeri was removed due to several objections to Ayatollah Khomeini and the officials' acts, especially the massacre of the political prisoners in 1988.

14. For the first three months in solitary imprisonment, one of my interviewees, Siavash, had no access to a toothbrush. He got a tooth infection after those three months.

15. This level of harassment and dehumanization is not specific to the IRI Regime; other states have also exercised this power over the bodies of their political prisoners. For example, it was the very incident of restricting prisoners' access to the bathroom and the frequent beatings on the way to the bathroom that sparked the Dirty Protest in the Irish prisons (1980–1981).

16. The connection between trauma and speech impediment is well established; see for example, Porges (2011).

17. Material used with permission from the Bamdad Foundation and Sholeh Wolpé.

18. There is extensive literature documenting the horrific effects of solitary on prisoners. See Kupers (1999, 2006); Rhodes (2004).

19. Morteza is one of my research participants who spent several years behind bars in the 1980s in Iran's notorious prisons. For security and privacy purposes, I refrain from presenting identifying information.

20. Material used with permission from the Bamdad Foundation and Sholeh Wolpé.

21. See Iranian People's Tribunal (2012, p. 23).

22. Scabies is not an infection, but an infestation. Tiny mites called *Sarcoptes scabiei* set up shop in the outer layers of human skin. The skin does not take kindly to the invasion. As the mites burrow and lay eggs inside the skin, the infestation leads to relentless itching and rashes.

23. The panopticon is a type of institutional building and a system of control designed by the English philosopher and social theorist Jeremy Bentham in the eighteenth century. The word "panopticon" is also used as a metaphor to refer to surveillance technology in modern times and totalizing institutions.

24. See Abrahamian (1999); Akhavan (2017); Sakhi (2017).

25. According to Wolpé, Forugh Farrokhzad is "arguably the most famous woman in the history of Persian literature, Farrokhzad was born in Tehran to a middle-class family of seven children. She married at seventeen and divorced within three years, painfully and unwillingly relinquishing her only son to her husband and his family. She never remarried. Instead Farrokhzad turned to poetry and film and led an independent life. Farrokhzad was a poet of great audacity and extraordinary talent. Her poetry was the poetry of protest—protest through revelation—revelation of the innermost world of women (a taboo subject until then), their intimate secrets and desires, their sorrows, longings, aspirations and at times even their articulation through silence. Her expressions of physical

and emotional intimacy, much lacking in Persian women's poetry up to that point, placed her at the center of controversy, even among the intellectuals of the time. On February 14, 1967, at thirty-two, she died in an automobile accident." You can read her poems in *Sin: Selected Poems of Forugh Farrokhzad*, edited and translated by Sholeh Wolpé (University of Arkansas Press). Used with permission from University of Arkansas Press and Sholeh Wolpé.

26. See *Sin: Selected Poems of Forugh Farrokhzad*, edited and translated by Sholeh Wolpé (University of Arkansas Press, 2010). Used with permission from University of Arkansas Press and Sholeh Wolpé.

27. Sakhi states (2017, p. 151): "By early 1988, the war with Iraq was going sour, Khomeini's health was declining, and, even after seven years of executions and forced conversions, there were still thousands of resistant others—dissidents and social justice activists—confined in prisons awaiting eventual release. [By later that summer], approximately 5,000 political prisoners had been executed and many more thousands were broken or neutralized, both inside and outside the prisons (Montazeri, 2000, pp. 625–640; Abrahamian, 1999, pp. 209–228; Iranian People's Tribunal, 2012). The objective was the annihilation of the Regime's revolutionary other, whether actual or potential, rendering them 'true converts' or annihilating them as completely as possible under the international conditions afforded by the ceasefire (Montazeri 2000, p. 1217). The executions of the internal other and capitulation to the external other were born as fraternal twins."

28. Following Margaret Price (2015), I refrain from using the word, "self-harming." Instead, I use "self-injuring."

29. As soon as Afshar shared his memory about this accessible communication strategy or access request, it brought to mind our Society for Disability Studies' conferences, held at the Ohio State University for the past few years. During the conference, we would use colorful stickers with different messages on them in order to communicate access needs and preferences in regard to communication with others. For instance, a green sticker might say "I like talking to others," and another one with a different color says, "I am not very talkative; please don't start new conversation with me."

30. Material used with permission from the Bamdad Foundation and Sholeh Wolpé.

CHAPTER 4

1. "In the case of theft, amputation is due only if the stolen goods exceed in amount or value the legal minimum (*nisab*). But there is no scholarly unanimity on what this 'minimum' is. The Shafi'i al-Qaffal cites the Zahiris, who claim that the minimum or maximum value of the stolen goods is immaterial for the criminal to deserve amputation. This Zahiri attitude renders amputation mandatory for any amount stolen, and for any motivation that might have led to it, disregarding all possible extenuating circumstances. The Zahiri position overlooks the probability that theft of small food items is sometimes driven by hunger and extreme poverty, for which other schools of law completely exempt the thief from criminal intention, hence from the punishment of amputation. Moreover, in cases of theft driven by hunger and poverty, other schools often condemn the society that allowed its members to fall to such a level of destitution" (Rispler-Chaim, 2007, p. 78).

2. In the next chapter, I discuss the intentionally caused disabilities that entail a monetary compensation to the victim (*diyat*), such as in the case of acid attacks.

3. This word is no longer used in Disability Studies discourse but since this is a direct quote, I have left it as is.

4. Material used with permission from the Bamdad Foundation and Sholeh Wolpé.

5. I discuss this thoroughly in the next chapter.

6. See William Montgomery Watt, quoted in Gerhard Endress, *Islam: An Introduction to Islam* (1988, p. 31).

7. See UN (2004).

8. See Statement of Kenneth Katzman, Specialist in Middle Eastern Affairs Congressional Research Service at Joint Economic Committee Hearing on Iran July 25, 2006 (Katzman, 2006).

9. The shame and stigma that Sabzichi talks about bluntly contradicts how Dols described the Islamic society's reaction to physical difference: "Islamic society did not form a correspondingly harsh judgment of the leper, prejudice and inhumane treatment of lepers and other disfigured individuals endured in Iranian and other Islamic communities" (Dols, 1983, p. 912).

10. It is not just Sharia that seeks deterrence. In *Discipline and Punish*, Foucault (1975) discusses the public spectacle as a means of deterrence in the French Judicial system in the 18th century as well.

11. See Al-Zuhayli (1989).

12. See Al-Husayni (1991).

13. See Sunaura Taylor's (2017) *Beasts of Burden: Animal and Disability Liberation.*

14. "The meaning of the body resides between bodies, between those who live through them, in them, and those who bring them to mind" (Titchkosky, 2005, p. 664).

CHAPTER 5

1. Able-mindedness is a term increasingly common in DS. Alison Kafer's *Feminist, Queer, Crip* explains its use "as a way of capturing the normalizing practices, assumptions, and exclusions that cannot easily be described as directed (exclusively) to physical functioning or appearance" (Kafer 2013, 184; emphasis in original).

2. In Iran, the government of the Islamic Republic mandates schools be segregated based on gender, and it is only at university that men and women can attend classes together, although they are expected to sit in different sides of the classroom. The same segregated system exists in the public transport system where men and women occupy different parts of the bus.

3. To contextualize Masoumeh's life story, it's worth mentioning that under Sharia law, which is the statutory law under the IRI, a woman can only file for divorce if the husband has committed certain crimes/misdemeanors, such as physical beating, heroin addiction, not paying for the household bills, etc. However, men can divorce their wives any time and for whatever reason they please. Furthermore, rape by a spouse is not considered a crime. After divorce, the custody of children above seven years of age is automatically granted to father or the paternal grandfather. These discriminatory custody laws are so effective in bringing abused women to the bargaining table after divorce and convincing them to surrender many of their rights in order to gain custody of their children.

4. I acknowledge that patriarchy is a universal phenomenon that is enacted in myriad forms, from the unrealistic portrayal of women's bodies on magazine covers and the gender wage gap to brutal practices such as Female Genital Mutilation to mandatory hijab/veil/Islamic dress code. However, what I am discussing here is how discrimination against women is facilitated by the rule of law, Sharia law, in this case. Men can legally engage in polygamy, while women can be murdered if seen with another man in bed by their husband, who can then walk with impunity. However, if the reverse happens, the wife will be charged with double homicide. Fathers can murder their daughters with impunity

under the guise of clearing their "honor," which happens in Iran and neighboring countries.

5. *Mehriyeh* or *Mahr* is a gift that the husband makes to the wife, usually at the time the couple get married. In Iran, a woman could ask for her Mahr to be paid to her at any time after marriage. If the husband refuses, the bride can file a lawsuit against him and have him go to jail or pay the Mahr in installments. As you will read in the story, often, Mehriyeh is the only way women ask for their rights under Sharia's family law.

6. This is a typical arrangement in Iran by which men agree to sign the divorce in return for being relieved of paying the mehriyeh, and it shows how discriminatory the divorce law is under Sharia.

7. Only five years of the previous sentence was enforceable.

8. This hadith can be found in: SaHeeH Bukhari: 29, 304, 1052, 1462, 3241, 5197, 5198, 6449, 6546 (FatH Al-Bari's numbering system); SaHeeH Muslim: 80, 885, 907, 2737, 2738 (Abd Al-BaQi's numbering system); Sunan Al-Tarmithi: 635, 2602, 2603, 2613 (Ahmad Shakir's numbering system); Sunan Al-Nasa'i: 1493, 1575 (Abi Ghuda's numbering system); Sunan Ibn Majah: 4003 (Abd Al-BaQi's numbering system); Musnad AHmad: 2087, 2706, 3364, 3376, 3559, 4009, 4027, 4111, 4140, 5321, 6574, 7891, 8645, 14386, 27562, 27567, 19336, 19351, 19415, 19425, 19480, 19484, 20743, 21729, 26508 (IHya' Al Turath's numbering system); Muwata' Malik: 445 (Muqata' Malik's numbering system); Sunan Al-Darimi: 1007 (Alami and Zarmali's numbering system). On the web you might consult these: Sahih Bukhari: Vol. 1:28, 301; Vol. 2:161; Vol. 7:124–126.

9. The way the Sharia courts calculate the bodily harm brings to mind the "soma-technologies of disability measurement" we discussed in Chapter 2 in respect to the disabled veterans' disability, although there is difference between the two. The percentage system in place to measure the severity of the veterans' disability was intended to determine the extent of the benefit the state was expected to provide for the veterans. The calculation of the harm done by acid, on the other hand, is needed so the exact same harm can be done on another person, which rarely takes place if the victim is a woman. The retributive logic behind it is that I will disable you as much as you disabled me, but if they cannot determine the extent of the harm, then you should compensate me financially. What is common between the two is the disabling state that keeps the veterans disabled by not providing adequate care for them, incentivizing them to remain unwell through the percentage system, while facilitating a women's disfigurement by running a gender apartheid system, assuring women's second-class citizenship, and letting acid throwers walk with relative impunity. I am not suggesting that a retributive justice system is fair or that male perpetrators should become disabled. What I argue is that the state facilitates people's becoming and remaining disabled by implementing sexist and ableist bureaucratic policies and enforcing violent laws that facilitate further wounding of both groups.

10. See Chapter 2 for the discussion of chemical injuries that the Iran–Iraq war veterans sustained.

11. The medical apparatus in Iran is pretty much doctor-centered as opposed to patient-centered whereby doctors are at the top of the social hierarchy. They rarely consider it necessary to explain to their patients the procedure they want to perform on them; nor do they often discuss their diagnosis with their patients in detail. Masoumeh mentioned that more often than not, she had to ask the doctors multiple times to get a brief answer about what they were thinking about her case.

12. See Azadi (2020).

13. Iran has a score of 24 this year, with a change of −1 since last year, meaning it ranks 149 out of 180 countries, according to the Transparency Index.

14. The amount is almost equal to $10 USD as of December 2020.

15. For qiṣāṣ to be carried out, the legal medical organization should issue proof certifying that the victim-patient's condition is stable and fixed so the court could issue a verdict concerning the severity of punishment for the perpetrator. This was a joke to Masoumeh and the medical team, because an acid attack means a lifetime battle with burns and an ever-changing body. The survivor has to go through as many as 70 to 100 surgeries, if not more, and the body changes as it ages. It is interesting that the Islamic Criminal Code is based on measuring the damage that has been done. Therefore, the injury should be "measured," and the damage determined, before the qiṣāṣ can be done. How to account for a body that is constantly changing and for a disability that goes through multiple junctures and healing/worsening phases? This is another ableist assumption embedded in Sharia law, among others that we discussed in the previous chapter.

16. This term was coined by the late Stella Young, an Australian disability activist who defined it as objectifying one groups of people, disabled people in this case, as a source of "inspiration" for another group of people, non-disabled people, for them to feel "better" about themselves.

17. Under the IRI, every cultural production including publication of text or multimedia has to go through the Ministry of Culture and Islamic Guidance to be "approved" before it can be mass-produced or published.

18. The IR state doesn't provide reliable statistics regarding the number of honor killings, femicides, child marriages, and acid attacks. This cover-up is part of the propaganda to protect their "holy image" as I explained earlier, because all of those issues are partially facilitated, if not caused by the patriarchal law of Sharia.

19. This discussion first appeared in *Human Rights on the Move* (pp. 139–148) edited by Wendy S. Hesford, Momar K. Ndiaye, & Amy Shuman. See S. Kazemi (2024b), Dislocated Selves, Incarcerated Rights: A Testimony by Sona Kazemi, used with permission of The Ohio State University Press. https://ohiostatepress.org/books/titles/9780814215685.html.

20. Susan Polgar, the Hungarian-born American chair of FIDE's Commission for Women's Chess, said she has "respect" for "cultural differences," even noting the "beautiful choices" of scarves Iranian organizers provided women in the past (Watson, 2016).

21. See Javaid Rehman, the Special Rapporteur on the situation of human rights in the Islamic Republic's most recent report to the UN Human Rights Council.

22. The state was initially anti-East and anti-West since the inception of the IRI, but it has gradually slipped into the arms of China and Russia. At this point, it can be designated pro-Russia and pro-China. There are many reasons for this inclination: one is the destruction of the Soviet Communist-led state, which the IRI saw as atheistic. And the second is the changes in the global political economy and geostrategic competition between the West and Russia/China.

23. This is about $200 USD as of December 2020 and amounts to a significant amount of money in Iran.

24. See Chapter 2.

CONCLUSION

1. I acknowledge that "speaking for" the other person can be interpreted as undermining the other person's self-determination and autonomy, given the historical oppression of disabled and mad people by not recognizing their "capacity" to speak/consent/decide for themselves. Here, I only use the term to amplify through proxy witnessing the lost voices of the dead or mad prisoners who never got a chance to tell their stories.

2. This discussion first appeared in *Routledge Companion to Literature and Social Justice* (pp. 305–314) edited by Masood Ashraf Raja and Nick T. C. Lu. See Kazemi and Karah (2023). Making Sense of the Disability Autonomy and Collectivity Binary: A Review of Informal Disability Justice Pedagogy (IDJP) across Cultures. Used with permission of Taylor & Francis Informa, from *The Routledge Companion to Literature and Social Justice*, edited by Masood Ashraf Raja and Nick T. C. Lu, 2023; permission conveyed through Copyright Clearance Center, Inc. https://www.taylorfrancis.com/chapters/edit/10.4324/9781003246428-27/praxis-sona-kazemi-hemachandran-karah.

3. In this section of the journal, we have been publishing papers and creative works in the authors' first language with an English abstract or full translation into English. See Kazemi & Karah (2021a, 2021b, 2021c).

References

Abbas, S. (2014). *At Freedom's Limit: Islam and the Postcolonial Predicament.* New York: Fordham University Press.
Abdorrahman Boroumand Center. (2017, November 15). *Amputation and Blinding Mohsen Sabzichi: A Victim of Punitive Amputation Speaks.* https://www.iranrights.org/library/document/3352
Abrahamian, E. (1999). *Tortured Confessions: Prison and Public Recantations in Modern Iran.* Berkeley: University of California Press.
Abrahamian, E. (2008). *The History of Modern Iran.* Cambridge: Cambridge University Press.
Abu Toameh, K. (2006, December 2). Gaza Women Warned of Immodesty: Unknown Group Threatens Arab Females Who "Violate Islam's Traditions." *The Jerusalem Post.* https://www.jpost.com/Middle-East/Gaza-women-warned-of-immodesty
Acid Survivors Trust International. (2024, Aug 30). https://www.asti.org.uk/learn/a-world wide-problem
Afkarnews. (2013, November 23). خبرهای خوش در مورد احراز جانبازی و شهادت. Afkarnews. خبرهای خوش در مورد احراز جانبازی و شهادت
Agah, A., Mehr, S., & Parsi, S. (2007). *We Lived to Tell.* Toronto: McGilligan Books.
Agamben, G. (1998). *Homo Sacer: Sovereign Power and Bare Life* (D. Heller-Roazen, Trans.). Redwood City: Stanford University Press.
Agamben, G. (2002). *Remnants of Auschwitz: The Witness and the Archive* (D. Heller-Roazen, Trans.). Zone Books.
Ahmadi, K., Fathi-Ashtiani, A., Zareir, A., Arabnia, A., & Amiri, M. (2006). Sexual Dysfunctions and Marital Adjustment in Veterans with PTSD. *Arch Med Sci,2*(4), 280–287.
Ahmadi, N. (2022, June 25). کشف اختلاس 5 هزارمیلیاردی بنیاد شهید! *Eghtesad News.* https://www.eghtesadnews.com/-بخش-اخبار-سیاسی-57/503945-کشف-اختلاس-هزارمیلیاردی-بنیاد-شهید.
Ahmed, S. (2000). *Strange Encounters: Embodied Others in Post-Coloniality.* London: Routledge.

Akhavan, P. (2017). Is Grassroots Justice a Viable Alternative to Impunity?: The Case of the Iran People's Tribunal. *Human Rights Quarterly, 39*(1), 73–103.

Alatas, S. F. (2003). Academic Dependency and the Global Division of Labour in the Social Sciences. *Current Sociology, 51*(6), 599–613.

Albright, D., & Burkhard, S. (2021). *Iran's Perilous Pursuit of Nuclear Weapons.* Washington DC: Independently published.

Al-Bukhārī, Ṣ. (2019, September). *Ṣaḥīḥ al-Bukhārī Hadith Collecetion.* Center for Muslim-Jewish Engagement. https://web.archive.org/web/20170610045306/http://cmje.usc.edu/religious-texts/hadith/bukhari/062-sbt.php#007.062.002

Alef.ir. (2010, March 30). مشکلات جانبازان زیر 50 درصد. http://alef.ir/vdcew78p.jh8f7i9bbj.html?6wml

Al-Husayni, S. J. (1991). *Al-'Uquba al-Badaniyya fi al-Fiqh al-Islami.* Cairo: Dar al-Shuruq.

Al-Khalil, S. (1990). *Republic of Fear: The Inside Story of Saddam's Iraq.* New York: Pantheon Books.

Althusser, L. (1968). *On the Reproduction of Capitalism: Ideology and Ideological State Apparatuses.* Verso Books.

Althusser, L. (2001). *Lenin and Philosophy and Other Essays* (Ben Brewster, Trans.). New York: Monthly Review Press.

Al-Zuhayli, W. (1989). *Al-Fiqh al-Islami wa-Adillatuh.* Jeddah: Dar Al-Fikr Al-Mouaser.

Amani, E. (2014, November 25). *No Justice for Survivors of Acid Attacks in Iran.* Payvand Iran News. http://www.payvand.com/news/14/nov/1157.html

Amnesty International. (2017). *Annual Report on IRAN 2015/2016.* https://www.amnesty.org/en/countries/middle-east-and-north-africa/iran/

Amnesty International. (2018, January 18). *Iran: Authorities Amputate a Man's Hand in Shocking Act of Cruelty.* https://www.amnesty.org/en/latest/news/2018/01/iran-authorities-amputate-a-mans-hand-in-shocking-act-of-cruelty/

Amnesty International. (2023, December 6). *Iran: "They Violently Raped Me": Sexual Violence Weaponized to Crush Iran's "Woman Life Freedom" Uprising.* https://www.amnesty.org/en/documents/mde13/7480/2023/en/

Anwary, A. (2003). Acid Violence and Medical Care in Bangladesh: Women's Activism as Carework. *Gender and Society, 17*(2), 305–313.

Arendt, H. (2018). *Thinking Without a Banister: Essays in Understanding, 1953–1975* (J. Kohn, Ed.). New York: Schocken Books.

Asad, T. (2003). *Formations of the Secular: Christianity, Islam, Modernity.* Stanford: Stanford University Press.

Austin, A., & Phoenix, L. (2005). The Neoconservative Assault on the Earth: The Environmental Imperialism of the Bush Administration. *Capitalism Nature Socialism, 16*(2), 25–44.

Azadi, P. (2020, August 17). *The Structure of Corruption in Iran.* Stanford Iran 2040 Project. https://iranian-studies.stanford.edu/news/publication-structure-corruption-iran

Bajoghli, N. (2015, July 22). *Iranian Vets Also Push for Nuclear Deal.* Payvand Iran News. http://www.payvand.com/news/15/jul/1140.html

Bakhash, S. (1984). *Reign of the Ayatollahs.* New York: Basic Books.

Bandyopadhyay, M., & Rahman Khan, M. (2003). Loss of Face: Violence against Women in South Asia. In L. R. Bennett, & L. Manderson (Eds.), *Violence Against Women in Asian Societies: Gender Inequality and Technologies of Violence* (pp. 61–75). New York: Routledge.

Bannerji, H. (1995). *Thinking Through: Essays on Feminism, Marxism and Anti-racism.* Toronto: Women's Press.

Bannerji, H. (2005). *Demography and Democracy: Essays on Nationalism, Gender, and Ideology*. Toronto: Canadian Scholars' Press.

Baradaran, M. (1995). *Simple Truth*. Essen: Nima Book.

Bargu, B. (2016). *Starve and Immolate: The Politics of Human Weapons*. New York: Columbia University Press.

Barker, C., & Murray, S. (2010). Disabling Postcolonialism: Global Disability Cultures and Democratic Criticism. *Journal of Literary & Cultural Disability Studies, 4*(3), 219–236.

Barnes, C. (2003). What a Difference a Decade Makes: Reflections on Doing "Emancipitory" Disability Research. *Disability & Society, 18*(1), 3–17.

Barnes, C. (2019). Understanding the Social Model of Disability: Past, Present and Future. In N. Watson & S. Vehmas (Eds.), *Routledge Handbook of Disability* (pp. 12–30). New York: Routledge.

Barnes, C., Mercer, G., & Shakespeare, T. (1999). *Exploring Disability: A Sociological Introduction*. Malden, MA: Polity Press.

Baruah, B., & Siddika, A. (2017, August 13). *Acid Attacks Are on the Rise and Toxic Masculinity Is the Cause*. The Conversation. https://theconversation.com/amp/acid-attacks-are-on-the-rise-and-toxic-masculinity-is-the-cause-82115

Bastani, H. (2019, December 25). 'من و محسن رضایی گفتیم کربلای ۴ فریب بوده تا تبلیغات خنثی شود'. BBC Persian. https://www.bbc.com/persian/iran-features-50911542

Bazna, M. S., & Hatab, T. A. (2005). Disability in the Qur'an the Islamic Alternative to Defining, Viewing, and Relating to Disability. *Journal of Religion, Disability & Health, 9*(1), 5–27.

BBC Persian. (2014, October 17). گزارش‌ها درباره 'اسیدپاشی به زنان' در اصفهان. BBC Persian. https://www.bbc.com/persian/iran/2014/10/141016_u08_isfahan_hijab_attacks

Behravesh, M. (2020, June 26). *Corruption Is a Job Qualification in Today's Iran*. Foreign Policy. https://foreignpolicy.com/2020/06/26/corruption-is-a-job-qualification-in-todays-iran/

Bell, C. (2006). Introducing White Disability Studies A Modest Proposal. In L. Davis (Ed.), *The Disability Studies Reader* (pp. 275–282). New York: Routledge.

Bengtsson, S. (2018). Building a Community: Disability and Identity in the Qur'an. *Scandinavian Journal of Disability Research, 20*(1), 210–218.

Ben-Moshe, L. (2020). *Decarcerating Disability Deinstitutionalization and Prison Abolition*. Minneapolis: University of Minnesota Press.

Bernstein, J. M. (2015). *Torture and Dignity: An Essay on Moral Injury*. Chicago: University of Chicago Press.

Birnbaum, N. (1960). The Sociological Study of Ideology (1940–60): A Trend Report and Bibliography. *Current Sociology, 9*(2), 91–172.

Borsay, A. (2002). History, Power and Identity. In C. Barnes, M. Oliver, & L. Barto (Eds.), *Disability Studies Today* (pp. 98–121). Cambridge: Polity.

Borshchevskaya, A. (2023, March). *Middle East Quarterly*. The Treacherous Triangle of Syria, Iran, and Russia. https://cdn-mef.meforum.org/8b/88/218d45306cd7d8bffb62abc32955/64208.pdf

Bozarslan, H. (2012). Revisiting the Middle East's 1979. *Economy and Society, 41*(4), 558–567.

Brincka, B. (2022). *A Quest for Belonging: Yazidi Culture and Identity Preservation in the Diaspora* [Master's thesis]. Ohio State University. http://rave.ohiolink.edu/etdc/view?acc_num=osu1654547256317513

Britannica, T., Editors of Encyclopedia. (2022, Jan 1). *Iran-Iraq War*. Encyclopedia Britannica. Encyclopedia Britannica. https://www.britannica.com/event/Iran-Iraq-War#ref344821

B'Tselem Report. (1994, July 15). *B'Tselem—The Israeli Information Center for Human Rights in the Occupied Territories*. Wayback Machine. http://www.btselem.org/download/199401_collaboration_suspects_eng.doc

Burke, H. S., Degeneffe, C. E., & Olney, M. F. (2009). A New Disability for Rehabilitation Counselors: Iraq War Veterans. *Journal of Rehabilitation, 75*(3), 5–14.

Burstow, B. (2015). *Psychiatry and the Business of Madness: An Ethical and Epistemological Accounting*. New York: Palgrave Macmillan.

Butler, J. (2006). *Precarious Life: The Powers of Mourning and Violence*. London: Verso Books.

Byman, D. (2008). Iran, Terrorism, and Weapons of Mass Destruction. *Studies in Conflict & Terrorism, 31*(3), 169–181.

Cambodian Acid Survivors Charity. (2010). *Breaking the Silence: Addressing Acid Attacks in Cambodia*. Phnom Penh: Cambodian Acid Survivors Charity.

Carrigan, A. (2010). Postcolonial Disaster, Pacific Nuclearization, and Disabling Environments. *Journal of Literary & Cultural Disability Studies, 4*(3), 255–272.

Chamberlin, J. (1990). The Ex-Patients' Movement: Where We've Been and Where We're Going. *The Journal of Mind and Behavior, 11*(3/4), 323–336.

Charlton, J. I. (1998). *Nothing About Us Without Us: Disability Oppression and Empowerment*. Berkeley: University of California Press.

Chen, M. Y. (2012). *Animacies: Biopolitics, Racial Mattering, and Queer Affect*. Durham: Duke University Press.

Chowdhury, E. H. (2005). Feminist Negotiations: Contesting Narratives of the Campaign against Acid Violence in Bangladesh. *Meridians: Feminism, Race, Transnationalism, 6*(1), 163–192.

Chowdhury, E. H. (2015, January). Rethinking Patriarchy, Culture and Masculinity: Transnational Narratives of Gender Violence and Human Rights Advocacy. *Journal of International Women's Studies, 16*(2), 98–114.

Clare, E. (2017). *Brilliant Imperfection: Grappling with Cure*. Durham: Duke University Press.

CNN. (2022, October 12). *Iranian Official Admits that Student Protesters Are Being Taken to Psychiatric Institutions*. CNN News. https://www.cnn.com/2022/10/12/middleeast/iran-schoolgirls-protests-institutions-intl/index.html#:~:text=Iranian%20official%20admits%20that%20student%20protesters%20are%20being%20taken%20to%20psychiatric%20institutions&text=As%20women%20burn%20headscarves

Connell, R. W. (2005). *Masculinities*. Oakland: University of California Press.

Corruption Watch. (2002, January 31). *Corruption Watch*. Radio Free Europe/Radio Libery. https://www.rferl.org/a/1342396.html

Corruption Perceptions Index. (2024). *Transparency International: The Global Coalition against Corruption*. https://www.transparency.org/en/cpi/2024/index/irn?utm_source=share&utm_medium=email&utm_campaign=share-button

Couser, T. (2012). *Memoir: An Introduction*. Oxfordshire: Oxford University Press.

Crow, L. (1996). Including All of Our Lives: Renewing the Social Model of Disability. In J. Morris (Ed.), *Encounters with Strangers: Feminism and Disability*. London: The Women's Press.

Das, A. K. (2020). The Ethics of Penal Amputation. *Indian Journal of Med Ethics, 2*, 143–148.

Davar, F. (2020, July 8). *Exclusive: Iran Agrees to Be China's Client State for the Next 25 Years*. IranWire. https://iranwire.com/en/features/7275

Davis, L. J. (1995). *Enforcing Normalcy: Disability, Deafness, and the Body*. London: Verso.

Defapress. (2016, June 14). ..خانواده شهید حسن مومنی در قلب تهران مفقودالاثر هستند/ «طوبی» شام ندارد. http://defapress.ir/fa/news/87518/-خانواده-شهید-حسن-مومنی-در-قلب-تهران-مفقودالاثر-هستند-طوبی-شام-ندارد

Dehghanpisheh, B. (2014, November 5). *Acid Attacks in Iran Sharpen Row Over Islamic Dress and Vigilantism*. Reuters. https://www.reuters.com/article/us-iran-politics-women-attacks/acid-attacks-in-iran-sharpen-row-over-islamic-dress-and-vigilantism-idUSKBN0IP15K20141105

Deleuze, G., & Guattari, F. (1987). *A Thousand Plateaus: Capitalism and Schizophrenia* (B. Massumi, Trans.). Minneapolis: University of Minnesota Press.

Dols, M. W. (1983). The Leper in Medieval Islamic Society. *Speculum, 58*(4), 891–916.

Dorey, P. (2010, July–September). A Poverty of Imagination: Blaming the Poor for Inequality. *The Political Quarterly, 81*(3), 333–344.

Dossa, P. (2008). Creating Alternative and Demedicalized Spaces: Testimonial Narrative on Disability, Culture, and Racialization. *Journal of International Women's Studies, 9*(3), 79–101.

DW. (2015, February 23). https://www.dw.com/fa-ir/قربانیان-اسیدپاشی-فراموش-شده-و-بدون-پشتیبانی/a-18275524

Ebert, T. L. (1996). *Lucid Feminism and After: Postmodernism, Desire, and Labor in Late Capitalism*. Ann Arbor: University of Michigan Press.

Edwards, J. O. (2012). *The Peace Education Project*. The Children's Peace Education. http://www.childpeacebooks.org/cpb/Protect/ourProject.php

Engelbrecht, C. (2022, November 19). *Hundreds of Protesters in Iran Blinded by Metal Pellets and Rubber Bullets*. The New York Times. https://www.nytimes.com/2022/11/19/world/asia/iran-protesters-eye-injuries.html

Entekhab.ir. (2016, January 28). برشی از زندگی ۲ جانبازی که می‌گویند فراموش شده‌اند. www.entekhab.ir: http://www.entekhab.ir/fa/news/249823/

Erevelles, N. (2011). *Disability and Difference in Global Contexts: Enabling a Transformative Body Politic*. New York: Palgrave Macmillan.

Esfandiari, G. (2014, October 22). *Hundreds of Iranians Protest Acid Attacks*. Radio Farda. https://www.rferl.org/a/iran-acid-attacks-protests-tehran-isfahan/26650881.html

Esfandiari, G. (2017, September 5). *Firestorm in Iran as Politician's Son Credits "Good Genes" for His Success*. Radio Free Europe/Radio Liberty. https://www.rferl.org/a/iran-aref-son-good-genes-firestorm/28718364.html

Evans, R. (2013, November 10). *Acid Attacks on Men Related to Gang Violence*. BBC World Service. https://www.bbc.com/news/uk-24835910

Fabris, E. (2011). *Tranquil Prisons: Chemical Incarceration under Community Treatment Orders*. Toronto: University of Toronto Press.

Fanon, F. O. (1965). *The Wretched of the Earth*. New York: Grove Press.

Fashnews. (2016, August 3). سر دواندن در کمیسیون به اندازه طول عمر!. Fash News. http://fashnews.ir/fa/news-details/48038/

FATF. (2020, February 21). *FATF Annual Report*. High-Risk Jurisdictions subject to a Call for Action. https://www.fatf-gafi.org/publications/high-risk-and-other-monitored-jurisdictions/documents/call-for-action-february-2020.html

Fledman, A. (1991). *Formations of Violence: The Narrative of the Body and Political Terror in Northern Ireland*. Chicago: University of Chicago Press.

Forti, S. (2015). *New Demons: Rethinking Power and Evil Today* (Z. Hanafi, Ed.). Redwood City: Stanford University Press.

Foucault, M. (1975). *Discipline and Punish: The Birth of the Prison*. Paris: Gallimard.

Foucault, M. (1976). *The History of Sexuality*. New York: Pantheon Books.

Frankel, G. (1990, September 17). *How Saddam Built His War Machine—With Western Help*. Washington Post Foreign Service. http://www.washingtonpost.com/wp-srv/inatl/longterm/iraq/stories/wartech091790.htm

Friedmann, L. W. (1972). Amputations And Prostheses in Primitive Cultures. In *Bulletin of Prosthetics Research*. New York: Department of Medicine and Surgery, Veterans Administration.

Fritsch, K. (2010). Intimate Assemblages: Disability, Intercorporeality, and the Labour of Attendant Care. *Critical Disability Discourses*, (2), 1–13.

Fritsch, K. (2015). Biocapitalism and the Neoliberalization of Disability Relations. *Canadian Journal of Disability Studies*, 4(2), 12–48.

Ghadarkhan, S. (2023, April 21). *Iran Wire*. A Very Dark Year for Iranian Children. https://iranwire.com/en/iran/115758-a-very-dark-year-for-iranian-children/

Ghai, A. (2012). Engaging with Disability with Postcolonial Theory. In D. Goodley, B. Hughes, & L. Davis (Eds.), *Disability and Social Theory: New Developments and Directions* (pp. 271–284). London, New York: Palgrave Macmillan.

Ghaly, M. (2010). *Islam and Disability: Perspectives in Theology and Jurisprudence*. London: Routledge.

Ghamari-Tabrizi, B. (2009). Memory, Mourning, Memorializing on the Victims of Iran-Iraq War, 1980–Present. *Radical History Review*, (105), 106–123.

Ghasseminejad, S., & Nader, A. (2020, April 17). Who Runs Iran's Propaganda Machine Abroad. https://en.radiofarda.com/a/who-runs-iran-s-propaganda-machine-abroad/30561872.html

Gibson, B. E. (2006). Disability, Connectivity and Transgressing the Autonomous Body. *Journal of Medical Humanities*, (27), 187–196.

Gilmore, R. W. (2007). *The Golden Gulag: Prisons, Surplus, Crisis, and Opposition in Globalizing California*. Berkeley: University of California Press.

Gleeson, B. J. (1997). Disability Studies: A Historical Materialist View. *Disability and Society*, 12(2), 179–202.

Golriz, D. (2009). Investment in Social Sciences: Key to a Democratic Iran. *Amsterdam Law Forum*, 2(1), 87–93.

Goodrich, N. H. (2013). A Family Narration of Disability Experience in Iran. *Review of Disability Studies: An International Journal*, 9(2&3), 54–62.

Gordon, M. R., & Engelberg, S. (1989, June 27). *A German Concern Sold Chemicals to Iran, U.S. Says*. New York Times. https://www.nytimes.com/1989/06/27/world/a-german-concern-sold-chemicals-to-iran-us-says.html?mcubz=3

Gorman, R. (2005). *Class Consciousness, Disability, and Social Exclusion: A Relational/Reflexive Analysis of Disability Culture*. Proquest. http://search.proquest.com.myaccess.library.utoronto.ca/docview/305378206/718A6E5DD701489EPQ/1?accountid=14771

Gorman, R. (2016). Disablement in and for Itself: Towards a "Global" Idea of Disability. *Somatechnics*, 6(2), 249–261.

Gorman, R. (2018). *Grieving Empire: Affect Aliens and Aesthetic Catharsis* [paper presented at the Historical Materialism Conference], Montreal.

Goss, J. L. (2019, December 18). *Role of Kapos in Nazi Concentration Camps*. Thoughtco. https://www.thoughtco.com/kapos-prisoner-supervisors-1779685

Gramsci, Antonio. (1971). *Selections from the prison notebooks of Antonio Gramsci*. New York: International Publishers.

Grech, S. (2009). Disability, Poverty and Development: Critical Reflections on the Majority World Debate. *Disability and Society*, 24(6), 771–784.

Grech, S. (2012). Disability and the Majority World: A Neocolonial Approach. In D. Goodley, B. Hughes, & L. Davis (Eds.), *Disability and Social Theory: New Developments and Directions* (pp. 52–69). London: Palgrave Macmillan.

Grech, S., & Soldatic, K. (2016). *Disability in the Global South*. Basel: Springer International Publishing Switzerland.

Haghgou, S. (2014). *Archiving War: Iran-Iraq War and the Construction of "Muslim" Women* [Master's thesis]. University of Toronto.

Haj, F. (1970). *Disability in Antiquity*. New York: Philosophical Library.

Hallajarani, F. (2014). *Redefining Disability in Iran through Entertainment Education*. Submitted to OCAD University in partial fulfillment of the requirements for the degree of Master of Design in Inclusive Design. Toronto: Creative Commons Attribution.

Hammami, R. (1990). Women, the Hijab and the Intifada. *Middle East Report, (164/165)*, 24–78.

Hamshahri Online. (2022, June 27). جزئیات تازه از پرونده اختلاس ۵ هزار میلیاردی در بنیاد شهید.. Hamshahri. https://www.hamshahrionline.ir/news/686496/-جزئیات-تازه-از-پرونده-اختلاس-۵-هزار-میلیاردی-در-بنیاد-شهید

Hande, M. J. (2017). *Disability (and) Care in Late-Capitalist Struggle: A Dialectical Analysis of Toronto-Based Disability (and) Care Activism* (1980863308) [Doctoral dissertation, University of Toronto]. Proquest Dissertations & Theses.

Hardt, M., & Negri, A. (2001). *Empire*. Cambridge: Harvard University Press.

Harris, S., & Aid, M. M. (2013, August 26). *Exclusive: CIA Files Prove America Helped Saddam As He Gassed Iran*. Foreign Policy Magazine. http://foreignpolicy.com/2013/08/26/exclusive-cia-files-prove-america-helped-saddam-as-he-gassed-iran/

Harvey, D. (2004). The "New" Imperialism: Accumulation by Dispossession. *Socialist Register*, (40), 61–86.

Hassanpour, A. (2015). Nation and Nationalism. In S. Mojab (Ed.), *Marxism and Feminism* (pp. 239–258). London: Zed Books.

Hesford, W. S. (2004). Documenting Violations: Rhetorical Witnessing and the Spectacle of Distant Suffering. *Biography*, 104–144.

Hiltermann, J. R. (2007). *A Poisonous Affair: America, Iraq and the Gassing of Halabja*. Cambridge: Cambridge University Press.

Hiro, D. (1991). *The Longest War: The Iran-Iraq Military Conflict*. New York: Routledge.

Hirsch, M. (2012). *The Generation of Postmemory: Writing and Visual Culture After the Holocaust*. New York: Columbia University Press.

hooks, b. (1994). *Teaching to Transgress: Education as Practice of Freedom*. New York: Routledge.

Hooper, J., & Goldenberg, S. (2002, December 17). *Germany Was "Key Supplier" of Saddam Supplier*. The Guardian. https://www.theguardian.com/world/2002/dec/18/iraq.germany

Human Rights Watch. (2018, June). *"I Am Equally Human": Discrimination and Lack of Accessibility for People with Disabilities in Iran*. Human Rights Watch. https://www.hrw.org/report/2018/06/26/i-am-equally-human/discrimination-and-lack-accessibility-people-disabilities-iran

IFP. (2018, July 18). *Gov't Pays Blood Money for 2014 Isfahan Acid Attacks as Culprits Not Caught*. Iran Front Page (IFP). https://ifpnews.com/govt-pays-blood-money-for-2014-isfahan-acid-attacks-as-culprits-not-caught/

The Independent International Fact-Finding Mission on the Islamic Republic of Iran. (2024, March 8). *Iran: Institutional Discrimination Against Women and Girls Enabled Human Rights Violations and Crimes Against Humanity in the Context of Recent Protests, UN Fact-Finding Mission Says*. United Nations. https://www.ohchr.org/en/press-releases/2024/03/iran-institutional-discrimination-against-women-and-girls-enabled-human

Ioannou, F. (2014, October 28). *The Slatest: Iranian Journalists Arrested After Coverage of Acid Attacks Against Women*. SLATE. https://slate.com/news-and-politics/2014/10/acid-attacks-against-iranian-women-protests-in-isfahan-arrest-of-journalists.html

IranPressNewsTube. (2012, June 11). *ضرب و شتم جانبازان در آسایشگاه توسط بنیاد شهید*. YouTube. https://www.youtube.com/watch?v=hntjVAXoj8I

Iran Tribunal. (2012, September 9). *On the Abuse and Mass Killings of Political Prisoners in Iran, 1981–1988*. Iran Human Rights Documentation Center (IHRDC). https://iranhrdc.org/wp-content/uploads/pdf_en/NGO_Reports/report_of_the_truth_commission_122530227.pdf

Iran Wire. (2019, April 9). *The IRGC Commercial and Financial Institutions: Khatam-al-Anbiya Construction Headquarters*. Iran Wire. https://iranwire.com/en/features/65741/

Iran Wire. (2023, April 17). *National Wave of Schoolgirl Poisonings Tortures Iran*. Iran Wire. https://iranwire.com/en/news/115639-national-wave-of-schoolgirl-poisonings-tortures-iran/

Irna. (2014, August 13). *معاون بنیاد شهید و امور ایثارگران: کمیسیون تعیین درصد جانبازی با نگاه مثبت پرونده ها را بررسی می کند*. Islamic Republic News Agency. http://vista.ir/news/16634930

Jack, I. (2017, February 11). *Acid Attacks Were a Stain on Victorian Britain. Now They Are Returning*. The Guardian. https://www.theguardian.com/commentisfree/2017/feb/11/acid-attacks-victorian-britain

Javanonline. (2014, January 15). *اعلام نحوه تعیین درصد جانبازان شیمیایی*. Javanonline.ir. http://javanonline.ir/fa/news/629773/اعلام-نحوه-تعیین-درصد-جانبازان-شیمیایی

Kafer, A. (2013). *Feminist, Queer, Crip*. Bloomington: Indiana University Press.

Kalantari, A. (2007). *Critique of Religious Violence: Essays on Islamism in Iran*. Retrieved from http://abdeekalantari.webspaceforme.net/archive/abdeekalantari/pdfs/Abdee_Kalantari_Book_Critique_of_Religious_Violence.pdf

Kalantari, A. (2016, September 25). *How Do We Understand the "System"? نظام را چگونه بفهمیم*. http://abdeekalantari.webspaceforme.net/archive/kalantari/pdfs/Abdee_Kalantari_Speech_at_Kevorkian.pdf

kaleme.com. (2016, August 15). *خودسوزی یک کارگر جانباز مقابل شهرداری؛ جنگ هنوز ادامه دارد*. kaleme.com. http://www.kaleme.com/1395/05/25/klm-247788/

Kalish, R., & Kimmel, M. (2010). Suicide by Mass Murder: Masculinity, Aggrieved Entitlement, and Rampage School Shootings. *Health Sociology Review, 19*(4), 451–464.

Kaplan, E. A. (2005). *Trauma Culture: The Politics of Terror and Loss in Media and Literature*. New Brunswick: Rutgers University Press.

Karah, H. (2019). Identity Politics and Practices of Exclusionism: A Review Via the Disability Lens. *Journal of Exclusion Studies, 9*(2), 154–163.

Kasaiezadeh, S. H. (2015, October 20). *گزارشی از وضعیت دارو و درمان جانبازان/ گزارشی از وضعیت تأمین داروی جانبازان شیمیایی زیر ۷۰ درصد؛ جانبازانی که در صف دارو شهید می‌شوند!*. Iranian Chemical Victims Blog. http://chemical-victims.blogfa.com/post-1391.aspx

Kasaiezadeh, S. H. (2016, July 23). *گزارش اسفبار از بنیاد شهید کشور آبروی بنیاد شهید باز هم رفت روایت تلخ روزگار یک جانباز دفاع مقدس ساسان همچنان آلکاتراز ایران/ پرونده امنیتی شد!*. Iranian Chemical Weapons Victims Blog. http://chemical-victims.blogfa.com/post-1407.aspx

Kashani-Sabet, F. (2010). The Haves and the Have Nots: A Historical Study of Disability in Modern Iran. *Iranian Studies, 43*(2), 167–196.

Katouzian, H. (2010). *The Persians: Ancient, Mediaeval and Modern Iran*. New Haven: Yale University Press.

Katzman, K. (2006, July 25). *Statement of Kenneth Katzman*. Iran Watch. https://www.iranwatch.org/sites/default/files/us-congress-jec-katzman-iran-energy-072506.pdf

Kazemi, S. (2017). Toward a Conceptualization of Transnational Disability Theory and Praxis: Engaging the Dialectics of Geopolitics, Third World, and Imperialism. *Critical Disability Discourse Journal*, (8), 31–63.

Kazemi, S. (2018). *Toward a Conceptualization of Transnational Disability Theory and Praxis: Entry Point, Iraqi Chemical Attack on Iran* (Order No. 10750974) [Doctoral dissertation, University of Toronto]. ProQuest Dissertations & Theses Global.

Kazemi, S. (2019a). Whose Disability (Studies)? Defetishizing Disablement of the Iranian Survivors of the Iran-Iraq War by (Re)Telling Their Resilient Narratives of Survival. *Canadian Journal of Disability Studies, 6th Edition, 8*(4), 195–220.

Kazemi, S. (2019b). Disabling Power of Class and Ideology: Analyzing War Injury through the Transnational Disability Theory and Praxis. *Disability Studies Quarterly, 39*(3), 1–20.

Kazemi, S. (2024a). Fetishization of the Disabled War Veterans in Iran through the Ideological Construction of "Living Martyrs." *Review of Disability Studies: An International Journal, 18*(4), 1–41

Kazemi, S. (2024b). Dislocated Selves, Incarcerated Rights: A Testimony by Sona Kazemi. In W. S. Hesford, M. K. Ndiaye, & A. Shuman (Eds.), *Human Rights on the Move* (pp. 139–148). Columbus: The Ohio State University Press. https://ohiostatepress.org/books/titles/9780814215685.html

Kazemi, S., Gold, E., Karah, H., & Hande, M. J. (2025). Transnational Disability Praxis: Archiving Survival, Resistance, and Resilience Amidst Ongoing Emergencies. In J. Barclay, & S. Stefanie Hunt-Kennedy (Eds.), *Cripping the Archives: Disability, History, and Power* (pp. 357–374). Chicago: University of Illinois Press.

Kazemi, S., & Karah, H. (2021a). Disability and Multilingualism: A Global Perspective. *Review of Disability: An International Journal, 16*(2–4), Editorial. https://www.rdsjournal.org/index.php/journal/article/view/1087

Kazemi, S., & Karah, H. (2021b). Disability and Multilingualism: A Global Perspective. *Review of Disability: An International Journal, 17*(1), Editorial. https://www.rdsjournal.org/index.php/journal/article/view/1056

Kazemi, S., & Karah, H. (2021c). Disability and Multilingualism: A Global Perspective. *Review of Disability: An International Journal, 17*(2), Editorial. https://www.rdsjournal.org/index.php/journal/article/view/1087

Kazemi, S., & Karah, H. (2022). "Madness As Response-Ability Against State Terror: A Case Study From Iranian Revolution." In M. H. Rioux, A. Buettgen, E. Zubrow, & J. Viera (Eds.), *Handbook of Disability*, (pp. 1–19). Singapore: Springer. https://doi.org/10.1007/978-981-16-1278-7_40-1

Kazemi, S., & Karah, H. (2023). Making Sense of the Disability Autonomy and Collectivity Binary: A Review of Informal Disability Justice Pedagogy (IDJP) across Cultures. In M. A. Raja, & N. T. Lu (Eds.), *The Routledge Companion to Literature and Social Justice* (pp. 305-314). London: Routledge.

Kazemi, Sona, & Karah, Hemachandran (invited, forthcoming). Cultural Imperialism and Life of the Mind: A Review of Cerebral Bias in Humanities Pedagogy and Beyond. In R. Gorman & B. Le François (Eds.), *Palgrave Encyclopedia of Critical Perspectives in Mental Health*. Palgrave MacMillan.

Kermani, H., & Tale'i, J. (2011, July 5). *An Interview with Ali Alfoneh*. Deutsche Welle. https://www.dw.com/fa-ir/٨%DB%B0-اسکله/a-6564896-غیرمجاز-زیر-نظر-برادران-قاچاقچی

Khalaji, M. (2014, June 11). *Ailing Official Highlights Concentration of Power in Iran*. The Washington Institute. https://www.washingtoninstitute.org/policy-analysis/view/ill-official-highlights-concentration-of-power-in-iran

Khorrami, M. M. (2015). *Literary Subterfuge and Contemporary Persian Fiction: Who Writes Iran? Mehdi Khorrami.* New York: Routledge.

Khoshnood, A. (2019). Poverty in Iran: A Critical Analysis. *Middle East Policy, 26*(1), 60–76.

Kim, E. (2011). "Heaven for Disabled People": Nationalism and International Human Rights Imagery. *Disability & Society, 26*(1), 93–106.

Kim, E. (2017). *Curative Violence: Rehabilitating Disability, Gender, and Sexuality in Modern Korea.* Durham, NC: Duke University Press.

Kirkup, J. (2007). *A History of Limb Amputation.* London: Springer-Verlag.

Kolářová, K. (2015). "Grandpa Lives in Paradise Now": Biological Precarity and the Global Economy of Debility. *Feminist Review,* (111), 75–87.

Konkle, M. (2008). Indigenous Ownership and the Emergence of U.S. Liberal Imperialism. *American Indian Quarterly, 32*(3), 297–325.

Korkman, Z. K. (2023). (Mis)Translations of the Critiques of Anti-Muslim Racism and the Repercussions for Transnational Feminist Solidarities. *Meridians: Feminism, Race, Transnationalism, 22*(2), 267–296.

Kupers, T. A. (1999). *Prison Madness: The Mental Health Crisis Behind Bars and What We Must Do About It.* Oxford: San Francisco.

Kupers, T. A. (2006). How to Create Madness in Prison. In D. Jones (Ed.), *Humane Prisons* (pp. 5–19). Oxford: Radcliffe Publishing.

Lansdown, R. (1997). *Visibly Different: Coping with Disfigurement.* Oxfordshire: Taylor & Francis.

Lawson, J. (1951). *History of North Carolina.* Richmond: Garrett & Massie.

Lenin, V. I. (1916, January). *Imperialism, the Highest Stage of Capitalism.* Marxists Internet Archive. https://www.marxists.org/archive/lenin/works/1916/imp-hsc/

Levi, Primo (1959). *If This Is a Man* (S. Woolf, Trans.). New York: The Orion Press.

Levi, Primo (1989). *The Drowned and the Saved* (R. Rosenthal, Trans.). New York: Random House.

Lifton, R. J. (1989). *Thought Reform and the Psychology of Totalism: A Study of "Brainwashing" in China.* Chapel Hill: University of North Carolina Press.

Littlewood, J. (2006, December 3). *Investigating Allegations of CBW Use: Reviving the UN Secretary-General's Mechanism.* Canadian Centre for Treaty Compliance. http://carleton.ca/npsia/wp-content/uploads/CC3.pdf

Makaremi, C. (2015). State Violence and Death Politics in Post-Revolutionary Iran. In A. Élisabeth, & D. Jean-Marc (Eds.), *Destruction and Human Remains: Disposal and Concealment in Genocide and Mass Violence* (pp. 180–198). Oxford: University Press Scholarship.

Maloney, S. (2015). *Iran's Political Economy since the Revolution.* Cambridge: Cambridge University Press.

Mannan, A., Ghani, S., Sen, S., Clarke, A., & Butler, P. (2004). The Problem of Acid Violence in Bangladesh. *The Journal of Surgery, 2*(1), 39–44.

Marx, K. (1845/1976). *Theses on Feuerbach.* Peking: Foreign Language Press.

Marx, K. (1852). *The Eighteenth Brumaire of Louis Bonaparte.* Marx Engels Archive. https://www.marxists.org/archive/marx/works/1852/18th-brumaire/

Marx, K., & Engels, F. (1932/1998). *The German Ideology, Including Theses on Feuerbach.* New York: Prometheus Books.

Mavroforou, A., Malizos, K., Karachalios, T., Chatzitheofilou, K., & Giannoukas, A. D. (2014). Punitive Limb Amputation. *Clinical Orthopaedics and Related Research, 472*(10), 3102–3106.

Mayer, A. E. (2000). A "Benign" "Apartheid": How Gender "Apartheid" Has Been Rationalized. *UCLA Journal of International Law and Foreign Affairs, 5*(2), 237–338.
McClintock, A. (1995). *Imperial Leather: Race, Gender, and Sexuality in the Colonial Contest.* Oxfordshire: Routledge.
McGovern, R. (2013, August 26). *CIA Helped Iraq Use Chemical Weapons on Iran.* RT America, YouTube. https://www.youtube.com/watch?v=Hk35suofbYQ
McGrouther, D. A. (1997). Facial Disfigurement: The Last Bastion of Discrimination. *BMJ: British Medical Journal,* (314), 991–992.
McKittrick, K. (2013). Plantation Futures. *Small Axe, 17*(3), 1–15.
McLaren, P., & Farahmandpur, R. (2001). Teaching Against Globalization and the New Imperialism: Toward a Revolutionary Pedagogy. *Journal of Teacher Education, 52*(2), 136–150.
McRuer, R. (2006). *Crip Theory: Cultural Signs of Queerness and Disability.* New York: New York University Press.
McRuer, R. (2010). Disability Nationalism in Crip Times. *Journal of Literary & Cultural Disability Studies, 4*(2), 163–178.
McRuer, R. (2018). *Crip Times: Disability, Globalization, and Resistance.* New York: New York University Press.
Meekosha, H. (2011). Decolonising Disability: Thinking and Acting Globally. *Disability and Society, 26*(6), 667–682.
Meekosha, H., & Soldatic, K. (2011). Human Rights and the Global South: the Case of Disability. *Third World Quarterly, 32*(8), 1383–1398.
MehrNews. (2012, September 23). *Narrating the Periods After the War/3 Million Dead and Disabled Resulting from 8 Years of War.* Mehr News Agency. http://www.mehrnews.com/news/1701485/Narrating the periods after the war/3 Million Dead and Disabled Resulting From 8 Years of War
Mesdaghi, I. (2006). *Neither Life Nor Death, Nazistan Na Marg, Prison Memoirs.* Stockholm: Alfabeth Maxima Publication.
Mesdaghi, I. (2012, November 3). شهادت ایرج مصداقی در ایران تریبونال. *Testimony of Iraj Mesdaghi in the Iranian People's Tribunal.* YouTube. https://www.youtube.com/watch?v=6ZqWXVJgBw
Meyer, S. (2014). The Social Model of Disability Under the Shadow of the Revolution: Ex-combatants Negotiating Identity in Nicaragua. *Qual Sociol,* (37), 403–424.
Meyer, W. J., Blakeney, P., Russell, W., Thomas, C., Robert, R., Berniger, F., & Holzer, C. (2004). Psychological Problems Reported by Young Adults Who Were Burned as Children. *The Journal of Burn Care & Rehabilitation, 25*(1), 98–106.
Middle East Eye and Agencies. (2015, February 14). *Acid Attacks on Iranian Women Linked to "Bad Hijab."* Midde East Eye. https://www.middleeasteye.net/news/acid-attacks-iranian-women-linked-bad-hijab
Mikaberidze, A. (2011). *Conflict and Conquest in the Islamic World: A Historical Encyclopedia.* Santa Barbara, California: ABC-CLIO.
Milani, A. (2012). *The Shah.* New York: St. Martin's Griffin.
Milani, A. (2018, February 23). *Iran Democracy Project, Hoover Institution, Stanford University.* YouTube. https://www.youtube.com/watch?v=Zh0uO0clpGA&feature=youtu.be&t=946&ab_channel=WorldAffairs
Miles, M. (2002). Disability in an Eastern Religious Context Historical Perspectives. *Journal of Religion, Disability & Health, 10*(1), 53–76.
Milton-Edwards, B., & Farrell, S. (2013). *Hamas: The Islamic Resistance Movement.* Hoboken: John Wiley & Sons.

Mingus, M. (2010, January 22). *Interdependency (Exerpts from Several Talks).* Leaving Evidence. https://leavingevidence.wordpress.com/2010/01/22/interdependency-exerpts-from-several-talks/

Mingus, M. (2011, May 5). *Access Intimacy: The Missing Link.* Leaveing Evidence. https://leavingevidence.wordpress.com/2011/05/05/access-intimacy-the-missing-link/

Mitchell, D. T., & Snyder, S. L. (2015). *The Biopolitics of Disability Neoliberalism, Ablenationalism, and Peripheral Embodiment.* Ann Arbour: University of Michigan Press.

Moghissi, Haideh. 1999. *Feminism and Islamic Fundamentalism: The Limits of Postmodern Analysis.* London: Zed Books.

Mojab, S. (2001). Theorizing the Politics of "Islamic Feminism." *Feminist Review, 69*(1), 124–146.

Mojab, S. (2015). *Marxism and Feminism.* London: Zed Books.

Mojab, S., & Gorman, R. (2007). Dispersed Nationalism: War, Diaspora and Kurdish Women's Organizing. *Journal of Middle East Women Studies, 3*(1), 58–86.

Mojab, S., & Taber, N. (2015, March). Memoir Pedagogy: Gender Narratives of Violence and Survival. *The Canadian Journal for the Study of Adult Education, 27*(2), 31–45.

Montazeri, H. A. (2000). خاطرات آیت الله حسینعلی منتظری: *khaterat Ayatollah Hosseinali Montazeri.* Retrieved from https://amontazeri.com/book/khaterat/volume-2/1164

Moore, A., & Kornblet, S. (2011). *Advancing the Rights of Persons with Disabilities: A US–Iran Dialogue on Law, Policy, and Advocacy.* Washington: The Henry L. Stimson Center.

Morris, J. (1991). *Pride against Prejudice: A Personal Politics of Disability.* London: Women's Press.

Murray, W., & Woods, K. (2014). *The Iran–Iraq War: A Military and Strategic History.* Cambridge: Cambridge University Press.

Najafi Mehri, S., Ebadi, A., Heravi Karimooi, M., Foroughan, M., & Sahraei, H. (2012). Experiences Living with Fatigue in Iranian Veterans Chemically Injured by Sulfur Mustard Gas: A Phenomenological Study. *Asian Nursing Research, 6*(4), 181–186.

Namehnews.ir. (2013, March 4). نگاهی به تعداد و دلایل خودکشی جانبازان.. Nameh News. http://namehnews.ir/fa/news/27648/

Nasr, E. A. (2014, November 12). جانبازان اعصاب و روان.. Bachehshemroon. http://anasr121.mihanblog.com/post/1250

Nice, G. (2013, December 10). *The Iran Tribunal—Professor Sir Geoffrey Nice.* YouTube. https://www.youtube.com/watch?v=upp4wMgNH0g&list=PLGk1hG9AHaOYaZV0EWcUrOgeQQo9-xU8N&index=38

NSA Archives. (2015, July 1). *The National Security Archive's Collection of Electronic Briefing Books (EBBs).* Electronic Briefing Books. http://nsarchive.gwu.edu/NSAEBB/index.html

O'Brien, R. (2005). *Bodies in Revolt: Gender Disability, and a Workplace Ethics of Care.* New York: Routledge.

O'Connor. (1989). Political Economy of Ecology of Socialism and Capitalism. *Capitalism Nature Socialism, 1*(3), 93–105.

Oftedal, P. (1984). *Genetic Damage Following Nuclear War: In Effects of Nuclear War on Health and Health Services.* World Health Organization. http://apps.who.int/iris/bitstream/10665/39199/1/9241561092_(p1-p82).pdf

Oliffe et al., J. L. (2015). Men, Masculinities, and Murder-Suicide. *American Journal of Men's Health, 9*(6), 473–485.

Oliver, M. (1983). *The Individual and Social Model of Disability.* London: UPSIA.

Oliver, M. (1990). *The Politics of Disablement: A Sociological Approach.* New York: St. Martin's Press.

Oliver, M., & Barnes, C. (2012). Back to the Future: The World Report on Disability. *Disability & Society, 27*(4), 575–579.

Oster, S. B. (2014). Impossible Holocaust Metaphors: The Muselmann. *Prooftexts, 34*(3), 302–348.

Packard, F. (1963). *History of Medicine in the United States*. New York: Hafner.

Pandolfo, S. (2018). *Knot of the Soul: Madness, Psychoanalysis, Islam*. Chicago: University of Chicago Press.

Parsipour, S. (1995). *Prison Memoir*. Stokholm: Baran Books.

Parvaz, N. (2002). *Under the Four O'clock's Bush: Zire Boute Laleh Abbasi*. London: Nasim Books.

Pearlman, L. A., & Saakvitne, K. W. (1995). *Trauma and the Therapist: Countertransference and Vicarious Traumatization in Psychotherapy with Incest Survivors*. New York: Norton.

Perlin, M. L. (1993). On Sanism. *SMU Law Review, 46*(2), 373–408.

Pervez, I. (1990). Islamic Banking. *Arab Law Quarterly, 5*(4), 259–281.

Phillips, J. W. (2006). Agencement/Assemblage. *Theory, Culture & Society, 23*(2–3), 108–109.

Phythian, M. (1997). *Arming Iraq: How the U.S. and Britain Secretly Built Saddam's War Machine*. Boston: Northeastern University Press.

Porges, S. W. (2011). *The Polyvagal Theory: Neurophysiological Foundations of Emotions, Attachment, Communication, and Self-regulation*. New York: W. W. Norton & Company.

Price, M. (2015). The Bodymind Problem and the Possibilities of Pain. *Hypatia, 30*(1), 268–284.

Priestley, M. (2001). *Disability and the Life Course Global Perspectives*. Cambridge: Cambridge University Press.

Puar, J. K. (2009). Prognosis Time: Towards a Geopolitics of Affect, Debility and Capacity. *Women & Performance: A Journal of Feminist Theory, 19*(2), 161–172.

Puar, J. K. (2017). *The Right to Maim: Debility, Capacity, Disability*. Durham: Duke University Press.

Quayson, A. (2012). *Cambridge History of Postcolonial Literature*. Cambridge: Cambridge University Press.

Quds Online. (2015). گزارش « قدس» از وضعیت تأمین داروی جانبازان شیمیایی زیر ۷۰ درصد؛ جانبازانی که در صف دارو شهید می‌شوند!. Quds Online. http://qudsonline.ir/news/317068/

Qutami, M., & Qutami, S. (2013). Exporting Democracy and Liberating Women: An Examination of a Debilitating Rhetoric. *English Language and Literature Studies, 3*(1), 122–133.

Radstone, S., & Schwarz, B. (2010). *Memory: Histories, Theories, Debates*. New York: Fordham University Press. http://www.jstor.org/stable/j.ctt1c999bq.

Raghfar, H. (2023, May 20). *At Least Half of Iran Below Poverty Line: Expert Economist*. Retrieved from https://www.iranintl.com/en/202305202022

Rajaee, F. (1997). *Iranian Perspectives on the Iran-Iraq War*. Gainesville: University of Florida.

Rajan, D. (2019). *A Pedagogy of Solidarity: Indigenous, Refugee Women and Women with Intellectual and Psychosocial Disabilities and Structural Violence* [Doctoral dissertation]. University of Toronto.

Rankin, S. K. (2019). Punishing Homelessness. *New Criminal Law Review, 22*(1), 99–135.

Rautman, M. L. (2006). *Daily Life in the Byzantine Empire*. Santa Barbara: Greenwood Publishing Group.

Rejali, D. (1993). *Torture and Modernity: Self, Society, and State in Modern Iran*. Boulder: Westview Press.

Rejali, D. (2007). *Torture and Democracy*. Princeton: Princeton University Press.

Rhodes, L. A. (2004). *Total Confinement: Madness and Reason in the Maximum Security Prison.* Oakland: University of California Press.

Ridley, R. T. (1986). To Be Taken with a Pinch of Salt: The Destruction of Carthage. *Classical Philology, 81*(2), 140–146.

Rispler-Chaim, V. (2007). *Disability in Islamic Law.* Dordrecht: Springer.

Robinson, E. (1997). Psychological Research on Visible Difference in Adults. In R. Lansdown, N. Rumsey, E. Bradbury, A. Carr, J. Partridge (Eds.), *Visibly Different: Coping with Disfigurement* (chap. 16). London: Butterworth- Heineman.

Robinson, J. P., & Goldblat, J. (1984, May). *Chemical Warfare in the Iran-Iraq War 1980–1988 SIPRI (Stockholm International Peace Research Institute) Fact Sheet.* Iran Chamber Society. http://www.iranchamber.com/history/articles/chemical_warfare_iran_iraq_war.php#sthash.x5VD8tIT.AqMyJREz.dpuf

Rothschild, B. (2000). *The Body Remembers: The Psychophysiology of Trauma and Trauma Treatment.* New York: Norton & Company.

Rumer, E. (2021, May 22). *Russia in the Middle East: Jack of all Trades, Master of None.* Carnegie Endowment for International Peace. https://carnegieendowment.org/files/WP-Rumer-MiddleEast.pdf

Russell, M., & Malhotra, R. (2002). Capitalism and Disability. *Socialist Register,* (38), 211–229.

Sadjadpour, K. (2019, October 3). *Iranian Supreme Leader Ali Khamenei Is One Despot Trump Might Not Win Over.* Time Magazine. https://time.com/5691642/iran-supreme-leader-ali-khamenei-trump/

Said, E. (1978). *Orientalism.* Vintage: Vintage Books.

Sakhi, S. (2014). *Ethics and the Resistant Subject Levinas, Foucault, Marx* [Doctoral dissertation, York University]. Proquest Dissertation and Theses. https://yorkspace.library.yorku.ca/server/api/core/bitstreams/85941bc7-fc88-4fd5-b817-84e7948db199/content

Sakhi, S. (2017). Ethical–Political Praxis: Social Justice and the Resistant Subject in Iran. In P. Vahabzadeh (Ed.), *Iran's Struggles for Social Justice: Economics, Agency, Justice, Activism* (pp. 145–164). London: Palgrave Macmillan.

Samarasinha, L. L. (2018). *Dreaming Disability Justice.* Vancouver, BC: Arsenal Pulp Press.

Samii, B. (2005, April 5). *Analysis: Corruption Becomes an Issue in Iran's Presidential Campaign.* Radio Farda. https://www.rferl.org/a/1058286.html

Samimi, M. (2014, September 29). *Iran Pulse: Iran's Disabled Veterans Lack Services, Access.* Al-Monitor. http://www.al-monitor.com/pulse/originals/2014/09/iran-veterans-iraq-war-disability.html

Schaffer, K., & Smith, S. (2004). *Human Rights and Narrated Lives: The Ethics of Recognition.* London: Palgrave Macmillan.

Schalk, S. (2018). *Bodyminds Reimagined: (Dis)ability, Race, and Gender in Black Women's Speculative Fiction.* Durham: Duke University Press.

Schalk, S., & Kim, J. B. (2020). Integrating Race, Transforming Feminist Disability Studies. *Signs: Journal of Women in Culture and Society, 46*(1), 31–56.

Shahidian, H. (2002). *Women in Iran: Gender Politics and the Islamic Republic.* Connecticut: Greenwood Press.

Shamlu, A. (2002). *Born upon the Dark Spear: Selected Poems of Ahmad Shamlu.* (T. B. Mohaghegh, Ed.) Contra Mundum.

Shickluna, D. M. (2020). *Remembering as Praxis: Reconceptualizing Structural and State-Sanctioned Violence, Oppression, and Trauma Through Radical Survival Narrative Pedagogy* (Order No. 28093657) [Doctoral dissertation, University of Toronto]. https://tspace

.library.utoronto.ca/bitstream/1807/103221/1/Shickluna_Dawn_Marie_202011_PhD_thesis.pdf

Shildrick, M. (2009). *Dangerous Discourses of Disability, Subjectivity and Sexuality*. New York: Palgrave Macmillan.

Shimrat, I. (1997). *Call Me Crazy: Stories from the Mad Movement*. Halifax: Press Gang Pub.

Shohadayeiran. (2016, August 3). "نماینده مجلس" به یک "جانباز" واکنش کوبنده "ادعای سهم خواهی می کنی؟!". Shohaday-e-Iran. http://shohadayeiran.com/fa/news/124504/-نماینده-یک-به-جانباز-کوبنده-واکنش مجلس-عکس

Sibley, N. (2022, October). *Policy Memo: How to Target Iran's Kleptocracy*. Hudson Institute. https://s3.amazonaws.com/media.hudson.org/How+to+Target+Iran's+Kleptocracy.pdf

Siddika, A., & Baruah, B. (2018). Can Understanding Phenomenology and Human Capabilities Help Us Address Acid Violence? *South Asia: Journal of South Asian Studies*, *41*(1), 153–172.

Sins Invalid. (2015, Sep 17). *10 Principles of Disability Justice*. Retrieved from https://www.sinsinvalid.org/blog/10-principles-of-disability-justice

Sluka, J. A. (2000). *Death Squad: The Anthropology of State Terror*. Philadelphia: University of Pennsylvania Press.

Sly, L., & Ramadan, A. (2014, February 28). *Syrian Extremists Amputated a Man's Hand and Live-Tweeted It*. Washington Post. https://www.washingtonpost.com/news/worldviews/wp/2014/02/28/syrian-extremists-amputated-a-mans-hand-and-live-tweeted-it/

Soldatic, K. (2014). Transnationalising Disability Studies: Rights, Justice, and Impairment. *Disability Studies Quarterly*, *34*(2), 1041–5718.

Soleiman Nia, A. (2012, December 29). فراموشی؛ روایتی از وضعیت جانبازان اعصاب و روان . YouTube. https://www.youtube.com/watch?v=5rj0UsUz-CI

Souryal, S. S., Potts, D. W., & Alobied, A. I. (1994). The Penalty of Hand Amputation for Theft in Islamic Justice. *Journal of Criminal Justice*, *22*(3), 249–265.

Spillers, H. J. (1987). Mama's Baby, Papa's Maybe: An American Grammar Book. *Diacritics: A Review of Contemporary Criticism*, *17*(2), 65–81.

Spivak, G. C. (1999). *A Critique of Postcolonial Reason: Toward a History of the Vanishing Present*. Cambridge: Harvard University Press.

Stecklow, S., Dehghanpisheh, B., & Torbati, Y. (2013, November 11). *Khamenei Controls Massive Financial Empire Built on Property Seizures*. Reuters Investigates. https://www.reuters.com/investigates/iran/#article/part1

Steinmetz, G. (2005). Return to Empire: The New U.S. Imperialism in Comparative Historical Perspective. *Sociological Theory*, *23*(4), 339–367.

Stone, D. A. (1984). *The Disabled State*. Philadelphia: Temple University Press.

Swanson, J. (2002). Acid Attacks: Bangladesh's Efforts to Stop the Violence. *Harvard. Health Policy Review Archives* *3*(1), 122–128.

tabnak.ir. (2009, July 29). . . . ؟ به دلیل جانباز دیگر یک خودسوزی؛ افتاد اتفاق قم شهر در/. www.tabnak.ir. http://www.tabnak.ir/fa/pages/?cid=57457

Talebi, S. (2011). *Ghosts of Revolution: Rekindled Memories of Imprisonment in Iran*. Stanford: Stanford University Press.

Tam, L. (2012). *Governing through Competency: Race, Pathologization, and the Limits of Mental Health Outreach*. Department of Sociology and Equity Studies in Education. Toronto: University of Toronto.

Tamim News. (2020, October 19). آیا گرداندن مجرمان در شهر قانونی است؟ .. Retrieved from https://www.tamimkhabar.ir/fa/news/42799/؟است-قانونی-شهر-در-مجرمان-گرداندن-آیا

Tarantelli, C. B. (2003). Life within Death: Towards a Metapsychology of Catastrophic Psychic Trauma. *International Journal of Psychoanalysis, 84*(4), 915–928.

Tavallaii, S. A., Ghanei, M., Assari, S., Dezfuli Nezhad, L., & Habibi, M. (2006). Risk Factors Correlated to Suicide in Deceased Iranian Veterans. *Journal Of Military Medicine, 8*(2), 143–148.

Tavana, M. H. (2014). Three Decades of Islamic Criminal Law Legislation in Iran: A Legislative History Analysis with Emphasis on the Amendments of the 2013 Islamic Penal Code. *EJIMEL: Electronic Journal of Islamic and Middle Eastern Law*, (2), 24–38.

Tehran News. (2019). .. فوق لاکچری ترین زندان دنیا در هتل اوین تهران APARAT. https://www.aparat.com/v/d31mxi6

Tehran Times. (2016, December 29). *Iran's President Rouhani Links "Grave-Sleeping" to Corruption*. Payvand Iran News. http://www.payvand.com/news/16/dec/1172.html

Thomas, C. (1999). *Female Forms: Experiencing and Understanding Disability*. Philadelphia, PA: Open University Press.

Timmerman, K. R. (1991). *The Death Lobby: How the West Armed Iraq*. Boston: Houghton Mifflin.

Titchkosky, T. (2005). Disability in the News: A Reconsideration of Reading. *Disability & Society, 20*(6), 655–668.

Titchkosky, T. (2008). "To Pee or not to Pee"? Ordinary Talk about Extraordinary Exclusions in a University Environment. *Canadian Journal of Sociology, 33*(1), 37–61.

Torbat, A. E. (2013, March 6). *Corruption in Iran: Clerics Plan to Hang Businessmen*. Wayback Machine. https://web.archive.org/web/20130306001653/http://www.informationclearinghouse.info/article34145.htm

Tucker, R. C. (1978). *The Marx-Engels Reader*. New York: Norton.

UNHCR. (2023, September 1). *Iran's Proposed Hijab Law Could Amount to "Gender Apartheid": UN Experts*. United Nations. https://www.ohchr.org/en/press-releases/2023/09/irans-proposed-hijab-law-could-amount-gender-apartheid-un-experts

United Nations. (1987, June). Peace and Security. Security Council Resolutions. http://www.un.org/en/sc/documents/resolutions/

United Nations. (2003, March 6). *Unresolved Disarmament Issues: Iraq's Proscribed Weapons Programs*. UNMOVIC. http://www.un.org/depts/unmovic/documents/UNMOVIC%20UDI%20Working%20Document%206%20March%2003.pdf

United Nations. (2004, September). *United Nations Handbook on Practical Anti-Corruption Measures for Prosecutors and Investigators*. Retrieved from https://www.unodc.org/documents/treaties/corruption/Handbook.pdf

United Nations. (2007, October 24). *Office of the UN Special Rapporteur on Disability: War, Armed Conflict and Disability: Challenges, Statistics, Facts*. Office of the UN Special Rapporteur on Disability. http://docslide.us/documents/war-armed-conflict-disability-ch-allenges-statistics-facts-office-of-the.html

Veisi, M. (2020, October 4). *The Friday Imam, the Head of the Suppression Network*. Iran International. https://iranintl.com/ای-در-راس-C8%80%2Eایران/یوسف-طباطبایی-نژاد؛-امام-جمعه-شبکه-سرکوب-استانی-اصفهان

Wacquant, L. (2009). *Punishing the Poor: The Neoliberal Government of Social Insecurity*. Durham: Duke University Press.

Walcott, J., & Mayer, J. (1986, November 28). *Declassified CIA documents, Wall Street Journal*. CIA. https://www.cia.gov/readingroom/docs/CIA-RDP90-00965R000504340006-3.pdf

Ward, S. R. (2014). *Immortal: A Military History of Iran and Its Armed Forces*. Washington DC: Georgetown University Press.

Watson, L. (2016, September 29). *Female Chess Players Forced to Wear Hijab as Governing Body Awards World Championship to Iran*. Telegraph. https://www.telegraph.co.uk/news/2016/09/29/female-chess-players-accuse-governing-body-of-sex-discrimination/

Welsh, J. (2009). *"It Was Like Burning in Hell": A Comparative Exploration of Acid Attack Violence* [Master's thesis], University of North Carolina at Chapel Hill.

WHO. (2011). *World Report on Disability 2011*. Retrieved December 16, 2016, from World Health Organization: http://www.who.int/disabilities/world_report/2011/en/

Wiesel, E. (2008). *The Night Trilogy: Night, Dawn, Day*. Hill and Wang.

Wolpé, S. (2007). *Sin: Selected Poems of Forugh Farrokhzad*. University of Arkansas Press. https://doi.org/10.2307/j.ctt1ffjm51

Wolpé, S. (2018). *Shole Wolpé's Official Website*. Retrieved from https://www.sholehwolpe.com/shamlou

World Population Review. (2024). *Crime Rate by Country 2024*. Retrieved from https://worldpopulationreview.com/country-rankings/crime-rate-by-country

Wright, R. (2014, January 20). *Iran Still Haunted and Influenced by Chemical Weapons Attacks*. The Time. http://world.time.com/2014/01/20/iran-still-haunted-and-influenced-by-chemical-weapons-attacks/

Wright, R., & Branigin, W. (2007, September 23). *Ahmadinejad Met with Protests, Criticism at Columbia University*. Washington Post. https://www.washingtonpost.com/archive/business/technology/2007/09/24/ahmadinejad-met-with-protests-criticism-at-columbia-university/14f8dd1e-096a-4dbf-9fde-fd79ecdf46a3/

Yousaf, F. N., & Purkayastha, B. (2015). Beyond Saving Faces: Survivors of Acid Attacks in Pakistan. *Women's Studies International Forum*, (54), 11–19.

Zarabadi, L. (2023). (Mis)translating the Life Stories of the "Heroes of the Year 2022: Women of Iran." *International Journal of Middle East Studies*, 55(4), 759–767.

Zubaida, S. (1995). Is There a Muslim Society? Ernest Gellner's Sociology of Islam. *Economy and Society*, [24(2)], 151–188.

Index

Abbas, Sadia, 16, 18
Abdorrahman Boroumand Center, 99, 111–113
Able-bodiedness, 55, 132, 148, 168
Ableism, 22, 29, 36, 81, 89, 100, 127–130, 146, 147, 171, 177, 182; ableist normative culture, 179; ableist society, 79, 165, 168, 170; ableist social norms, 27; ableist tradition, 120
Abrahamian, Ervand, 44, 57, 66, 70, 76
Access, 26, 33, 93–96, 105, 112, 122, 123, 130, 152–154, 158, 165, 167, 168, 182
Accessibility, 119, 153, 156, 182
Access intimacy, 94, 95
Accommodation, 75, 152, 154, 167, 176
Acid, 15, 26, 27, 101, 128–131, 139–148, 150, 153, 157, 159, 160, 163, 164, 168, 170, 171
Acid attack, 2, 6, 9, 13, 14, 25–27, 128–130, 133, 135, 139, 141, 142, 145–149, 159, 161, 162, 164, 171, 183
Acid Survivors Trust International (ASTI), 131
Activism, 15, 40, 41, 56, 64, 158, 164, 180
Adultery, 21, 104, 106
Afghanistan, 20, 22, 102, 108, 162. *See also* Taliban
Africa, 7, 10, 101, 117

Agamben, Giorgio, 14, 68, 79, 87, 88, 97, 125
Alinejad, Masih, 164–166
Alobied, Abdullah I., 100, 106, 108, 114, 116, 119, 119, 120, 126
Amani, Elahe, 130, 133, 159, 160–162
Amputation, 100, 101, 105–107, 112, 118, 121, 125, 126
Anthropocentrism, 25
Anwary, Afroza, 131, 134, 135, 163
Arendt, Hannah, 97, 177, 178
Asia, 7, 10, 101
Assemblage, 25, 26, 41, 60
Association for the Support of Acid Victims (EHGHA), 129, 159, 164
Ataei, Masoumeh, 39, 130, 135–148, 150–158, 160, 164–171
Australia, 7, 11, 55, 67, 68
Austria, 44
Azadi, Pooya, 108, 109, 160

Bangladesh, 134, 142, 164
Bannerji, Himani, 23–25, 37, 58–60, 63, 64, 166
Bargu, Banu, 14, 88, 91, 125, 150, 176
Barnes, Colin, 25, 34, 37, 38, 166, 178
Ba'th party, 44, 47
Belgium, 44, 162

Bengtsson, Staffan, 106, 118–120
Bernstein, Jay M., 12, 67, 87, 100, 117, 121, 123, 125, 171, 183
Biosovereignty, 14, 15, 88, 125, 150, 176; biopower, 87; bio-surveillance technologies, 39
Blanchot's paradox, 78
Bleeding wounds, 99, 126
Blood money, 142, 144. *See also* Diya
Bodymind, 6, 7, 12, 27, 65, 66, 70, 72, 78, 80, 87, 89, 90, 94, 97, 116, 121, 123, 125, 125, 127, 139, 158, 169, 176, 179
Body-Without-Organ, 25, 27
Britain, 44, 115, 131, 162
Burning wounds, 15, 128; burns, 47, 57, 71, 128, 133, 144, 146, 152, 157, 159; burn victim, 154, 179; burn survivors, 113, 179, 183, 184; chemical burns, 130, 150
Burstow, Bonnie, 48, 81, 89, 179

Cambodia, 134; Cambodian Acid Survivors Charity, 131
Canada, 11, 55, 67, 68, 167, 168
Capital, 23, 25, 30, 31, 39, 44
Capitalism, 5, 13, 24, 28, 29, 31–33, 36, 37, 40, 43, 46, 104, 107, 118, 129; capitalist economy, 3, 29, 64, 108; capitalist relations, 23; transnational capitalist modes of production, 36
Care, 8, 13, 15, 17, 34, 35, 40, 46, 48–50, 53–55, 57, 58, 60, 61, 63, 65, 81, 94–96, 119, 127, 167–170, 179, 180, 182; collective, 15, 16, 40, 65, 95, 96, 174, 175; electroconvulsive therapy, 186n; infrastructures of, 3, 15, 35, 94, 97, 129, 169, 180, 182, 183; inseparability of disability and, 3; medical, 71, 154, 167
Care activism, 163, 179
Care assemblages, 25
Chemical weapons, 44, 45, 47, 50, 57
China, 4, 7, 10, 17, 44, 84
Chowdhury, Elora Halim, 130, 131, 132, 134, 139, 144, 146, 150
City of Esfahan, 130, 140, 150, 151, 159–163
Clare, Eli, 6, 34
Class, 5, 9, 12, 22, 23, 25, 28–31, 38, 43, 46, 100, 107, 118, 129; consciousness, 40, 177; global relations, 2, 27, 38, 45; society, 3, 46, 60, 64, 84, 126, 130
Colonialism, 5, 11, 36, 37, 148
Communism, 46, 83

Convention on the Rights of Person with Disabilities (UNCRPD), 34, 35
Cruelty, 101, 117
Culture, 20, 22, 23, 57, 59, 64, 85, 120, 133, 134, 148, 162
Cure, 12, 15, 33, 34, 54, 55, 147, 168, 170, 176, 177; cure seeking, 55, 168; curative culture, 55, 168; curative politics, 13

Das, Anjan K., 117, 125
Defetishizing, 2, 3, 64, 175
Dehghanpisheh, Babak, 109, 110, 133, 159, 160
Dehumanization, 86, 149, 150
Dehumanizing practices, 127, 182
Deleuze, Gilles, 25–27, 146
Delusion, 75, 76
Democracy, 101, 107
Depression, 91, 96, 178
Dialectics, 31, 36; dialectical and historical materialism (DHM), 3, 13, 20, 23–25, 28–30, 32, 33, 41, 65, 98, 107, 178; dialectical relation, 32, 37, 125
Diaspora, 37, 129, 168
Dignity, 100, 103, 117, 118, 121, 123
Disability: consciousness, 2, 15, 39, 175, 177; creation of, 2, 38, 170; defetishize, 1, 8, 65; dialectic of, 7, 15, 35, 176; identity, 8, 54, 63, 175, 76; justice, 3, 15, 35, 39, 40, 122, 123, 176; praxis, 127, 177, 182; relations, 130, 166; fetishization of, 2, 43, 126; imposed, 100; production of, 4, 12, 13, 54; understanding of, 2, 3, 12, 13, 15, 25, 36, 64, 184
Disability-care dialectic, 65, 94, 97, 176
Disability model, 13, 35, 39
Disability oppression, 33, 36, 38
Disability percentage, 50, 52, 56
Disability rights, 11, 158, 163
Disabled Veterans and Martyrs' Foundation (DVMF), 50, 51, 52, 62
Discrimination, 21, 107, 130, 137, 143, 161
Disfigurement, 15, 29, 55, 108, 168
Divine punishment, 107, 156
Divorce, 136–139
Diya or the financial compensation, 142, 143, 155

East, 44
Eastern Europe, 7, 10
Education, 37, 96, 114, 117, 137

Emancipation, 136, 137, 139
Environmental destruction, 15, 32, 36, 38
Epileptic prisoners, 72, 76
Equality, 118, 119
Erevelles, Nirmala, 2, 11, 12, 27, 29, 35, 37
Esfandiari, Golnaz, 105, 133, 161
Ethnicity, 9, 28, 46, 63, 127
Europe, 7, 11, 44, 68, 101, 178
European colonization, 101, 117
Exclusion, 9, 119
Execution, 83, 84, 116, 117, 124, 142
Experience, 28, 173; of disabled survivors, 28; embodied, 170; lived experiences of violence, 23; marginalized, 28; personal, 28, 66
Exploitation, 9, 29, 31, 59, 61, 103, 118, 123
Eye burns, 130, 151

Facial disfigurement, 130, 133
Fascism, 2, 46, 85, 88; clerical, 182; clerical-fascist dictatorship, 102
Fear, 17, 130, 142, 160, 163
Female genital mutilation (FGM), 2, 15, 115, 122, 127
Femicide, 141
Feminine aesthetics, 171; compulsory aesthetics of femininity, 152
Femininity, 183
Feminism, 158; feminist consciousness, 130, 157; feminist imperialism, 5, 21; feminist mission, 19; feminist of color approach, 186n
Fetishization, 8, 60, 61, 126, 127, 179
Feudalism, 46, 118
Financial Action Task Force (FATF), 109
Financial independence, 139, 146
Fiqh (Islamic jurisprudence), 101, 105, 106
Flogging, 102, 122
Form, 30, 32
Forti, Simona, 86, 87
Foucault, Michel, 16, 85, 88, 115, 117, 124, 125, 155
France, 44, 162
Freedom, 26, 76, 78, 108, 136, 161, 180; of choice, 162; of expression, 17, 63, 158; of the press, 158
Friedmann, Lawrence W., 101, 106, 107
Fritsch, Kelly, 7, 25

Gaping wounds, 13, 42
Gaza, 162, 163

Gender, 6, 9, 12, 13, 17, 28, 29, 135, 148, 175; gender-based violence (GBV), 2, 4, 9, 11, 15, 23, 37, 128, 129, 135, 147, 167, 169, 170; gender-related problems, 135; gender apartheid, 18, 55; gendered segregation, 161; gendered violence, 21, 41; gender politics, 134
Genital burning, 139
Genocide, 2, 5, 21, 54
Germany, 67
Ghamari-Tabrizi, Behrooz, 45, 47, 62
Globalization, 39, 134, 135
Global North, 1, 7, 8, 10, 12, 27, 30, 33, 34, 36
Global South, 1, 2, 7-10, 12, 13, 28-30, 34-36, 38, 41, 131, 158, 166, 181, 182
Gorman, Rachel, 4, 5, 7, 11, 12, 21, 27, 35, 40, 166, 173
Guattari, Félix, 25, 27, 146

Hadiths, 99, 142
Haghgou, Shirin, 56-60, 62-64
Hande, Mary Jean, 7, 27, 28, 183
Hassanpour, Amir, 46, 47
Headquarters for Executing the Order of the Imam (HEOI), 109, 110
Healing wounds, 15, 173
Healthcare, 12, 33, 34, 37, 54, 133, 168
Hegemonic masculinity, 132, 135, 146
Hegemony, 24; anti-U.S-hegemony, 18; pro-Islamic hegemony, 18; Western hegemony, 20
Higher education, 135, 137
Hindu nationalism, 59
Historical materialism, 24, 29
Hodud (Islamic judicial apparatus), 102, 104, 111, 113, 115
Holocaust, 76, 79, 117, 159
Homelessness, 14, 103
Homicide, 142, 143
Homophobia, 22
Human body, 100, 103, 114, 120
Human bodymind, 1, 121, 123
Human dignity, 108, 122, 126
Humanity, 118, 122, 123, 175, 177, 180
Human rights law, 121
Human Rights Watch, 153
Hussein, Saddam, 44, 62

Ideology, 12, 22, 25, 30, 31, 34, 36, 43, 46, 59, 60, 61, 63, 99, 103, 107, 121, 126, 127, 134, 147

Imaginary access, 156
Imam, 112, 126; Friday Imam, 160; infallible Imam, 111
Immigrants, 21, 96; anti-immigrant rhetoric, 21; disabled immigrant, 167, 169; displacement, 179; forced migration, 5; immigration law, 37; migration problems, 96; precarious immigration status, 7
Imperialism, 1, 2, 4, 5, 10, 11, 17, 20, 23, 28, 31, 36, 37, 40, 43, 45, 104, 129, 149; imperialist expansion, 20, 37; imperialist feminism, 21; imperialist power, 20, 30
Imprisonment, 63, 65, 77, 82, 101, 116, 117, 122, 129, 142, 184
Impunity, 128, 129, 134, 135, 163, 170, 176
Incarceration, 2–4, 13, 15, 29, 67, 74, 111, 122, 127, 175, 183
Inclusion, 119, 169
India, 21, 59, 101, 134, 137
Iran, 1, 4, 5, 7, 10, 15–22, 26, 43–47, 49, 50, 55, 60, 62, 63, 66–71, 73, 80, 84, 86, 97, 102, 104, 105, 108–113, 121, 124, 129, 133–135, 137, 142, 147, 150–152, 155, 159, 160–168, 174, 176, 177, 179, 180
Iranian diaspora, 55, 67, 152
Iranian People's Tribunal, 68, 69, 71, 73; Truth Commission, 69, 70
Iran-Iraq War (1980–1988), 1, 8, 13, 17, 176
Iraq, 5, 43–45, 47, 57, 62, 111
Islamic Revolutionary Guard Corps (IRGC), 46, 107, 109, 110
ISIS, 18, 21, 113, 114, 161
Islam, 17, 18, 22, 62, 84, 85, 91, 100, 102, 104, 108, 116, 121, 127, 133, 134
Islamic Code of Conduct, 162
Islamic code of sharia, 124
Islamic criminal code, 113, 142–144, 176
Islamic dress code, 163; bad hijab, 159, 162; bad veiled women, 129; bad veiling, 17, 162, 163; bad veilers, 159, 160; burqa, 155; veil, 21, 22. *See also* Sexist dress
Islamic imperialism, 22
Islamic law, 22, 103, 118, 120, 133, 134, 184; Islamic hodud, 105; Islamic jurisprudence, 133. *See also* Fiqh; Islamic jurists, 99; Islamic justice, 114, 119
Islamic Republic of Iran (IRI), 68, 74, 84, 85, 87, 90, 91, 95, 102, 107, 109, 111, 112, 124, 128, 133, 143, 144, 158, 161, 163, 178
Islamic society, 111, 177
Islamic state, 21, 84, 102, 110, 125, 126, 134, 159, 160, 170
Islamic state terror, 21, 22
Islamism, 182; Islamic fundamentalism, 19; Islamic history, 118; Islamic ideology, 21, 135
Islamophilia, 22
Islamophobia, 17, 18, 22
Israel, 20, 45
Israeli Defence Forces (IDF), 55
Italy, 162

Jack, Ian, 101, 102, 131
Ja'fari school, 111
Japan, 100
Jazayeri, Shahram, 105, 112
Jihad, 56, 57, 111
Judeo-Christian traditions, 106, 116
Judicial limb amputation, 102, 104
Justice: justice-seeking movements, 68, 70, 178; restorative form of justice, 117; retributive justice, 104
Justice Sword of Islam, 162

Kafer, Alison, 147, 148, 169, 170
Kalantari, Abdee, 85, 102, 165
Kaplan, Ann, 174, 183
Karah, Hemachandran, 2, 10, 12, 15, 16, 35, 39, 40, 70, 122, 175, 176, 180, 182, 183
Kazemi, Sona Hill, 2, 10–12, 15, 16, 35, 39, 40, 42, 43, 45, 54, 70, 115, 122, 136, 175, 176, 180, 182, 183
Khan, Rahman, 130, 135
Khomeini, Ruhollah, 67, 71, 109, 110, 161, 162
Kim, Eunjung, 9, 11, 12, 54, 55, 168, 169
Kirkup, John, 100, 106, 107, 114
Kleptocracy, 29, 60, 109, 151; theocratic-kleptocracy, 14
Korkman, Zeynep, 18, 19

Labor, 30, 31, 39, 55, 84, 101; child, 111; free form of, 60; hyperexpoitation of, 13; indentured, 36, 37; power, 107, 108, 119; slave, 117; social division of, 30, 35, 40, 107
League of Arab Nations, 44
Legitimacy, 56, 58, 125
Levi, Primo, 14, 66, 68, 87, 174
LGBTTQI persons, 159
LGBTTQI+ Movements, 182
Libya, 45

Living corpse, 128
Living martyr, 13, 43, 59, 60, 61, 63, 64, 176
Luxemburg, Rosa, 5

Madness, 9, 13, 65–67, 69, 70, 73, 74, 77–81, 85, 86, 88–91, 93, 97, 98, 176, 184
Mad studies, 6, 98
Mannan, Ashim, 130–133
Marginalized body, 36; lower-class criminals, 107; marginalized disabled people, 166; second-class citizens, 47, 122, 142
Martyrdom, 49, 56–58, 62
Marx, Karl, 24, 26, 28, 31, 37, 38, 40, 41, 46, 59, 158, 178, 181
Maryland, 153, 154
Masculinity, 131, 132, 146, 183
Materiality, 99, 147
Material reality, 37, 53, 59, 60, 64, 65, 134, 139, 176
Mavroforou, Anna, 100, 101, 106
McClintock, Anne, 148, 149
McRuer, Robert, 25, 55, 100, 155, 168
Medical model, 32, 33, 35, 49, 176
Meekosha, Helen, 9–12, 35
Mehr, Najafi, 47, 84
Mehriyeh (mahr), 137, 138
Memoir, 68, 77, 78, 91
Memory, 66, 175
Mental disability, 48, 52, 53, 55; mental health concerns, 92, 96, 167; mental health crises, 13, 86, 94, 176
Mesdaghi, Iraj, 73, 80, 84–86, 92, 94
Middle East, 1, 2, 10, 16, 18, 20, 21, 34, 36, 44, 47, 106
Militarism, 28
Mingus, Mia, 15, 92, 94, 95
Misogyny, 16, 20, 29, 128, 146, 171; misogynist Islamic theocracy, 19; misogynist law, 18; structures of, 17
Mojab, Shahrzad, 36, 39, 136, 175
Montow, 141, 162
Moral injury, 121, 123
Morality Police Force, 159, 160, 162
Muselmann, 14, 79, 87
Muslimization, 14, 85, 86, 88
Muslim-phobia, 17, 20, 21, 127
Muslims, 21, 22, 85
Myanmar, 21

Nationalism, 11, 23, 28, 43, 46, 129; cultural, 56, 58–60, 63; fetishization of, 46; nationalist sentiments, 44; nationalist violence, 10
Nation-building, 12, 43, 149
Nation-state, 13, 23, 46, 58, 64
Naturalization, 182
Nazi fascism, 88; concentration camps, 87; Kapos, 84, 85; Nazi Extermination Camps, 79, 84, 86, 87
Nia, Ahmad Soleiman, 48, 54
Nicaragua, 45
Nigeria, 102
Non-disabled, 25, 147, 157; disabling a non-disabled, 102, 122, 126; non-disabled body-mind, 69, 80; non-disabled person, 156
Nonnormative: nonnormative behavior, 77, 81, 82; nonnormative method of communicating, 94; nonnormative suffering, 87
Normalcy, 34, 36, 121, 154
Normative culture, 130, 132, 148, 149
North America, 7, 10, 16, 18, 19, 101, 178
North Korea, 45

Obsessive compulsive disorder, 69
Oil, 110, 111; oil supply, 44
Organization of Iranian People's Fedai Guerillas (OIPFG), 67
Oliver, Mike, 25, 32, 33, 37, 38, 107
Oppression, 7, 28, 32, 34, 39, 47, 59, 86, 146, 147, 158, 166, 168, 173, 175, 179; axes of, 9; disability, 33, 36, 38; gender, 38; oppressive hijab law, 162; oppressive order, 162
Organization of Paykar for the Emancipation of the Working Class, 68
Organization of Razmandegan for the Freedom of the Working Class, 68
Organization of Revolutionary Workers of Iran (Rah-e Kargar), 67
Orientalism, 21, 116
Oster, Sharon B., 79, 174

Pahlavi monarchy, 65, 75
Pakistan, 102, 115, 134, 137; Pakistani Taliban, 134
Parsipour, Shahrnoush, 70, 77, 78
Patriarchy, 1–3, 20, 23, 28, 29, 36, 98, 128–130, 132, 135, 139, 146, 182; Patriarchal society, 131, 152, 157
People's Mujahideen Organization of Iran (MKO), 67

Percentage system, 52, 55, 56
Personal experience, 28, 66
Peru, 100; Peruvian law, 101, 102
Police force, 134; police brutality, 15, 37
Political consciousness, 16, 37, 39–41, 158, 174, 178, 183
Political dissidents, 14, 55, 67, 70, 80, 88
poor, the, 36, 100, 101–104, 107, 110, 119, 121, 126, 127, 177; disabling the poor, 14, 120
Potts, Dennis W., 100, 106, 108, 114, 116, 119, 120, 126
Poverty, 7, 10, 13, 14, 22, 26, 30, 32, 37, 43, 49, 99, 102–104, 107, 110–112, 114, 118, 121, 126, 127, 152, 179
Power, 10, 29, 56, 65, 66, 69–71, 74, 87, 90–92, 99, 105, 109, 110, 124, 125, 132–134, 136, 137, 160, 162; core in the system, 160; dynamics, 12; imbalance, 28, 49; political, 125, 150; relations, 10, 25, 46, 58, 64, 115, 119, 158, 166, 173; structures of, 5, 8, 9, 170, 174
Praxis, 3, 12, 15, 39, 40, 166, 175, 180, 183
Price, Margaret, 6, 170
Prison: Ghezelhessar prison, 71, 72, 77, 86; Gohardasht prison, 72, 83; literature, 189n; mad prisoners, 8, 67, 69, 79, 81, 82, 86–88, 90, 92, 93, 95; memoirs, 70; political prisons, 12, 84, 85, 87, 89, 96, 174; survivors, 93, 174, 178; system, 84
Process of defetishization, 3, 64
Prophet Mohammed, 99, 106, 125, 126, 142
Puar, Jasbir K., 4, 7, 11, 12, 38, 45
Punitive-judiciary system, 124, 125
Punitive limb amputation (PLA), 2, 4, 9, 11, 14, 29, 36, 54, 55, 99–108, 110–118, 121–127, 175
Punitive system, 120

Qisas, 100, 105, 106, 115, 142–146, 155
Queer, trans, Black, Indigenous, people of color (QT/BIPOC), 9
Queer people, 19
Quran, 103, 106, 112, 119, 133, 143

Race, 6, 9, 28, 29, 37, 38, 175; racial apartheid, 122, 180; racism, 7, 21, 63, 86
Refugee, 96
Rehabilitation, 33, 119, 176
Resilience, 39, 78, 180, 182
Resistance, 38, 62, 85, 89, 90, 91, 98, 125, 142, 159, 163, 174, 180, 182, 183

Response-ability, 69, 90, 177
Retaliation, 104, 143
Rich Kids of Tehran, 111
Rispler-Chaim, Vardit, 102, 103, 105, 106, 114, 115, 118–120, 126, 143
Robbery, 102, 103, 106, 118, 126
Rotten wounds, 98
Ruling class, 46, 107, 112
Russia, 4, 7, 10, 21

Sabzichi, Mohsen, 112, 113, 126
Said, Edward, 116, 182
Sakhi, Shokoufeh, 14, 65, 66, 69, 84–89, 91, 125, 177, 178
Saudi Arabia, 20, 102, 108, 115, 121, 124, 137
Second-class citizenship, 22, 161
Sexism, 22, 63, 85, 130, 146, 171
Sexist dress, 162
Sexuality, 9, 17, 29, 135, 137, 146, 148, 157, 170
Shamlou, Ahmad, 42, 78, 81, 97, 104
Sharia Law, 15, 18, 21, 101, 108, 111–113, 116, 120, 125, 127, 135, 137, 142–144, 162, 163, 177, 182
Silence, 17, 42, 43, 45, 49, 61, 70, 72, 83, 161, 172
Social justice, 33, 169, 177–179
Social media, 129, 167, 179; Facebook, 153; Instagram, 129. *See also* Rich kids of Tehran; social media accounts, 164
Social model of disability, 9, 25, 33
Social relations, 2, 3, 5, 8, 15, 23, 24, 27–29, 31–33, 36–40, 42, 44, 46, 55, 59, 64, 65, 94, 107, 115, 147, 166, 168, 175, 177, 181, 182
Solitary confinement, 72, 76, 80, 83, 93, 94, 112
Soma-technologies of disability measurement, 14, 15, 43, 50, 54, 176
Souryal, Sam S., 100, 106, 108, 114, 116, 119, 120, 126
South Africa, 20, 122, 180; apartheid regime, 122
Soviet Union, 7, 44, 45
Stigma, 99, 120, 126, 132, 157
Stoning, 102, 112, 122
Sunni-Islamic state, 124
Survival, 38, 39, 85, 118, 182; survival ego, 85, 88
Swanson, Jordan, 130, 131
Switzerland, 44, 67, 109
Syria, 20, 45, 111

Talebi, Shahla, 65, 68, 74, 85, 96
Taliban, 113, 134, 135, 162; in Afghanistan, 134
Tavvabism, 14, 88; tavvab-making process, 85; tavvabs, 83, 84, 85, 87, 90
Tehran, 57, 90, 92, 111, 145, 150, 153, 155, 161
The Hague, 68
Theocracy, 2, 3, 11, 28, 29, 36, 43, 46, 59, 97, 107, 129, 133, 139, 170
Theocratic nationalism, 20, 31
Third World, 7, 33, 130
Titchkoshy, Tanya, 123, 156
Torture, 2, 4, 6, 11, 12, 22, 23, 29, 63, 65, 67, 68, 71–75, 78, 84–88, 90, 91, 93, 94, 101, 117, 121–124, 127, 129, 130, 143, 171, 175, 176, 183, 184
Toxic masculinity, 129, 132; toughness, 131, 132
Transnational Disability Model (TDM), 13, 14, 23, 33, 35–38, 40, 42, 43, 64, 65, 175; transnational disability praxis, 9, 16, 122, 129, 166, 173, 178, 180; transnational disability solidarity, 12, 183; transnational disability theory, 2, 3, 8, 41, 56, 121, 122
Transnationalism, 36, 37, 39, 46; transnational infrastructure of care, 39, 176, 180; transnational political consciousness, 3, 64; transnational solidarity, 15, 39, 122, 127, 166, 175, 182
Trauma, 13, 30, 48, 53, 61, 66, 78, 122, 171, 179, 181, 183; physical and psychological, 132; post-traumatic stress, 43, 47, 96, 178, 179; transgenerational, 7, 9; vicarious traumatization, 183
True Islamic Hijab, 163
Turkey, 4, 5, 10, 18

Unconventional weapons, 43, 45
Undesirable, 131, 144, 148, 149, 170
Unemployment, 43, 53, 107
United Kingdom, 7, 11, 22, 67, 131, 164, 165, 167, 169
United Nations, 34, 42, 44
United States, 4, 5, 7, 10, 11, 17, 20, 44, 45, 55, 67, 68, 115, 117, 130, 132, 153, 154, 159, 167; U.S.-imposed economic sanctions, 19; U.S. imperialism, 19
Universal Declaration of Human Rights, 121
Universal disability identity, 35
Universal healthcare system, 154, 168
UN Security Council Resolutions, 42

Veterans, 8, 42, 43, 47–54, 56–58, 62, 176; disabled, 14, 34, 40, 47, 49–51, 54–58, 60, 61, 63, 81, 176; disabled war veterans, 49, 50; mentally disabled, 47, 48; war, 46, 165, 184
Violence, 2, 3, 7, 11, 13, 15, 19, 23, 28–30, 32, 35, 36, 38, 40, 41, 45, 54–56, 65, 72, 80, 98, 121, 123, 125, 126, 130, 131, 135, 139, 144, 149, 157, 158, 160, 161, 163, 164, 166, 168–170, 172, 173, 175, 179, 180–182; acid, 130, 132, 167, 179; domestic, 2, 149; colonial, 12, 101, 117; curative, 9, 54, 168, 169; gender, 130, 134, 177; state, 4, 7, 9, 11, 67, 76, 91, 117, 127, 130, 175, 181; structural, 13, 176, 181, 182
Visible disfigurement, 132, 133
Vitriolage, 130
Vitriol morality police, 129
Vulnerable war casualty, 180

Wacquant, Loci, 102–104
War, 4, 6, 7, 11, 13, 21, 23, 28, 32, 36–38, 41–45, 47, 49, 51–64, 88, 106, 118, 121, 174–176, 184; violence of war, 13; war on terror, 19; war story, 59, 62, 64
Welsh, Jane, 130, 131
West, 17, 20, 21, 22, 35, 44, 62, 164; Western world, 10, 11
White Cane Center, 153
Whiteness, 35, 175
Wholeness, 100, 103, 115, 119, 121–123, 126, 127, 177
Witnessing, 15, 16, 156, 166, 173–175, 177, 183, 184; active witnessing, 9, 15, 16, 35, 173, 176, 178; bearing witness, 173, 174; present witness, 15; proxy witnessing, 66, 174
Womanhood, 17; body and sexuality of women, 129, 137, 138, 140, 157; women's solidarity, 165
Women survivors, 167, 171, 180; stoning of women, 21, 104; violence against women, 129; wounding women, 141
World Health Organization (WHO), 107, 108
Wounded, 8, 29, 34, 40, 52, 63, 70, 90, 121, 123, 129; becoming wounded, 27; wounded bodymind, 8
Wounding, 7, 28–30, 32, 36, 122, 123, 147, 170; problem of, 8; violent, 27

Xenophobia, 46, 47

Yazidis, 21, 114
Yemen, 111
Younessi, Ali, 161

Zakat, 119
Zarabadi, Ladan, 18, 19
Zarrab, Reza, 112

Sona Kazemi is Assistant Professor of Race, Gender, and Sexuality Studies at the University of Wisconsin–La Crosse. She is the 2018 honorable mention for the Irving K. Zola Award for Emerging Scholars in Disability Studies from the Society for Disability Studies and associate editor for the Global Ideas section of *Review of Disability Studies: An International Journal.*

www.ingramcontent.com/pod-product-compliance
Lightning Source LLC
Chambersburg PA
CBHW030121240426
43673CB00041B/1351